YESTERDAY'S FACES

YESTERDAY'S FACES

VOLUME V
Dangerous Horizons

Robert Sampson

Library of Congress Catalogue Card No.: 82-73597

ISBN: 0-87972-513-3 Clothbound
        0-87972-514-1 Paperback

Cover design by John Stats, Jr.

To Walker Martin, this overdue acknowledgement of his
enthusiasm and patient help for a very long time.

Acknowledgements

My thanks to Carolyn Davis and the George Arents Research Library, Syracuse University, for their support and help over all these years.

Additional thanks to Tom and Ginger Johnson of *Echoes* and John P. Gunnison of *The Pulp Collector*.

My warm appreciation to Ed Keniston and Cynthia Lindsey for innumerable cover photographs, some used here.

My particular thanks to all those friends who helped whenever I had a problem, which was often, opening their collections and notebooks, providing ever more checklists, giving generously of their time and knowledge.

For all that continuous special detailed help, thanks to Rick Lai, A.H. Lybeck, Steve Miller, Richard Minter, and Leonard Robbins.

For help on so many series, no matter how obscure and odd, thanks to Nick Carr and Diggs LaTouche.

For the wonderful and continuing flow of their articles and for the integrity of their scholarship, thanks to Jack Adrian, Randy Cox, and Will Murray.

For their guidance through the complicated world of Edgar Wallace, my thanks to John Hogan and Chris Lowder.

For those final facts about George Worts, special thanks to Richard Bleiler.

And thanks to Jack and Helen Deveny and Earl Kussman, who share with me this curious passion for yesterday's fiction.

Certain material in this volume has appeared, in rather different form, as follows: "On the Bum," *Echoes* #15, Vol. 3, No. 5 (October 1984); "Trails of Death," *The Pulp Collector*, Vol. 1, No. 3 (Winter 1986); "Adventuress," *The Pulp Collector*, Vol. 3, No. 1 (Summer 1987); and "Cowpunchers of Desolation" (as "The Wild Wild West"), *The Armchair Detective*, Vol. 21, #3 (Summer 1988).

Covers reprinted by permission of Blazing Publications, proprietor and conservator of the respective copyrights and successor-in-interest to Popular Publications, Inc., The Frank A. Munsey Co., Red Star News Company, Butterick Publishing Company, and Pro-Distributors Publishing Company for *Adventure* (copyright © 1910 and 1924, The Ridgway Company; copyright renewed 1938 & 1966, and 1952, Popular Publications; and copyright © 1935, Popular Publications, renewed 1963). *All-Story Weekly* (copyright © 1919 The Frank A. Munsey Co., copyright renewed 1947, Popular Publications). *Argosy* (copyright © 1934, The Frank A. Munsey Co., renewed 1962, Popular Publications). *Short Stories* (copyright © 1923 Doubleday, Page & Co., renewed 1951, Short Stories, Inc.). *Young's Magazine* (copyright © 1922, renewed 1950, C.H. Young Publishing Co.). *Snappy Stories* (copyright © 1924, New Fiction Publishing Co.). *Big Story Magazine* (copyright © 1929, Western Stories Publishing Corp.). And Conde Nast Publications, Inc, for *The Popular Magazine* and *Top-Notch Magazine*, (copyright © 1905, 1916, 1920, renewed 1933 and 1961, 1944, and 1948 respectively by Street & Smith Publications).

Contents

To The Curious Reader   1

Invocation   3

Chapter 1
Fighting Captains   6

Chapter 2
Dragons to the East   33

Chapter 3
Out of Africa   62

Chapter 4
The Pathless Trail   93

Illustrations   107

Chapter 5
Adventuress   121

Chapter 6
Cowpunchers of Desolation   132

Chapter 7
Right in Your Own Backyard   152

Afterword   178

Notes   181

Bibliography   188

Magazine Appearances of Series Characters   190

Index   206

To The Curious Reader

Adventure fiction was the supreme offering of the pulp magazines. They published little else. In the usual sense, the adventure story is an account of danger and excitement in distant places. But there is no need to hold such narrow limits. You may find adventure in the tropics or among ice floes. You may also find it when you turn the ignition key or open the front door. For adventure is an unexpected thing with golden teeth and opal eyes. It can appear this instant, offering opportunity and terror. You need not wait. It scratches at the door.

This book is concerned with series characters who sought adventure through the early pulp magazines. Adventure is meant in the widest sense. It is spelled with a capital "A" and given unlimited charter to take risks, face hazards, grapple with the unexpected at any time or place.

That is in keeping with the practice of the pulps. In them, adventure fiction wore many hats. It was western story and war novel. It appeared as interplanetary tale, sea story, mystery, or a mixture of them all. Each was a special form of the adventure story; each a fraction of the grand subject.

The Argosy was the first. It had been published in various formats since 1882, with the dime novels its only competition until 1903, when *The Popular Magazine* was introduced. Soon after, similar magazines began to multiply. During that interesting period between 1903 and 1910, inexpensive, all-fiction magazines began appearing quietly, testing the market, like mice exploring by night. These pioneers were unillustrated, containing 200 pages of small type packed double column.

In 1905 *The All-Story* was published, followed in 1906 by *The People's Favorite*, the *Railroad Man's Magazine,* and *The Monthly Story Magazine* (which was retitled *Blue Book* in 1907). *The Cavalier* was issued in 1908. Two years later, in 1910, *Top Notch* arrived and *Adventure,* soon to become the symbol of excellence in popular fiction. That same year, *Short Stories,* a quality magazine of reprint fiction, was converted to a pulp and began its extended career.

These magazines published adventure fiction in all its forms. They spun out series about adventures occurring close to home, excitement and conflict flaring in your own backyard. Other series were built around jobs that tickled the imagination of the period—firefighting, deep-water diving, performing on the vaudeville stage. Still other series featured such new inventions as the telephone, the motion picture and the camera, the gasoline automobile.

If a subject promised to interest the public, it got into the magazines. Each subject was spread with the glittering lacquer of action and conflict, and swept the reader into lives quite unlike his own.

1

After the long day's work, when the newspaper was discarded and the after-dinner silence set in (unbroken by the sound of radio or television), the adventure fiction magazine opened the walls of your well-known room. Out of the pages emerged a new world, hot with color. In that world, life was larger than the one you knew. The air bit more sweetly and the heart grew large out there.

No longer were you another face at the mill, another farmer on the fields. You found yourself to be unique, competent in action, undaunted by the strange. You saw mountains thrusting at a foreign sky. You observed the savannah rolling under a sun as hot as secret thoughts. You traveled beneath fleshy leaves along trails twisting toward strange destinations. You moved easily into the past, that black ocean. You learned the way of life on the open range and shared the violent lives of men who swept, under sail, among islands of promise and dread.

Out there, in rough country beyond the law, mortal danger set the tone. Unfamiliar men watched you approach. They stood arrogant and deadly, their thick shoulders tense, knives glinting in their hands, or heavy pistols. Their feet set against Texas prairie, the schooner's deck, the frozen tundra, the clay of Chinese valleys. They were powerful men, measuring you with frigid eyes. Frequently they were terrible sons of evil.

In adventure fiction some complexity of character was allowed. But it was never necessary to ponder who was evil and who was not. Evil was a hunting thing. Greed powered it. Murder was its tool, out there under the leaf canopy, at the base of the thrusting mountains. Evil threw its challenge. By accepting it, you faced struggle and blood. So much was at stake. Your hard-won wealth. Your life. Her life, perhaps.

For there was always the essential woman. Through the stories, women slip ambiguously, danger clinging to them like a dark ornament. A few were alluring, if deadly. More were charming, the essence of grace and purity. All had a universal tendency to get captured by uninhibited men. But that merely added to the excitement and the satisfaction of your eventual victory.

Through the decades, to an ever increasing readership, the magazines spun out their tales of adventure. The sentences were short, the action fierce. Often the central characters were as predictable as a mortgage payment. But not all. From the hundreds of series published between 1903 and 1930 rose characters of originality and force. We will meet a selected number of them in this book. Not all. Not many. Only a selected few.

We will begin with an Irish adventurer, the quintessence of the romantic soldier of fortune. We will sail with captains of the sea. We will wander the South Sea of 1870, the Far East, the Africa of the 'Teens, and plunge into the violence of South American politics and the terror of South American jungles. Then we will ride the dangerous hills of the American West.

From these places, we will return to adventure closer home—to sports and politics, the world of entertainment, and the extraordinary things that happen to men and women living just down the block.

Cowboy and captain, hunter, fireman, explorer, adventurers all. Their lives rolled like thunder through the pulp magazines. They impressed their personalities on the fiction to come. They stand immense behind today's characters, joining far-separated generations as a single, evolving whole.

Invocation

The Argosy. Adventure. Short Stories. The All Story. Action Stories.
The wind was nor-east and blowin' strong. By the time we was abreast of Djaheyrtill the tops of the waves was whippin' off like cream...

Dear Editor: I have just finished the first issue of *Romance* and I want to tell you...

In Canada, Jervis LaChambret's hate waxed ever stronger, a raging ember. Yellow eyes asquint in the Mexican twilight, he hastily blew out the candle and drew his knife.
Islands. Fetid jungle. The waterless horror of the Green Hell.

"Irregular Brethren" by H. Bedford-Jones. A story of an Oriental Masonic Lodge and of a weird adventure of one of its members in the wilds of interior Borneo.

Rippling muscles knotted under deep-bronzed skin as he
William Wallace Cook, Charles Wesley Sanders, H.V. Reed, J. Allan Dunn, Albert Payson Terhune, Frank H. Shaw, Scott Campbell, W. Beale Baldwin, W.C. Tuttle, Hilary Blake, Frank Packard, Talbot Mundy.

The Trail Ahead: A trip around the map—that will be the mid-April *Adventure*, which comes to you on March 18.

Scarlet and purple coral glowed weirdly beneath the keel of our tiny vessel as a brimming wave swept us into the smooth jade lagoon.
Blue Book. The Popular Magazine. Pep. People's Favorite. The Frontier.

"With Rope and Brand" by William McLeod Raine. A spirited story of big men in a big country, where words are measured by deeds.

...the black night stabbed with pistol flame, the silence broken by curses and crashing shots.

SENATOR MARTIN Says: "I have used *Hayner Whiskey* for medicinal purposes in my family and have found it very satisfactory. I believe it to be a number one medicinal whiskey."
4 FULL QUARTS. $3.20.

Cruel mouth sneered bloody froth at lips. "It is the deadly Patolle, a tiny fish but each spine drips with deadly venom. As you will discover to your cost, Americano."

The Cavalier is issued monthly by the Frank Munsey Company, 175 Fifth Ave., New York.

"I saw a woman with wistful eyes who seemed to yearn for something that was not hers."

"Red Toll" by Hugh Pendexter.

"Untempered Steel" by Burt L. Standish.

"Blood Money" by Rafael Sabatini.

Before me, a Notary Public, in and for the State and country aforesaid, personally appeared Ormand G. Smith who, having been duly sworn according to law, disposes and says that he is the president of Street and Smith Corporation, publishers of *The Sea Stories Magazine...*

Top Notch, Golden Book, World-Wide Adventures, Thrill Book.

Gold! In the flickering torchlight, it seemed alive. A deadly reptillian stench. Low vapors danced omniously over the black surface of the swamp that morning as "Nevermore shall you return but remain with me, Francois Hamilton, in my tiny cabin above the pines."

F. Marion Crawford, Arthur O. Friel, Hulbert Footner, George Surdez.

When you finish reading a magazine bearing this notice, place a 1 cent stamp on this notice, mail the magazine, and it will be placed in the hands of our soldiers, sailors and marines. *No Wrapping. No Address.* A.S. Burleson, Postmaster General.

Huge fragments of heavy wood hurtled past his head, but by a miracle they missed him. The perfume of sun-warmed woods. Silver blades and rancid yak butter. Gleaming fangs snapped, and then...

Complete Stories, Cowboy Stories, War Stories, Submarine Stories.

To Be Continued Next Week: Don't forget this magazine is issued weekly, and that you will get a continuation of this story without waiting a month.

Captain Dingle, James B. Hendryx, George F. Worts, L. Patrick Greene.

Locked together they tumbled into the clearing's ooze. He was on top, underneath... Whenever a fist wrenched free it drove into its enemy's face. In the budding dawn she mocked him...rosy tiny clouds on the distant horizon... Beef Deveny hauled the fore and main sheets amidships, while

All-Story Cavalier Weekly, Everybody's, Western Story Magazine.

Law Study At Home. *Gov't Positions.* Diamonds Cash or Credit. *Dandruff It's A Danger Sign.* Let Me Make You A Master Salesman. Another $50 Raise. *For Extra Heavy Beards.*

...across the rocky ravine but before he could fire again scarlet and purple lotus languidly and the silver-maned wolf slavering jaws If I don't get through Note to Old Dad heavy automatic smoking on table through shattered windows the perfume of the tropics and rose pearls in a pool of gore standing high above the silent crater reeled forward shrieked battered silently they sprinted into deeper shadow the pounding of their hearts gray waves of rain as he whispered huskily top gallants splitting the smell of blood and gold lies over Caracara where green jungle stinks of fever and the red parrots twirl like images in a thundered pounded husked pale still features seemed foam bubbles in clipper's wake as he clapped the younger man on the back white light along the razor edge...

It's a queer story.

Chapter 1
Fighting Captains

1—

(Colonel Terence O'Rourke) was tall, but the effect of tallness was not impressive until one drew near to him, so broad were his shoulders and so solid his build...he was all thew and sinew—a fact which produced in his bearing an air of lithe, active alertness.

Moreover, he was deep in the chest, lean at the flank, trim of leg. His head was of a good shape, the close-clipped dark hair curling the least trifle—not offensively; his skin was well browned, features lean and eager, eyes a warm blue-gray, and of a lively habit. At the time he affected clean lips and chin. There's the O'Rourke for you.[1]

A big laughing powerful Irish lad with a huge heart, striding forth into this good world to get a bit of his own and, yes, to give a bit, too. Red-headed Danny, his young valet and friend, frisking cheerfully behind. Ah, and the adventures they did have. Surely your heart should be an iced stone would it not lift with the glory of those hard fights, a fine Irish lad against odds and be damned to the Devil!

He is a contemporary D'Artagnan. His past gleams bright with the romance of excitement and danger. He holds an honorable discharge from the French Foreign Legion, owns a sword won in Cuba and a Captain's commission once held under the Greek flag. In his pocket bulges a gem-studded gold watch presented by the president of a South American republic.

The watch is hocked in the first story to pay O'Rourke's room rent. But the only lasting gift of glory is scars.

Colonel Terence O'Rourke is an early figure in the fiction of Louis Joseph Vance (1879-1933), who also created the more celebrated figure of The Lone Wolf. Vance was a regular contributor to the early *The Popular Magazine*, first appearing in 1903. "O'Rourke, Gentleman Adventurer," was published as a 4-part serial in that magazine, March through June 1904. Next followed "The Further Adventures of O'Rourke," a series in six loose parts, July through December 1904. A final series, "O'Rourke the Wanderer," ran from November 1906 through February 1907. Most of the 1904 stories were collected in the book, *Terence O'Rourke, Gentleman Adventurer* (1905), a pleasing treasure to be grasped quickly when found in used book stores.

And isn't O'Rourke as fine a fighting gentleman as ever your eye did see? With rapier if possible, for he was near the greatest that ever lifted blade. With pistol or rifle if he must. And always with the image of the dearly beloved, Madame la Princesse Beatrix de Grandlieu, a white coal in his heart.

...her profile stood in clear, ivory-like relief, clean cut and distinguished as a cameo—
and perilously beautiful; her full lips were parted in the slightest of smiles, her eyes were
deep, warm shadows, the massed waves of her hair uncovered, exquisitely coiffured...[2]

O'Rourke meets her during the first serial. He is a penniless soldier-of-
fortune and she is a jewel of French aristocracy, radiant and inaccessible. But
in grave danger. Her weakling brother, Leopold Lemercier, has fallen victim
to a gang of parasites, headed by that cynical rogue, Prince Felix de Grandlieu.
Forced by her brother to contract marriage to Prince Felix, Beatrix has discovered
an elaborate plot to secure the Lemercier fortune.

Brother Leopold has been persuaded to mount an expedition to the North
Coast of Africa, there to set up The Empire of the Sahara. He would reign
as Emperor—until Felix arranges his death, then marrying Beatrix and
swallowing her fortune.

In this moment of danger, she can trust only an old family friend, Monsieur
Adolph Chambret, a brilliant hand with a pistol. And the O'Rourke, himself,
who meets her after he leaps into her cab to escape the police.

He was escaping the police because he slapped down Monsieur Chambret
for an incivility. And so, coincidence on coincidence, off we go to Africa, in
a seethe of mutual hostility. They take along forty mercenaries, most of whom
will be shot dead before story's end.

There follows a satisfying quantity of plots and treachery, panting action
and rifles pounding under a scalding sky. The Empire of the Sahara is not
to be had without cost. Tribute must be paid to the Tawar a scalding sky. The
Empire of the Sahara is not to be had without cost. Tribute must be paid to
the Tawareks—the pirates of the desert, whose territory is being invaded. And
before you know it, Beatrix has been abducted by them. But O'Rourke gets her
back, almost killing himself by his exertions during the rescue.

In the end, Chambret kills Felix in a duel and the dream of empire
disintegrates as the Tawareks attack, gunning down virtually everyone in the
cast but the sustaining characters. O'Rourke generals the retreat to the ship,
but precious few of the party ever see France again. Leopold, whose folly caused
it all, receives no hurt; only dented expectations.

This is the giddy whirl of day dream. Your heart grows large as the sky
and the world spreads out its promise, a many-colored feast. The engaging hero,
powerful and young, seeks his fortune in perilous ways. Women flush at the
sight of him and touch their hair. He is a master of battle, touchy of his honor,
a commander born.

He bulked so big, so masterful, this Irishman who seemed to mean every word that
he uttered; his bearing was so assured, his control of himself, as well as of others, so
indisputable...[3]

This man is no lumpish clerk with cigarette breath, tallying up the days
to retirement. O'Rourke is in superb physical condition. If he suffers wounds,
he rises, splendidly bloody, to new exertions. If necessary—for adventure is
suffering as well as joy—he can drive himself beyond human endurance. As

when, having rescued Beatrix from the Tawareks, he runs long miles across the desert beside her camel. They strain toward sanctuary:

> He lost the sense of motion in his legs—nearly lost consciousness. (The desert) reeled dizzily about him, swirling like a maelstrom in a blood-red flood. His heart labored mightily, beating with trip-hammer blows upon the walls of his chest; and his lungs were like twin crucibles brimming with molten metal.
>
> An inquisition could have devised no torture more sublime; practically the man was already dead; only that something which was death-defying in his make-up, that determination almost superhuman, held him upon his feet, and kept those digging into the sand and spurning it to the rear...[4]

No adventure worthy of the name is enjoyed without suffering. It is necessary. If the hero is to stand forth, immense and wonderful, his challenges must be equally immense. All is magnified. His successes are bought in agony. If he falls, he must rise to more terrible exertions.

> He had been lying motionless, deep down in the silent depths of an ocean of recuperative unconsciousness; complete inertia had been numbing his every faculty; he had slept the sleep that follows a prolonged struggle with death—slumbers which should have lasted for hours.
>
> Yet to him the crack of that first Mauser (Desert natives are attacking) had been like the crack of a whiplash to a drowsy horse. The second report had not sounded before he was on his feet—reeling, it is true, but nevertheless standing.... He did not know that he was too weak to move about alone, so he did not hesitate to exert himself.[5]

This is the stuff of romantic adventure, and O'Rourke is a sublime example of that interesting fictional form. He is a chivalric hero, born too late for the Roundtable, but conducting himself in this modern world of Mausers and steam ships as if King Arthur watched.

As any knight, O'Rourke has embraced a quest. This is the heart of the series and all the adventures pulse to its beat. O'Rourke's quest is to become worthy of the beloved Beatrix. Financially worthy is what is meant. He is poor, poor; she glitters with diamonds. She would throw aside her wealth for him, but he will have none of that. First he must earn his fortune; then he will claim her.

And so she waits, tapping her brocaded shoe in irritation at the idealistic simplicity of men. While The O'Rourke strides forth in quest of fortune.

He has every gift save that of making money. His standards of honor, and a habit of befriending those in trouble, keep him poor—as honor and a warm heart tend to do. But he does find adventure.

After the Sahara episode, he travels to the little European duchy of Lutzelburg ("In Which O'Rourke Returns To The Sword," July 1904). There, Prince George, a base scoundrel, has kidnapped the seven-year old heir to the throne; he seeks to force the child's mother, the Duchesse, into marriage. (Forced marriage is a common series menace.) As O'Rourke strides to the rescue, he is trapped in a tavern and nearly killed. Saved by the Duchesse, disguised as a bar maid, they flee directly into another of the Prince's traps. Unfortunately for the Prince, he elects to dispatch O'Rourke with rapiers. It is an error of judgment. And fatal.

Next to Cairo ("In Which O'Rourke Serves The King," August). There he discovers a conspiracy to murder the British Resident and launch an uprising against the English. But being neither an assassin nor intriguer, O'Rourke smashes the plot.

In Tangier ("In Which O'Rourke Plays Providence," September), he wrecks a blackmail scheme that would force a lovely young widow to marry a skulking fellow. "In Which O'Rourke Pays A Debt" (November), he rushes off to India to aid a friend trapped by the politics of revolution.

These are splendid adventures, all, brimming with plots and evil schemes by evil men, and the hot iron sniff of danger. Only O'Rourke's audacity and quick Irish wit keeps him alive. But he finds no fortune.

Which descends upon him unexpectedly, manna from the generous author, in the final story of the 1904 series, "In Which O'Rourke Sheathes His Sword" (December). His tight-fisted uncle dies, leaving O'Rourke with O'Rourke Castle, all its lands, and all its debts. It is, however, enough for marriage.

But now his true, patient love, Madame la Princesse, has been abducted by the soft, twisted Duke Victor. Across Europe O'Rourke hurries to the sinister castle looming in the dusk. There he fights hand-to-hand with a big, hard fellow in an echoing corridor before a door that opens to a sheer drop down a cliff. Soon after the big fellow pitches through that door of doom, Duke Victor dies by gun fire.

And afterward, it's through the secret passage to the car where la Princesse crushes a scented handkerchief in her anxiety. And away across France, driving fast for the border, as the Lone Wolf would drive in ten years, toward marriage and joy and the conclusion of the series.

Successful series, however, do not conclude so tamely, and successful heroes have been known to return from death or even marriage. So it is no overwhelming surprise to discover that, like an aging stage star, O'Rourke returns again to the pages of *The Popular Magazine*. The encore is in four parts, titled "O'Rourke, The Wanderer" (November 1906 through February 1907). And, since married heroes are tedious fellows, the stories turn back in time to when O'Rourke was still single, still young, still poor.

A common thread connects the stories: O'Rourke seeks to return an enormous ruby to its owner in India and secure a large reward. Not for himself. Heaven forbid that a romantic Irish adventurer should benefit from his exertions. He does it for Nora, daughter of his old friend in the Foreign Legion, O'Mahoney of Galway.

In the first story, "The Pool of Flame" (November 1906), O'Mahoney gets killed by desert bandits. O'Rourke has a strenuous time finding the ruby, which has been hidden, which has been stolen, which is in the possession of merciless men. What with one thing and another, O'Rourke finds himself at the lip of another duel—this time for possession of the ruby. Thus:

Together, each bearing a naked blade, they left the dining-room, strode across the veranda and down a short step, to the lawn. The vicomte stood aside quickly, bringing his feet together and saluting in the full glare of light.

O'Rourke whipped hilt to chin with consummate grace, his heart singing. This was work such as he loved. The night was pitchy black, the windows barred it with radiance. In the dark spaces between, a man might easily blunder and run upon his death. Somewhere in the shrubbery away from the house a nightbird was singing as though its heart would break. There was a sweet smell in the air.

His blade touched the vicomte's with a shivering clash, musical as glass.[6]

In the next scene, O'Rourke is heading East with the ruby in his pocket.

These adventures, swaggering and wonderful, are densely packed with such devices as the penny dreadfuls and dime novels used to extend their little stories one chapter more. Through O'Rourke's world move the stereotyped characters of yesteryear, neatly updated if hardly changed from the original appearances in Dumas—the plotting nobleman, quick to strike at your back; the aristocratic maiden, a pink and white prize; the comic assistant; the deadly enemy who becomes a warm friend; the young girl in danger; the intrigue for power; the struggle, the trap, the duel, the battle; and the shining teeth of danger.

O'Rourke's adventures pulse with movement and menace. In this he is entirely modern. When action comes, it is brief, deadly. The story prepares for fifteen pages and completes in two.

It is gloriously romantic stuff. It flies along in a clear prose so deceptively simple that you forget how ruthlessly Vance exploits all the conventional devices of action fiction, outraging probability, echoing Dumas and Stevenson and Conan Doyle, and pouring forth his glib and satisfying story, an admirable example of pre-war pulp writing.

2—

The fifty-year era of the pulp magazines began quietly enough in the early 1900s. At that time, inexpensive, all-fiction, action-oriented publications printed on coarse, wood-pulp paper, began to dot the news stands, thrusting up their titles like anemones bursting through the snow.

The Argosy was there to greet them.

The Argosy was the favored magazine of publisher Frank A. Munsey. It was his first born, founded in 1882 as a vehicle for his hopes and soaring aspirations. The magazine nearly died in founding, for no sooner did Munsey arrive in New York City and spend most of his money for manuscripts, than his backers bowed out. Left with forty dollars and a mass of unpublished fiction, Munsey persuaded a small publisher to take on the new magazine, imposingly titled *The Golden Argosy, Freighted with Treasures for Boys and Girls.*

Beneath this mass of title, like a very small girl in a very large hat, was a diminutive pamphlet of eight pages, dated December 9, 1882, and priced at 5¢. The first issue contained serials by Horatio Alger, Jr. ("Do and Dare; or a Brave Boy's Fight for a Fortune") and Edward S. Ellis ("Nick and Nellie; or God Helps Those Who Help Themselves").

The Golden Argosy was not quite a magazine, not quite a dime novel, most certainly not a pulp magazine. Relentlessly oriented to a juvenile market, it stumbled on for six years, surviving the publisher's bankruptcy, lack of funds, and lack of credit. The publication continued because Munsey willed it to continue and exerted himself fanatically. And performed inspired footwork to keep it alive.

With the December 1, 1888, issue, the name was changed to *The Argosy*—recognizing, as Munsey said, that it was no longer a child's publication but an adventure magazine. And still it languished until Munsey's grand success with *Munsey's Magazine* in 1893. Soon after, he renovated *The Argosy* to an adult, 10¢ publication, issued monthly. But the great days did not begin until 1896, when *The Argosy* became an all-fiction magazine, the paper pulp, the editor, Matthew White, Jr.

With these changes, circulation swelled. From 9,000 copies in 1894, the magazine rose to 80,000 following its 1896 facelift; by 1907, circulation had increased to nearly 500,000, and it was earning a profit of $300,000 a year.[7]

These figures did not go unnoticed by other publishers. And as a natural consequence, other anemones began to bloom.

There were at first precious few of them.

Around 1905 there were perhaps 6,000 magazines published in the United States. Of these, fewer than 400 offered fiction in whole or part, and more than 200 of these were priced at 10¢ a copy or less. The pulp magazine was a decidedly minor magazine type, jostling for an audience in a sea of competitors. The pulp was unique only in the meager quality of its paper and the casual vigor of its fiction.

Between 1903 and 1910, several enduring pulp titles appeared. Chief among these were *The Popular Magazine* (1903), *All Story* (1905), *The Monthly Story Magazine* (also 1905, becoming *Blue Book* in 1907), and *The Cavalier* (1908). In 1910, as Halley's Comet glared portentously in the sky, threatening wonders, came *Top Notch* and *Adventure*. That same year, the quality reprint magazine, *Short Stories*, converted to a pulp and, touched by comet dust, embarked on its long career.

These magazines offered a heady mixture of fiction—mystery, sports, western, mixed with tales of action and conflict around the world. The pulps had a strong tendency to fictionalize on subjects of proven public interest. This led to concentrations of stories about Africa, where European powers contended for colonial empires, and lost civilizations glimmered behind the horizon, *a la* H. Rider Haggard. Or about the South Seas, temptingly strewn with pearls and cannibals and volcanic islands bright as emeralds. Or the Northwest of the American continent, dark with forest, where gold glowed in Klondike streams and harsh men fought for wealth. Both India and China were popular settings. The descriptions were largely drawn from *The National Geographic* and the adventures from the imagination, but if events were not as they really were, they were as they should be.

Pulp fiction also fed the public appetite for stories about the French Foreign Legion. And about soldiers of fortune, explorers of unmapped places, and drivers of automobiles, aeroplanes, and steam engines. For any new mechanical device was good for a series, given a smattering of technical jargon and a few performance statistics. It was applied engineering set to prose—technological fiction. Meaning adventure fiction written around a central gadget.

The fiction itself was in the romantic tradition—wonderful tales filled with action and incident and gilded with realistic description. The hero, solitary and self-reliant, faced peril and action and again peril. Danger escaped on one page rose ferociously on the page following. It all occurred in fascinating places drawn in clear, solid prose pictures, so real that you could see the rocks and smell the dust and taste the water.

We have seen how these merits shine through the adventures of Terence O'Rourke, the splendid Irishman, wanderer in far places. O'Rourke was the concentrated essence of the pre-war adventure hero. His generosities and elevated sense of honor, his physical endurance, his relaxed attitude toward death—these characteristics he shared with other adventurers in the magazines that followed *The Popular Magazine.*

3—

The first issue of *The Popular Magazine,* dated November 1903, contained 96 pages of fiction suitable for boys. The stories, about sports and adventure and uncomplicated motives, could have snuggled comfortably into dime novel pages. The editor, Henry Harrison Lewis, had long experience as a Street & Smith dime novel editor and writer.

The magazine began with the conventional editorial hope that it would "be read by every boy in the United States," and it was dedicated to pleasing "boys and 'Old Boys'," a sentiment which seems dreadfully cute after all these years.

Almost at once it became clear that only 'Old Boys' were buying the magazine. Possibly boys of 1903 found it difficult to raise ten cents a month. They did not buy—although their older brothers and fathers did.

Editorial re-direction was immediate, a sudden, single jerk, like the tightening of a slack rope. By the fourth issue (February 1904), you notice that the Table of Contents has been swept clear of such familiar boy's fiction writers as Gilbert Patten and Edward Stratemeyer.

Other changes had occurred. The second issue contained 128 pages; the third issue 194.[8] Fiction suitable for an adult readership cautiously peeped out and by the February 1904 issue, the conversion was complete, as adult fiction poured into *The Popular.*

From early 1904, most issues of the magazine contained up to four serials, five or more short stories, plus one to three series stories, and several inaccurately called "Complete Novels." Advertisements massed at the front and back of the magazine.

By the end of 1904, such familiar writers as E. Phillips Oppenheim and Richard Marsh were publishing serials. They were followed by "Ayesha," H. Rider Haggard's immensely successful sequel to *She.* H. G. Wells contributed "The Crowning Victory," later published as *Love and Mr. Lewisham.* B. M. Bower provided a serial, "The Lonesome Trail," and Vance and George Bronson-Howard offered quantities of adventure fiction. If you watched closely, you could also find occasional poems by Theodore Dreiser.

Of the many series springing up in the magazine, a few continued remorselessly through the years. Scott Campbell wrote about Felix Boyd, the brilliant detective, who was half Sherlock Holmes and half Nick Carter. B. M. Bower began her endless chronicles of the Flying U ranch, realistic cowboys in sentimental adventures. George Bronson-Howard introduced his extended series about Norroy, fashion plate and secret agent, who will be discussed later in a later volume.

More modest series rose to sparkle for a few stories, then vanish. The first of *Popular*'s series told of the Derelict Hunters (beginning January 1904), young men seeking fortune by salvaging out-of-luck ships. Other series over the next years included Faraday Bobbs, a freelance newspaper correspondent (six 1906 stories); and the remarkable Geoff, soldier of fortune in Latin America (twelve stories, 1906-1907).[9]

And there were sea captains, busy at everything but ships.

Sea captains gripped readers' imaginations with a force probably proportional to their distance from the sea coast. To a man fettered by animal husbandry or factory employment, the captain's life seemed ideal: Freedom, responsibility, mastery, endless travel among thundering foreign names, and skies that were far, indeed, from the stores selling *The Popular Magazine*. That such a free-flowing existence was not experienced by professional captains made little difference. The captain was seen as a free agent, living a challenging life, each second bright with excitement.

The line between sea captains and fighting naval heroes was vaguely drawn. In 1904, the name of Commodore George Dewey, Hero of the 1898 Manila Bay action, rang glorious. And school histories celebrated the accomplishments of Commodore Perry, who opened Japan to trade in 1854, after firing his guns in Tokyo Bay.

The adventures of these American heroes were paralleled by swarms of lesser captains passing through the pages of fiction. They appeared in widely read books—Stevenson's *Treasure Island* (1883), Conrad's *Youth* (1902) and *Typhoon* (1903), London's *Sea Wolf* (1904). They also appeared in dime novels and story papers, through which valiant captains faced storms, fierce natives, and pirates in all their vivid multitudes, while brave boys constantly quelled mutinous crews and saved the ship as it reeled toward the reef.

The captain, already an accredited fictional hero, moved directly into the new all-fiction pulp magazines.

As, for example, Captain Bantam, whose five-story series, "Captain Bantam, Kingdom Jumper," appeared in *Popular* during 1904-1905. The series, written by William Wood, has a great deal to do with colonialism and little with the mechanics of ship handling.

Captain Jacob Bantam, that acerb man, undertakes an expedition to seize an African kingdom—any African kingdom. It is good business, and he is backed by a London syndicate.

Bantam is harsh, sudden, full of bluff. He commands an old tub, the *Dione*, stuffed with obsolete rifles and ammunition. His adventures are small, some only incidents. As in "Saving the Cargo" (December 1904), in which a British destroyer stops the *Dione*. The hold is crammed with contraband weapons.

Whereupon Bantam lies. Yes, he does. He claims he is carrying the weapons to a British military expedition. The dim English accept his word and sail away. And that's the story, plus considerable description of Bantam's tense nerves.

In Central Africa, after adventures, Bantam accidentally locates a desirable territory ("In the Reign of King Bantam," March 1905). The king is fleeing with the treasury, having traded his country for Bantam's ship. But during a storm, the king drowns and Bantam finds himself appointed Commissioner of the territory by edict of the British military expedition that has been sniffing around since series' beginning. Commissioner is a peculiar job for a sea captain entirely unskilled in a Commissioner's arts. But it will pay Bantam a pension.

No sooner has Bantam exited, scowling, into the deeps of Africa, then Commander John Kelly McTurk, USN, enters. His series was written by Charles John Cutcliffe Wright Hyne (1865-1944). Better known as Cutcliffe Hyne, he was an English novelist and author of the highly popular Captain Kettle series. Since Kettle was a direct influence on both Bantam and McTurk, a few explanatory words might be useful.

At least ten collections of Captain Kettle stories were published as books between 1898 and 1932. Most stories had appeared in English magazines, although an eight-story series was published in *The Black Mask*, November 1926 through June 1927. Captain Owen Kettle is a fierce little pepper-pot with a razor for a tongue and the self-confidence of a god. He is a licensed sea captain, an enthusiastic versifier, and the founder of the Wharfedale Particular Methodist church. Wearing a red, Kentucky colonel beard and mustache, he fumes aggressively through adventures gently warmed by comedy.

Money problems fret Kettle. His wife and daughters require support; his farm's mortgage is past due; financial disaster looms. In Morocco, a pious sheik cuts off Kettle's right leg after he refuses to convert to Mohammedanism. But Kettle rises above such woes. Aided by Mr. McTodd (a ship's engineer with a fondness for drink) and Mr. Fanner (a clever young consumptive), Kettle forces trade concessions in Morocco. Gradually he becomes wealthy. He receives an English title in an accidental sort of way.

Success does not change him. He remains a hot-tempered bantam rooster, quick to anger, hasty in speech, rigid of opinion, a vivid personality.

Many of his characteristics, scarcely changed, slipped over into the character of Commander McTurk, "an American citizen and a United States naval officer first and all time."

"The Trials of Commander McTurk" ran in *Popular* from September 1905 through May 1906, a total of nine stories. Tall, powerful, with a red wrinkled face and a red, wrinkled temper, McTurk traveled on sensitive missions for his country. Complications swarm around him.

In the February 1906 story, "The Sultana," he:

—encounters a tornado off the African coast.

—travels through treetops like Tarzan, eight years before Tarzan:

To pass through the unfathomable slime and mud of a mangrove swamp is a thing impossible; to pass over the top of it among the desperately close fabric of the branches, in a stew of heat, in a maze of mosquitoes, is a feat generally accounted hopeless for a white man. But, in spite of his great height, commander J.K. McTurk was a man of enormous strength and activity...[10]

Later, he confronts savages, battles through a black maze filled with murderous tribesmen, is faced with the choice of marrying the Sultana or being killed, and escapes through the jungle by night.

All this in twelve pages. He lived life to its fullest.

McTurk and Bantam rush through their shallow little stories undisturbed by any taint of reality. They are beyond realism. For realistic prose imposes limitations and demands not only character depth but character change.

It is not intended that Bantam and McTurk meet these awesome standards. They are impervious to change, and their kindly authors, skillfully gripping the reader's fragile attention, slide past all limitations. Both characters consist of a few vivid traits selected for instant recognition. They are sketched with bold hand, then sent forth to do their little dance and sing their little song. They entertain, although they do not penetrate the heart.

Later characters did. Hurricane Williams came close. But Williams appeared in 1919 and a great deal had happened by that time.

4—

The First World War had happened by that time.

The War, that bloody surprise, cracked the serenity of the new century. Intense passions, social outrage, angers struggling for voice roiled slowly under that serenity, as deep infection heats and pulses under rosy skin. But for a time, the illusion of health persisted.

No one anticipated war. Certainly not the millions who would be eaten by it. Least of all by the national leaders—the Kaisers and Czars and Kings and Royal This and Exalted That. All stood confident in their power and yapped ceaselessly at each other, like puppies at transgressing birds. They maneuvered for national advantage. They defended national honor in the iron-necked, unlaughing way with which men usually defend intangibles and abstracts, those bloody shadows.

So the puppies yapped. And presently, posturing, unbending, fearsomely innocent in their guile, they tripped into war. Then men rose in the chilled hours of morning, and filed patiently by columns into the machinery of killing.

It was wonderfully successful, that machinery, a triumph of applied engineering: The artillery, the machine-gun, the field telephone, the entrenching tool, the grenade, the semi-automatic rifle, the gas, the airplane, the submarine, the barbed wire, the high-explosive deluge. Using these elements, and new industrial techniques, and new transportation techniques, the masters of the Armies shaped a splendid machinery.

They did not understand what they had created. In their dry old brains, filled with yesterday's wars, flickered dreams of high accomplishment: massed charges sweeping the enemy away, ceremonial surrenders. The military masters found honor and glory in this, and pride, combustible commodities at best.

So for honor and glory and national pride, young Germans, Russians, Italians, French, British hurled themselves against massed modern automatic weapons of high efficiency.

They did not succeed. They did not stop trying. An entire generation of European men was obliterated, whose talents might have guided the 1930s on more reasonable paths. Their atoms nourished the fields. They nourished little else.

After the killing, the dry old brains remained, planning new error. They did not recognize that. Honor whispered to them in its silver voice and national advantage glowed in their minds. It was unthinkable to them that they might err. Power justifies itself and is never seen to be in error.

So Western Civilization sampled lunacy and found it good.

Which leads to another story, not yet completely told. Such a disaster as the First World War spreads its consequences like an evil haze down the decades, depositing malignancy on every leaf. But this is not an account of the war and its consequences. Enough that war came. A great many valuable young men died for no purpose. And the confidence of the survivors in the wisdom of their leaders grew thin and sour. For a few years.

5—

The war chopped across popular fiction, changing much. It introduced tones of darkness and unease. It whispered doubt. It gave rise to harsh new attitudes and introduced coldly controlled characters, wary and unsentimental as sharks, who moved through society but were not of it. The social stability that pre-war characters assumed as a matter of course no longer existed. The world had become irrational. It had washed in blood. And now its leaders, beslimed with gore, proposed to resume pre-war politics as if nothing at all had happened. To some writers and some fictional characters this was intolerable.

Others ignored these unsettling dichotomies. The war was over and life went on and four years of organized murder merely added a host of minor conventions to their fiction. Thus Germans customarily were rendered as bull-necked sadists wearing monocles. The Colt .45 automatic was glorified. Every well-regulated hero was assigned a military background in either Intelligence or aviation, with an officer's rank and a cluster of brave medals. Military tactics wormed into the fiction. Black Star and the Gray Phantom conducted mass robberies with full military discipline. Bulldog Drummond battled crime with a hard-fisted cadre of ex-servicemen. The aerial bomb, the hand grenade, the airplane became well-worn plot devices. Violence sensibly increased, as the importance of death diminished.

At war's end, there came a turn from contemporary problems to historical fiction, a form in general eclipse since the turn of the century. By 1919, the pulp magazines found eager readers for adventure fiction set in the past. Zorro rode Old California trails. Those prominent seamen, Hurricane Williams and Captain Blood, set sail in *Adventure* magazine.

Captain Blood hunted the Caribbean of the 1690s in stories of buccaneers and swooping attacks on Spanish treasure ships and passionate, romantic struggle. By contrast, the Hurricane Williams series, set in the South Seas of the late 1870s, was agonized stuff, leanly grim, with alienation hollow under the sentences. Williams was a post-war hero, whatever his dates.

6—

An excellent young man named Clive Stanley came to the South Seas in the mid 1870s. He was brilliant, wealthy, of good family, and ability flared in him like a solar storm. He fell in love with a married woman. She was of great beauty and hated her husband. She was also intelligent and subtle and, because in 1919, beautiful women devoted themselves to twisting men artfully and shattering their lives, Lania fled with Clive. Leaving the husband dead behind them.

She loved Stanley briefly. Then she grew tired. "She always grew tired." After that, she began to fear him a little. The authorities came and took him away. Eventually they hanged him.

The hangman bungled the job and left too early. A fellow convict cut down Stanley, still alive. Another convict named Brundage buried a dummy and Stanley escaped to the Solomon Islands.

He turned native. He grew bitter, untrusting, savage as the cannibals with whom he lived.

After some years, a slave-hunting schooner anchored off the island. Stanley took over that ship. Renaming himself Williams, he began a new life. Even by the reckoning of that lawless time and place, he was an outlaw.

Now Hurricane Williams was, for reasons of his own, an exile.... He hated white men with an intensity that could not have endured without being perpetually nourished by memories.... It was sheer bitterness that made him hate his race, yet he knew, though he might try not to acknowledge it within his own thoughts, that there were men other than the treacherous, dishonest, brutal, sneaking fellows it seemed his fortune to have always encountered.[11]

Williams was the "most hated and despised white man in the South Sea Islands," for he would have nothing to do with other whites. Accompanied only by Tongans and Samoans, he wandered the immensities of the South Pacific, trading, fishing, raiding. While legends grew around his name.

They called him Hurricane because, when he fought, he struck without warning, with violence and power, lashing out with the terrible intensity of a man indifferent to consequences:

Dan McGuire: "I had seen Hurricane in fights of all kinds. I never knew him really to be taken off guard, unaware. That was probably because he was always tense, always strained, always suspicious, and had the remarkable faculty of throwing himself in any direction as suddenly as an arrow leaves the bowstring."[12]

He preferred the physical blow to a weapon. He was quick and exceedingly strong, a "fierce-eyed, short bearded (man), with hair unevenly carelessly cut short. And he stood firm-footed, legs apart, like a statue of bronze. Every muscle was tense, and the body, though not huge, or even big, was gnarled with the knotted muscles which were supple and smooth in his quieter moods."[13]

He was deeply burnt by the sun. Customarily he wore only trousers cut off at the knees, and carried only a sheath knife with a lanyard attached. In the sunlight, his body shone as if cast from molten bronze.

After a long time, this metallic facade softens slightly. He permits himself to trust three men: the convict Brundage, an old man, lean and wrinkled; the red-headed Dan McGuire, a flippant alcoholic, easily touched by women; and Francisco, lounging and sudden with the knife. Only these three.

The story of Hurricane Williams ran intermittently in the *Adventure* magazine from 1919 to 1931. It includes four serials and a novel, all later published in book form. These were written by Gordon Young, born in Missouri, 1886, and one of the major contributors to *Adventure* from 1917 to the late 1940s. Young was of that select group of *Adventure* magazine writers—among them L. Patrick Greene, Harold Lamb, and Talbot Mundy—who brought to the post-war adventure story a spare toughness. Their characters were hard men competing in settings where danger and violence were customary. Young, himself, mixed sentiment, melodrama, and ice-edged pragmatism into fiction filled with hardboiled attitudes, if not hardboiled diction. He was at least three years ahead of *The Black Mask*, and his series character, Don Everhard, directly influenced Carroll John Daly and the first of the hardboiled detectives.[14]

Like Everhard, the character of Hurricane Williams sent ripples down the years. His example showed in numerous later South Seas stories, particularly those written by Albert Richard Wetgen for *Action Stories* featuring Typhoon Bradley and Shark Gotch.

Gordon Young's third major series character was Red Clark, one of those tough roving cowboys with a dash of Hopalong Cassidy in his background. Clark was Young's most popular character, being featured in most of the later serials and books. Young continued to write through the 1940s. His final book was published in 1948, the year he died in Los Angeles.

The later novels were less complex than the Hurricane Williams series. In those stories, Young wrote of deeply flawed men and women. They moved through complicated melodramas told in prose like an eagle's stare, coldly harsh. Most of the characters are human trash, mindless as sharks and as rapacious. Their lives are records of treachery, greed, murder, drunkenness, and betrayal. The few sympathetic characters, palely shining in this darkness, are themselves flawed. The civilization that sustains them also leaves them defenseless before men consumed by self interest. These characters live in a world of horror. It is set in sunshine and blue water among islands like gems, ringed by white beaches. The sand is slobbered with blood.

Williams first appeared in a short story, "The Unlisted Legion" (First May 1918, *Adventure*). He developed to a major character in the four-part serial, "Savages" (Mid-July through First September 1919).[15]

In this story, young Gilbert Lang comes to the South Seas, hunting the man and woman who killed his brother. Seeking information, Gilbert arrives at the island of Hurricane Williams.

Gilbert does not particularly care for Williams, "a peculiarly unfriendly man and disagreeable as well as at times terrifying.... Williams had been constantly blasphemous.... It was natural that Gilbert Lang would almost invariably mistake discourtesy, such as was continuous in Williams—for a kind of repulsiveness of character."[16]

Williams' personality will be modified in later stories. From a crusty sourball, harsh and gruff, he will slowly change to the more conventional grim-mouthed hero, whose locked lips hide his personal tragedy. Crusty sourballs are hard to sympathize with.

Now the boat of Winston Willerby arrives at the island. Willerby is a trader and self-made power in the South Seas, deeply corrupt. Accompanying him are Paul Du Beque, Lania Du Beque (Paul's cousin), and a collection of social parasites. Willerby is a thoroughly rancid villain and has many naughty plans. Anticipating that Williams will interfere with these, Willerby invites Gilbert to the ship, proposes that he betray Williams into their hands. Gilbert refuses, is beaten up and chained in the hold.

Paul goes to Williams with a plausible tale of Gilbert's planned treachery. This does not surprise Williams, treachery being what he expects. He does not trust Paul, either. When lured aboard Willerby's ship, and trapped there, Williams promptly attacks:

Then it happened as men who know of him say it always happened with Williams. As the hurricane strikes with scarcely a warning for those who are not watchful, Williams struck. He half wheeled; an arm flashed out; Du Beque was down unconscious for minutes and sickened for days to come...

Williams glanced quickly to right and left; then he rushed straight into the huge fist of Willerby, taking a glancing blow on the neck and going on right up against him. A hand, steel-fingered, closed on Willerby's full throat, and a blow like the drive of a piston smashed into his face. He dropped.[17]

Through a hammering of rifle fire, Williams escapes the ship. From that moment it is blood war between him and Willerby. It is war richly spiced with double- and triple-crossing, for, with the exception of Williams and Gilbert, the other characters act only for personal advantage and lash at each other like wounded snakes, more savage than the island cannibals.

Through this twisting account of betrayal and violence, the story of Clive Stanley and his faithless wife is slowly exposed. Williams is revealed as Stanley; Lania as his wife. Williams had hung for her crime, the murder of the husband; loving her, he had accepted the guilt and punishment. She had borne him a daughter. By then she hated him and told him that the baby died. She lied easily. Thereafter, she thought him safely dead and drifted on, under a variety of names.

Her victims were many, for her beauty—and that something which lies beyond beauty and gives it witchery—was great; and in the hot South Seas islands, where passions are deadly and lives cheap, she had played recklessly, proud of an evil power that had not seemed to her at all evil... She had not been deliberately cruel but utterly heartless; and had thrown broken men away as a wealthy child discards broken playthings.[18]

While Willerby attempts to destroy Williams, Lania sets herself to seduce Gilbert, although she is guilty of his brother's death. Before she succeeds, a native girl, who is very fond of Gilbert, slashes Lania's face, leaving a scar from ear to chin across her left cheek. Then Williams confronts her. Seeing her disfigured, he lets her live. Punishment for her and punishment for Willerby, who is blinded during the final fight with Williams.

This is grand opera in prose. Magnified passions rage and flare. Emotions stalk like figures in a storm, fury and hatred and cruelty. The quietest page trembles with repressed violence. It is melodrama, but tightly plotted melodrama, emotion flowing like molten steel, searing as it touches.

"Savages" does not complete the story, which is continued in the 1923 serial, "Hurricane Williams' Vengence." Before that, other Williams' adventures are published.

"Wild Blood" (four-part serial, Mid-March through First-June 1920).[19] The story is told in first person by Dan McGuire, a friend of Williams, a lounging, ragged, red-headed alcoholic whose favorite pose is that of a beach comber. He is trained in navigation and is a competent man in a fight. Like Williams, he is wanted by the authorities for various crimes— poaching pearl shell, piracy, and other small change of South Seas life.

Williams and McGuire, both using aliases, are hired by an Englishman named Davenant to help him raise a crew. He wants them to take over a ship to which he claims title. Afterward they are to raid a pearl bed on an island near Dakarn. They do so.

On board is a girl named Dula, Davenant's niece. She has come to the South Seas to kill her father, believing him to be a monster. She is wrong about him. But most girls in this series believe other people's lies and get themselves into terrible problems as a result. In this series, girls exist to complicate the plot and expose their femininity to horrid outrage. Since this is a bleak world filled with appalling people, the girls often get more than they, or the reader, anticipate.

Off the ship sails to the pearl beds, through a haze of double-crossing, murder, and intrigue. By the end of the story, you wonder that the Pacific hasn't become permanently red.

"Storm Rovers" is, if anything, even more brutal. It was published in the Mid-December 1920 *Adventure* as a full-length novel.

The incompetent captain of the *Marianne* has shipped a crew of thugs and a cargo of one-half million in gold. The captain is promptly lost overboard during a storm. Williams whips the crew into shape and sets his course for the island of Kakaruta, a 2000-foot live volcano off New Georgia in the Solomon Islands. A faulty compass and a storm brings the ship onto a reef near the island. The ship sinks. "The curse that had ever followed and touched Williams again and again fell. He, who simply would not be thwarted or crushed, was ever and ever struck by hazardous luck."

Williams sends Brundage and McGuire to Honolulu to buy a schooner. There they learn that Captain Gorvhalsen of the *Heraldr* plans to sail to the volcano, trap Williams, and grab the gold sunk in the *Marianne*. Both Brundage and McGuire ship with him.

The *Heraldr* is an unlucky ship. It carries a load of passengers, including another of those vamping, man-teasing women, Jeanne Vaughn, a high fever in a tight dress. McGuire attempts to quench his hunger for her in gin, that balm of hurt minds. He does not have much success.

At this point, the Captain loses control of the crew. Mutiny, like an explosion of gasoline vapor. And not the pleasant little B-picture kind of mutiny with a well washed crew and gentlemen clicking swords and crying "Damme!" at each other. This mutiny seems the real thing—a brutal riot, crazy with blood, where men in mindless frenzy shriek and tear and hack blindly at each other. Brains and vomit on a bloody deck. The pound of bare feet. Blundering violence through a haze of black powder smoke. Sunlight on a bright axe edge, and bright blood spraying across a white door.

It is not romantic or even picturesque. It is foul and sordid and very terrible. It gets worse.

The Captain is paralyzed from the hips down, his spine chopped by an axe. The mutineers gamble for the women. Jeanne poisons herself and dies contorted, her mouth foam-ringed. Attempting to save the remaining passengers, McGuire and Brundage trap the mutineers in a cabin. Another grisly fight at close quarters. Brundage is killed. McGuire and a few remaining souls seal themselves into a cabin, waiting for the final attack. And night falls.

By then, the ship is near Tinakala and in the darkness, Hurricane Williams boards the floating slaughter-house. Three-quarters of the mutineers are helplessly drunk; he subdues the remaining ones mainly by force of personality.

It is, at best, a temporary stalemate. The ship, still filled with mutineers, is a cocked trap. At this moment appears the schooner, *Francis Vore*, come searching after Williams.

To save the passengers, Williams surrenders the *Heraldr*. He and McGuire are arrested and chained in the hold. But Williams escapes to set the ship on fire. Both men are believed killed in the blaze. Who knows for sure?

In both "Wild Blood" and "Storm Rovers," Williams is held rather in the background. Large portions of the story pass without his presence. When he does appear, the impact of his personality is magnified by anticipation. In "Hurricane Williams' Vengence," however, he is on stage through more than half the story. It seems that he did not, after all, die on the *Heraldr*.

"Hurricane Williams' Vengence" (four-part serial, May 30, June 10, 20, 30, 1923, *Adventure* magazine) completes the tragedy begun in the 1919 "Savages." Williams, McGuire, and the big red-headed Red Delaney, have been framed for the murder of a bishop and others on a missionary ship. All a plot by Slade Willerby, son of the blinded Winston Willerby. Only four men know the truth of this plot and it is Williams' task to hunt them down and secure their confessions.

He has terrible luck, as usual. As each man is captured, he dies in some freak accident. The opportunity to prove the innocence of the framed men dwindles away, until only Slade Willerby is left.

Woven into this bloody sequence is a second plot—how Williams' long lost daughter returns to the South Seas, hunting her mother. The daughter's name is Doris Stanlea, raised in a convent, to which a treacherous nursemaid had taken her when still a baby.

Doris finds her mother, Lania, living alone, shielding her scarred face, on a remote island. Too late, Lania learns that Slade Willerby has seen Doris and plans to have her. To protect the girl, Lania enlists the help of La Salle, a naturalist, who is friendly with Williams. In no time at all, the pages grow thick with plots: Lania plans the murders of Willerby and Williams; Willerby plans the murder of Williams and the abduction of Doris; Williams struggles to keep at least one witness alive; and the rest of the cast murder and double-cross with high abandon.

After bloody pages, Williams boards Willerby's fleeing ship. In the cabin, he finds Doris dead, a knife driven into her heart. Willerby insists she committed suicide; Lania claims that Willerby murdered her. In spite of Willerby's confession before witnesses that Williams was innocent of the missionary murders, his life is forfeit. Williams hangs him from the yardarm. Unable to face her future, Lania kills herself. And the story ends in a somber glow, like light from the gates of Hell, Willerby's ship slowly sinking as he hangs by his neck against a full tropical moon.

As mentioned before, this is grand opera without music. The tragedy is unrelieved. If the evil die, the innocent are also destroyed. The Furies strike impartially at everyone; there is no provision for goodness; no safety anywhere.

Williams survives. His experiences would drive any man insane and perhaps he has gone far in that direction. McGuire believes so.

> ...Williams had a mad sense of justice. In fact, McGuire believed that he was streaked with madness; his eyes seemed filled with a kind of piercing madness; and the way he drove himself, appearing never to sleep, never to rest, his manner of seeming always at the verge of anger and the tense, fierce repression with which he held himself, or his sudden fierceness and headlong hurtling when he let himself go, was very like a kind of madness.[20]

Half-crazy heroes have limited audience appeal. After "Hurricane Williams' Vengence," the series paused long. In 1925, Williams made a brief appearance in *Siebert of the Islands*, a story not published in *Adventure* because it contained an excess of women and their slippery ways. Dan McGuire is the real lead in *Siebert*, as he is in "Wastrel," a five-part serial published in *Adventure*, April 15 through June 15, 1927.

Williams finally returned in 1931 in a four-part serial. "If There Be Courage" (June 1 and 15, July 1 and 15, 1931, *Adventure*) is a step back in time to before the death of Brundage. The story turns about a former pirate who has changed his name and settled down. He befriends Williams, who drifts on-scene in an open boat, his luck out, as usual. Seems that a renegade trader, aided by a collection of evil Chinese, has captured Williams' ship, enslaved his crew, and done what should not have been done, if he expected to live beyond the serial's conclusion.

Again we are treated to a smoking mixture of treachery, murder, and dual identities. Sea ruffins endanger a beautiful girl; a chest of treasure lies concealed in a catacombs; and many guns fire constantly. In spite of these agreeable matters, the story seems deflated and tired. Williams appears quite sane.

By 1931, the South Seas adventure story had shifted to other hands. These later writers were less interested in grand opera than in wild west shoot-outs in steamy climates. Young's character-oriented horror stories modified to action adventures that employed boats instead of horses and the Pacific Ocean, rather than the open range. The heroes were muscled, fast-gun artists. Few of them, with the possible exception of Shark Gotch, showed any complexity of character.

Williams, himself, is less complicated than tangled. In him, several conventional character strands wind together without ever melting to a single personality. He is at once the bronze avenger, the bent hero, the embittered loner, the icy leader of men, and the tormented hero. Young never quite decides which. Most often, most vividly, Williams is the tormented hero.

Unlike the classical tormented hero, Williams has not defied the gods. He has stolen no holy fire. Merely he made an ill-judged marriage and a sentimental sacrifice.

The punishment for this is immense. All out of proportion to the offense. In the Hurricane Williams series, however, innocent error is punished as ferociously as original sin.

As a result, Williams spends much time knotted by paroxysms of romantic emotion. He glares and glowers and simmers and strikes. The man he was is never shown; the man he has become is presented in degraded images of early Romanticism. The mouth strains wide, denoting anguish. The eyes glare. The tense body trembles with the effort of endurance.

Before Williams, pale men grappled their silent secrets in the dime novels; and after him, they did the same in the silent movies. Williams was of a type— a bit more bronze, more powerful, more swift, more savage, more feared. But a familiar type.

It was a type the pulps honored by continuing for twenty years. They omitted Young's emotional intensity, while keeping his version of the South Seas and the human piranha hunting there. Few writers echoed the demoniac bleakness of Young's stories. These operas in serial were too intense. After awhile, even catharsis becomes tedious.

If the world of Hurricane Williams is a November sleet storm, the world of Captain Peter Blood is afternoon in bright July. Beneath these opposites whisper quiet similarities. Each series recoils from the mass homicide of the First World War, where a single death was statistically unimportant, except, perhaps, to the statistic himself. Each celebrates an individual alienated from his society and shaping his destiny in lawless places.

The Williams stories are soaked in post-war cynicism and despair. Those about Captain Blood abandon the Twentieth Century completely and retreat two hundred years to the Spanish Main—a locale as brutally blood-soaked as Flander's fields. Although two hundred years effectively filters out the sordid, leaving as residue only a romantic glowing.

Here then, richly colored by time's deceitful palette, stands Captain Peter Blood, gentleman buccaneer, on the deck of his red-hulled ship, the *Arabella*. The 1680s sun presses weightily against the ruffled Caribbean. But Blood is untouched by external heat.

He is a tall, slender man, clean shaven, swarthy as a dark Spaniard. He is elaborately dressed in the Spanish style, heavy lace at throat and wrists. On social occasions, a great black wig covers his black hair. He appears a Spanish grandee, although black eyebrows and bright blue eyes reveal that, like O'Rourke, he is an Irish rover. His voice is low, pleasant, if often metallic. When speaking English, his words are flavored by a drawling Irish accent. More usually he speaks Castilian, the pure lisping Spanish of the nobility. His accent and language changes, as needed, to fit the role he wishes to play.

For he plays many roles. It is forced on him, both the Spanish and English having set a price on his head.

Around Blood move his trusted companions. Little Jeremy Pitt, the shipmaster, whose detailed notes in the ship's log were to be such help to author Sabatini, two hundred years later. There stands Old Wolverstone, a giant with one eye, rumbling in the ear of Nathaniel Hagthorpe, who is a pleasant gentleman of 35, too mild appearing to be an officer of buccaneers. And trotting busily along the deck is Nicholas Dyke, short and sturdy, intent on business, once a petty officer in the British navy.

These men stare toward the horizon, where blue water cuts the frail transparency of sky. Eagerness draws their faces. Extending a telescope, Blood leisurely inspects an awkward galleon lumbering alone near the horizon. Spanish, clearly. Heavy with cargo.

The telescope snaps shut. "Pursuit, gentlemen," says Blood, tersely opening another episode.

Of sudden attacks and escapes. Of ungainly ships foaming before the Caribbean wind. The hard thud of iron cannon. Gray banks of smoke, the shatter of wood and slash of splinters, and hand-to-hand combat under the furnace of the sun. Cut and thrust with edged weapons and edged wits. For no man speaks the whole truth and Blood's suave trickery is as effective a weapon as his seamanship.

The stories glint with images. Ragged men barefoot on sand as white as soap powder. Treacherous Spanish, their eyes hot with cupidity. Drunken seamen howling in the waterfront den. Spanish gold, irregular red chunked gold, in clinking sacks, the weight of them bending a man's back. And women come drifting through the action. They are imperious, beautiful, frightened, disdainful, trying a buccaneer's honor and his temper. So the passionate adventure races among the green islands of the West Indies. It is not particularly realistic, but it is intensely exciting.

Nine episodes from the life of Captain Blood appeared in *Adventure* from First June through Mid-October 1921. Each story was subtitled "A Tale of the Brethren of the Main"—the word "brethren" implying a cozy closeness among thieves and throat-cutters which is denied by the details of every story. The series was written by Rafael Sabatini, a master of that fantasy form, the historical romance.

Sabatini (1875-1950) was born at Jesi in Central Italy. His English came early, learned from his mother, Anna, an Englishwoman who had married a dazzling Italian and been swept away to his dazzling, curious country. Sabatini was born with the itch to daydream on paper. His first book, *The Tavern Knight* (1904), is sufficient proof that, from the beginning, his imagination hunted in the past. Later he would write a few histories— *The Life of Cesare Borgia* (1912) and *Torquemada and the Spanish Inquisition* (1914). But he was a novelist born; his primary interest was the historical romance, the tale of adventure, crowded with costumes and splendid deeds under a younger sun. His heroes were agile-witted men, excelling in action, while history boomed around them. His books touched such diverse subjects as the American and French Revolutions, Old England, the Middle East, the Caribbean, Old Rome, and antique Venice. And if these novels were more nearly adventure romance than history, what difference has that ever made?

Sabatini took up residence in England. During the First World War, he worked in the Intelligence Department of the War Office and books continued to race from his mind. Among these was *The Sea Hawk* (1915), reprinted by *Adventure* in 1922 and becoming a best seller in 1923. *Scaramouche* (1921) also became a best seller—after rejection by six publishers. *Captain Blood* was published as a book in 1922. It was followed by two short story collections,

The Chronicles of Captain Blood (1931, also titled *Captain Blood Returns*), and *The Fortunes of Captain Blood* (1936).

Blood's history is thoroughly dramatic, almost as if it were fiction, although Sabatini assures us that it is biography. Born in the mid-1600s, Peter Blood was educated at the Trinity College in Dublin, becoming a doctor at the age of 20, those being casual times. Since Irish blood craves far skies, he promptly went to sea. He served with the Dutch under their great admiral De Ruyter. From this genius, Blood learned seamanship. From campaigning against the Spanish, he also learned to be wary of that nation, for he spent two years in a Spanish prison.

Returning to England in 1685, he was immediately caught up in the Monmouth Rebellion, one of those factional struggles with which England lacerated herself every few decades, in the finest tradition of European politics. Because he treated a wounded gentleman who happened to be on the losing side, Blood was arrested as a traitor and shipped as a slave to Barbados. This is a West Indies island in the Lesser Antilles.

There he was purchased for ten pounds—the small price rankled him—by Colonel Bishop of the Barbados Militia and an important planter on the island. Also a man of consummate arrogance, pride, and temper.

He did not choose Blood; his niece, Arabella, did. Arabella has all the virtues of a heroine, being young, beautiful, intelligent, and sympathetic. The plot also requires her to be imperious and disdainful, for the function of a plot is to introduce two young people who should be married, then separate them until the last chapter. In spite of plot requirements, Arabella is a thoroughly nice young lady. She selects Blood. The ten pounds are paid, and the story foams giddily onward.

A doctor was too valuable to remain a field hand. Blood has soon treated the Governor for gout and his wife for indisposition. His reputation swells. He ministers to Bishop's slaves. And he plots escape.

And does escape, as told in "The Rebels Convict" (*Adventure*, First June 1921). Spanish pirates attack the town, force its surrender. The authorities flee. The Spanish come ashore and give themselves over to the fleshy pleasures of victory. Blood sees opportunity. "Sluggishness of decision was never a fault of Blood's. He leapt where another crawled." That night, he collects twenty slaves and captures the ill-guarded Spanish ship. When the Spanish return the following morning, they meet the blast of their own guns.

So Blood acquired freedom and the red-hulled *Cinco Llagas* (later renamed the *Arabella*), and sailed for the safety of the buccaneer stronghold at Tortuga.

Subsequent stories tell his adventures as a fledgling buccaneer. He grows successful. Five ships serve him and finally a thousand men. He inflicts a major disaster on the Spanish ("Maracaybo," Mid-July 1921). He is taken prisoner by two toughs for the reward on his head ("Blood Money," First August). And he saves Arabella and Lord Julian when they have been captured by the merciless Spanish admiral, Don Miguel de Espinosa ("Lord Julian's Mission," Mid-September 1921).

Lord Julian has been sent by the English Secretary of State to offer Blood a commission in the King's service. This because Blood commands a famous mass of buccaneers who prey exclusively on the Spanish, and England wishes to reduce tensions with Spain. At first Blood refuses the commission, his pride aflame because Arabella has called him a thief and pirate. Later he accepts to save the lives of his men—and to confound Bishop, recently appointed the Deputy-Governor of Jamacia.

From this point, matters ascend into heady daydream. Blood shatters a powerful French fleet, although he loses the *Arabella*. He comes at last to an understanding with Miss Arabella Bishop. (Remarkably enough, she loved him all the time.) Colonel Bishop is stripped of his position, and Blood is appointed the Deputy-Governor of Jamaica.

From slavery to governorship has taken just three years.

The nine stories of the Brethren of the Main were promptly rewritten into the book, *Captain Blood*. This was a major revision, on the order of converting a bungalow into a condominium. In one part of the work, the ten-page story, "Lord Julian's Mission," was artfully expanded to sixty-six book pages, Chapters XVIII through XXI. Other parts of the nine-story sequence were freely interchanged or reserved for later use, and characters and continuity were altered wonderfully.

All to good effect. *Captain Blood* became a minor classic, known both as a successful novel and a successful moving picture. Its version of Caribbean derring-do was stamped permanently upon fiction. Every dashing buccaneer of later vintage carried something of Captain Blood—or of Errol Flynn, who played Blood in the 1935 motion picture.

How curious that English popular fiction should be so deeply marked by an Italian writer who loved the past.

8—

The magazine through which Hurricane Williams and Captain Blood pursued their stressful courses was *Adventure*, that distinguished pulp. The magazine was published for sixty years, beginning November 1910 and ending April 1971. During that period, it printed a continuous stream of action fiction, solid as a granite floor, by an imposing catalog of writers. A library of novels spun from its pages. To be published in *Adventure* was a mark of professional competence. The standards were high, the competition keen, the editorial requirements severe:

We want only clean stories. Sex, morbid, "problem," psychological and supernatural stories barred. Use almost no fact-articles.... Use fiction of almost any length; under 3000 (words) welcome.[21]

What these requirements did not state—perhaps it was not necessary to state—was that the fiction was addressed to adult males. Women were welcome to buy the magazine; in fact, the covers from 1914-1916 give the impression of a magazine containing fiction to probe a woman's heart. But covers are a hazardous indicator of a magazine's contents. Inside *Adventure*, the stories were for men about men in a man's world. Pastel feminine emotions were discouraged. Fiction depending on the unsteady complications of male-female relationships were flatly refused. *She* could motive a man's behavior. *She* could be saved from peril. *She* could scheme her schemes. Or *she* could perish dramatically. But *she* was a subordinate element to the main narrative, like cartridges or gin. The essential thrust of an *Adventure* story lay elsewhere.

Pulp stories are never written by women; they are written by men for men. Their style is rougher, more inclined to exaggeration; their theme fighting, either for or against the law; and their substance violent physical action. They are designed to fill the gap, as best they can, in the lives of American men who sit in offices and get their exercise by attending prize fights and baseball games. There is little love interest in the pulps, and when there is, it is companionate and never, never leads to human reproduction. Pulp stories are, by and large, very moral within their limitations.[22]

At *Adventure*, the main thrust was to show character through action, men coping with difficulty and danger. If there was violence along the way, so much the better. In spite of the physical emphasis, the stories required high levels of craftsmanship. As Editor Arthur Sullivant Hoffman wrote:

As to its literary quality (*Adventure*'s fiction) has pretty well proven itself. During my time it had to struggle against the feeling of both the critics and the general public that no action story could be literary. That is, of course, absurd and if any critic or college professor or woman's club is rash enough to uphold that half-baked idea I'll take great joy in meeting him, her or it on purely academic grounds and demolishing the absurdity. If action, however violent, evolves from character there is no higher literary expression and the ultimate crystallization of character is likely to lie in physical rather than psychological action.[23]

These high ideals did not eliminate a good deal of melodramatic action for its own sake. But they restricted the more improbable extravagances of the writers, a breed inclined to improbable extravagances. *Adventure* wanted character exposed by action, and if it sometimes got caricature, just as frequently it got character of some complexity.

Although Hoffman's opinion of *Adventure* quality was high, a less enthusiastic opinion was given by P.G. Wodehouse. In commenting on a story written by his friend, William Townend, which had been rejected by Hoffman, Wodehouse said:

I think Hoffman's criticism of the other story you sent me was sound enough from his viewpoint. It's a very good story...but it was too gray for *Adventure*. You had your characters struggling against Life and Fate and all that sort of thing, and what *Adventure* wants are stories about men struggling with octopuses and pirates. The *Adventure* public doesn't want to feel uneasy.... You make them think about life, and popular magazine readers don't want to.[24]

Literary quality and majesty of theme to one side, *Adventure* was also known for its authenticity of place and accuracy of detail. Hoffman "took pride in keeping *Adventure*, not withstanding its wildest flights of tale-telling, as strictly accurate as a Baedeker."[25]

(The pulp magazines) demanded a strict factual basis of truth behind their exaggerations. A pulp writer could, if he wished, make his hero pick off an enemy at a thousand yards range, but he had to mention by name the brand of the gun and ammunition that it would take to turn that trick. Only the brand of the hero's eye and nerve was taken for granted.

The readers of the old *Adventure Magazine* knew guns, boats, fishing tackle, the most distant islands and continents, the insides of volcanoes, and the solar regions as intimately as they knew their pants pocket. The slightest mistake relating to mechanics and the great outdoors drew instant and bitter protests from its readers.[26]

Adventure readers scattered the world and each was instantly ready to battle author error with scorching letters. They took a proprietary interest in the magazine and its precision of detail. They represented a major success of Hoffman's policy to involve readers with the magazine. Originally he aimed at the narrow commercial goal of nailing down repeat customers. But that goal shriveled away as the magazine became a club, a mail-box, an information exchange, and a rallying point for men from the world's remote corners. The response was astonishing—and quite gratifying to the Circulation Department. It happened this way.

The first issue of *Adventure*, dated November 1910, was a 15¢ monthly, edited by Trumbull White. At that time White was the editor of *Everybody's Magazine*, a publication of considerable contemporary reputation.

Both *Adventure* and *Everybody's* were among the magazines published by The Ridgway Company. Ridgway had been purchased in 1909 by the Butterick Publishing Company, a formidable power with thirty-two magazines. Among them was the influential *Delineator*, which had begun as a fashion magazine and gradually expanded its coverage to include home departments, articles, and fiction. The fiction staff included Arthur Sullivant Hoffman, an associate editor, soon to become *The Delineator*'s Managing Editor.

When *Adventure* was created, Hoffman assisted Editor White with part of the editorial work.

Hoffman: The original intention was to make (*Adventure*) a magazine of outdoor action but of better grade than other "pulp" magazines so that it might appeal to readers of higher intelligence than was attributed to pulp readers in general. It was from the beginning, I think, better than most other pulps.[27]

In the spring of 1911, White returned to *Everybody's* and Hoffman became editor. Thus began one of the happiest combinations of man and magazine in the record of American publications. "Hoffman," wrote T.S. Stribling, "was the grandest editor that I ever knew. He wore his hair and eyes and ears so that he looked continually surprised. He was a high-tempered man of endless patience and goodness of heart."[28] And his mind churned with ideas: *Adventure* was to become a quality pulp.

Unfortunately his budget was very small. Since he was unable to pay premium word rates to established writers, Hoffman systematically began to encourage new writers. Adventure's pages soon glowed with fiction by writers whose reputations would soon rise, whose work would soon be sought by editors and readers, whose books would cascade from the press. Talbot Mundy had already published his first story in *Adventure*, April 1911. A freshet of other writers followed: L. Patrick Greene, J. Allan Dunn, Harold Lamb, T.S. Stribling, Hugh Pendexter, Ralph Perry, Gordon Young, Arthur B. Reeve, W.C. Tuttle, H. Bedford-Jones, Walter Coburn, George Surdez, Arthur O. Friel, Raoul Whitfield, F.R. Buckley, Albert Wetjen, and, because lists are tedious, a startling array of others.

Most of these writers are ill-remembered today, fame being as transient as love. But for twenty years they were notable presences in pulp magazine fiction.

Even as he brought new writers to the magazine, Hoffman also began a studied wooing of his readers. With the June 1912 issue, he established the department "The Camp-Fire." Located in the back of the magazine, "The Camp-Fire" published a fascinating mixture of readers' letters, comments by the writers, and extensive editorial bursts by Hoffman. He held firm opinions about law, manliness, politics, and fiction, and he was willing to express these at length and defend them against the world.

Soon "The Camp-Fire" budded off subordinate departments. "Lost Trails," first appearing April 1913, listed the names of those who had dropped from sight and names of those anxious to renew old friendships. "The Trail Ahead," added May 1914, announced coming fiction. "Ask Adventure," beginning in 1917, was an elaborately set up question and answer bureau on "Outdoor Life and Activities Everywhere." A slowly changing staff of experts, each covering specific geographical regions, fielded such questions as where to boat in Eastern Tennessee, what hunting equipment to take to Borneo, the meaning of "chuni," and whether you could earn a living hunting and trapping in Southern Alaska.

The answers were terse, factual, detailed, and left in the heart of the soft city fellow stinging regret that he had accumulated so many wives and responsibilities.

In 1915, with the European war blazing nicely, Hoffman proposed the formation of an American Legion—that is, more accurately, an availability list of men having military and technical training. If war came, that list would be provided to the government.[29] Exactly how the government was to use this information was unclear. Nevertheless the idea was endorsed by all the living ex-Presidents (Theodore Roosevelt and William Taft) and ex-Secretaries of War or The Navy. Indirectly, Adventure's Legion seems to have contributed to the more formal organization of the American Legion, some years later.

Informal organizations bloomed mightily around "The Camp-Fire." If the American Legion were engendered there, so was the proposal to form a fighting group of red-headed men. An American League for Citizenship was suggested in 1918, its function to sniff out profiteering and German spies. Identification cards and buttons were provided below cost to readers, with serial numbers on file in the editorial offices. Mail drops ("Camp Fire Stations") were set up for the convenience of readers at the beginning of the 1920s. And all readers participated in a concerted effort to collect old ballads and songs; this was suggested in the First August 1919, issue, with a department titled "Old Songs" appearing in 1922.

Assisting Hoffman in these editorial and social science chores were men later to come to some prominence, among them Sinclair Lewis, Elmer Davis, and two future *Adventure* editors, William Corcoran and Anthony Rud.

The magazine editorial office was on an upper floor of the Butterick Building, near New York City's Italian quarter. According to T.S. Stribling:

The lower stories of the Butterick Building were full of presses and smutty men and women. As the elevator went up, you could glimpse huge machines on many floors, but, finally, in the upper stories you reached a region of pale persons pruning proofs.

When I got off on *Adventure*'s floor, I...picked my way uncertainly through corridors and rooms, avoiding the female editorial force of the *Delineator* and *Everybody's*. They were excellent women for an *Adventure* writer to avoid. They seemed so sophisticated and tired and superior that for any visitor of less rank than a woman novelist even to address one, much less to attempt a conversation, was vanity...

Then I would reach the *Adventure* offices, and there would be Arthur Hoffman and the *Adventure* boys who read the manuscripts, arguing. They would argue bitterly and learnedly about any outdoor topic under the sun: guns, bowie knives, Mayan hieroglyphics, Pennsylvania pepper pots...and the dentition of the Solomon Islanders.[30]

During one visit, Stribling reported "One of the boys began telling about an African chieftan who had come into the *Adventure* office with gun and knives and all the regalia. The boys had asked to see an African dance. The black man began his dance which grew wilder and wilder, and presently he began throwing his knives and firing his gun there in the office. Nobody objected. They let him finish his dance in peace, if it were peace..."[31]

Under Hoffman's editorship, *Adventure*'s popularity translated directly into increased frequency of issue. With the Mid-September 1917, issue, twice-a-month publication began. Later this increased to three-times-a-month, beginning with the October 10, 1921, issue. After certain page and price fluctuations, the magazine stabilized at 192 pages for 25¢. It returned to twice-a-month issuance with the April 8, 1926, issue.

The following year, Hoffman resigned, accepting the editorship of *McClure's Magazine*, a position he held from April 1927 to June 1928.[32]

After a series of editors, *Adventure* became a monthly (June 1933, 128 pages, 15¢). It was sold to Popular Publications in mid-1934. The magazine remained a pulp, still featuring work by many of the original writers, until the March 1953 issue.

With the collapse of the pulps in the 1950s and the rise of the sensational, sex-tinged male magazines, the character of *Adventure* changed permanently. The magazine survived, although at dreadful costs. In 1953, it became bimonthly, combining fiction, fact articles, and photographs. During the 1960s, the pages filled with views of nude girls. In the final stages, by then a grotesque caricature, it became a 50¢ digest magazine of 130 pages. The final issue, dated April 1971, contained still competent fiction embedded in a suggestive leer of advertisements and cartoons struggling to be risque. Volume 148, No. 1.

For all its present reputation, *Adventure* was only one title among swarms on yesterday's news stand—just as the sea captain, rollicking through pulp pages, was only one character type among many. Still, there was a plentitude of captains. In *Sea Stories*, every third hero was one. Even in less specialized magazines— *New Story Magazine, Action Stories, Outdoor Stories, Romance*—captains appeared with frequency, bringing a sniff of sea air among tales of trappers, ball players, and horse riders.

If sea stories over-emphasized the captain, it was likely the writer's fault. Writers favored captains, since they enjoyed freedom of movement, a necessity in short fiction. Far fewer stories were written about common seamen and mates, for those professions were limited by duties and discipline, and, lacking sufficient opportunity to shoot and scheme and hazard all, were unpromising subjects for action adventures.

Most usually, the adventuring captain story conformed to one of two general situations. In the first, the captain was a sort of floating businessman, responsible to higher authority. On routine business, he got into a tight spot but lucked through, depending on muscle and firepower as often as wit.

That is the pattern of the Bantam and McTurk tales. These were cast as problem stories, a typical pulp fiction form. The problem story begins in action, burdens the main character with a major difficulty, confronts him with danger, adds ever more trouble, and resolves in a shout of action. That useful sequence, like an articulated skeleton, supported fiction in all high-action magazines, from mystery-adventure to war to sports.

With minor modifications, that skeleton also supported several *Adventure*'s later captain series. During the early 1920s, Arthur D. Howden Smith told of woman-hating Captain McConaughy who repeatedly saved the fortunes of the Red Funnel Lines—although it was managed by a woman—although, perhaps he may have liked her a trifle. During the same period, John Webb wrote a more extended series about that hard-nosed little martinet, One-Two Mac— Captain James McGuire—of the *Hawk*, who battered his way around the Caribbean through contemporary stories stuffed with guns and fists.

The second story situation used many of these same elements, although in a different frame. In these, the captain was a wronged man. Embittered, outcast, he often walked lawless ways. In deference to the reader's feelings, this captain robbed only those more spiritually soiled than himself. He was not a justice figure, punishing when society failed to do so. The wronged captain sneered at society and its laws. He lived by his own stark code of justice. If he also protected the innocent and battered the wicked, that is what you did in a 1920s magazine.

Both Captain Blood and Hurricane Williams were wronged captains. As we have seen, Blood eventually re-entered society, gleaming with grace. Williams remained teetering at the lip of piracy, following his own hard code to the last.

During the 1930s, the wronged captain's criminality was reduced and his violent habits accentuated. Albert Richard Wetjen wrote two series in this vein. Barring the lead character, these series were as similar as straight pins. One featured the wispy little ice-hearted fast-draw artist, Shark Gotch, one of the most fascinating of the 1930s series characters. The other series featured a simplified clone of Hurricane Williams, named Typhoon Bradley, also a fast gun, but big and hard as a granite ledge.

The Gotch and Bradley series had a tendency to melt together at the edges. Both men appeared in "The Vengence of the Shark" (*Wide World Adventures*, September 1929). Even after the two series split apart, constant cross-over references to friends, enemies, and shared events kept them loosely associated.

Both men were opposed by equally competent villains. Bradley spent his days fighting the nearly continuous crimes of Gentleman Harry, Gotch in battling Larsen of Singapore. At the end of the latter series, Larsen kills Gotch, who then kills Larsen, a decisive conclusion. Bradley, however, continued unkilled into the 1940s. Both series were published in *Action Stories*, with occasional excursions into other magazines.

The scene for both series was the South Seas, out around the Gilbert and Marshall Islands, with infrequent forays to the Far East. As described by Wetjen, this area was a wet Wild West. No law out there. Only ferocious men struggling for wealth. The fastest gun, the thickest muscles, the most agile mind survived. Although the stories are slabs of violence, bloody as fresh-cut steaks, they are told in prose of a curious charm, as if a story-teller hunched by a low fire were recalling days of myth. The stories are stripped, lean, compressed, tight with suspense and harsh encounter. And full of death. Death by gun, by knife, by fist, by club. Whisky and powder smoke, betrayal doubled and redoubled, blood on gold coins, men dying white faced under a red sky on a red sea in a scarlet world of killing.

These shadows of Hurricane Williams no longer troubled themselves to reveal character through action. By the mid-1930s, action had become the prime purpose. Character had hardened to caricature. The caricatures, sharply defined, existing for violence, fought and bled and died. It was a shallow existence, if an exciting one.

Turn the pages of a 1939 *Action Stories*. The fiction is a succession of gun fights, fist fights, captures, escapes, formalized as a minuet. Twenty years of competitive magazine faction have brutalized the action story. You think of Hoffman, seeking factual accuracy and literary quality in the upper floors of the Butterick Building. How distant those editorial voices arguing exact facts. How remote Hoffman's quest for excellence seems.

These shadows of the 1930s need not trouble us. They are the ghosts to come. In our present, the 1920s, the sun is warm, the future confident, and we are untroubled by the great mechanisms of history working silently behind the light. The Great War is over. The severe depression of 1920-1921 is easing. Prohibition is the law of the United States. Problems glower on every side, but the future shines.

One small element of that promising shine is the magazine industry. Each month sees a new title among the pulps stacked in the railroad station or clinging, like bright shingles, to a street vendor's stand.

In the adventure magazines, a fine new crop of series characters have risen. They are horizon followers, explorers of far places. They push past familiar boundaries to distant fringes of the world. They tread Africa and Alaska. They sniff suspiciously at China. They pry through Amazon jungles. Danger is routine out there. A man's life is a small thing, easily lost. Or so the magazines tell us.

So let us turn next to those adventurers who push forward toward dangerous horizons and share, if fleetingly, their violent lives.

Chapter 2
Dragons to the East

1—

"It is chiefly to get back at (the managing editor of the *Clarion*) that I am writing the true story of my adventures. He it was who first played me up for a hero in his sheet—that terrible, blasting reputation of which I have never been able to rid myself."

"Fancy it! Plantagent Hock a hero. A little insignificant five-feet-five piece of manhood, with tow-colored hair and spectacles; philosophically minded, and with an affection for French bonbons. Hero! Why, that would made an elder in the Mormon Church laugh. And laughing is not their long suit. They're too much married."[1]

The voice is that of Plantagent Hock, reluctant adventurer through a brief series of five stories in *The Popular Magazine*, March through July 1907. The author was George Fitzalan Bronson-Howard (1884-1922), who enjoyed a remarkably varied career. He was a war correspondent for the *London Daily Chronicle* during the Russian-Japanese War, a reporter for the *New York Herald*, a dramatic critic for the *New York Morning Telegraph*; he contributed to the *Sunset Magazine, Popular, The Green Book, The Century*, and the *Smart Set*. In 1913, he served with US Intelligence and the British Ambulance Corps in France. Between 1907 and 1922, he published ten books, had a number of plays produced in New York City, and contributed a stream of articles and fiction to American and European publications. During 1914-1916, he wrote and directed silent moving pictures in Hollywood. He died in 1922 at the age of 38.

Bronson-Howard's most enduring contribution to popular fiction was the dapper figure of Norroy, a diplomatic agent (which is to say, spy) for the US government. Norroy appeared irregularly in *The Popular Magazine* until the 1920s, outwitting deadly foreign nationals in short stories, serials, and novelettes. (His career will be discussed in the next volume to this series.) The first collection of his adventures, *Norroy, Diplomatic Agent* (1907) was published the same year that Plantagent Hock make his appearance.

Both characters are touched by Bronson-Howard's peculiar reverse magic. Norroy seems to be a languid fop, inconsequential and foolish, a hero whose iron is concealed. Hock seems inconsequential, detests action, stumbles unwillingly through his adventures, and is a determined anti-hero.

For the last thing that Plantagent Hock wishes to do is have adventures. He is a dramatic critic sent by the *Clarion* to the Philippines as a Special Correspondent. That was the beginning of his ill luck. It continued every moment he was out of the United States. From the beginning, recorded in the March 1907 "The Lady of Luzon," trouble erupted around his simplest actions.

It is all because, as he explains, he keeps forgetting the Eleventh Commandment: "Thou Shalt Not Butt In." It is the work of the "Romance-wraith," he remarks, which keeps beckoning him to assist ladies in distress. After which, rolling disaster.

The endangered ladies that Hock meets are not the usual dainty wisps of femininity. They are, instead, raucous-voiced hussies who pour his whisky down the sink, berate him for smoking, and shove guns into his neck at exactly the wrong time. They are as feminine as a wad of sandpaper. It is sad. But nothing in Hock's world turns out the way the Romance-wraith promises.

The *Clarion* relishes his calamities. He may fumble grandly, blunder, stumble, get humiliated with distressing frequency. Each time, the *Clarion*, with a god-like imperviousness to the facts, writes him up as a hero. All over the United States, readers snatch up newspapers to read of his latest wonderful doings. It is clear proof that the newspaper business hasn't changed all that much.

In "A Custom of the Country" (May), he does a favor for Senorita Ana; that, he discovers to his horror, means that he is engaged to her. He can only escape by applying white paint to his face and claiming that he has become a leper.

In full flight from the senorita, he gets washed from a boat during a storm ("Jonah Number Two," June). He sputters up on one of the Visayan Islands, where stand a man and woman arguing fiercely. Since woman must be protected, he fights in her defense. It is another violation of the Eleventh Commandment. As a result, he finds himself aboard a tiny, coal-burning launch, heading out across the immense ocean toward Singapore, with the woman holding a pistol on him and a coast-guard boat in hot pursuit.

Seems that the launch is carrying $25,000 in payroll funds stolen from the Army by Captain Somers—that man back at the island. When the Coast Guard shells the launch, Hock is knocked out. The woman tells the Coast Guard that he, P. Hock, that insignificant fellow with tow-colored hair, is Captain Somers. She then vanishes. And Hock is kept tightly jailed for weeks until a newsman from a rival paper identifies him and writes a humorous story about his troubles.

Equally bad luck waits for him in China. The *Clarion* sends him there to investigate reports of a massacre of missionaries. On the way by river, he is overtaken by the houseboat of a mandarin, whose wife, a loud, vulgar, white woman, has just lost her temper and slapped her mother-in-law. In China, that crime is punished by whipping with rods until death.

Naturally she flies to Hock for protection. And that is the reason he discovers himself racing along the river, chased by the mandarin and a swarm of murderous, sword-swinging lackies. There follows a brutal fire fight described in cold, harsh detail—no light humor at this point. Before annihilation, they are saved by the intervention of the Emperor of China and George Bronson-Howard. Hock ends up with a wounded side, a sore head, and a short temper.

Then he discovers that the awful woman who caused all this trouble thinks that he acted like a hero and wants to cuddle him.

At this point the series stops, as if it fell down a hole. Bronson-Howard proceeded with other things, and whether Plantagent Hock ever got back to the *Clarion* isn't revealed. We hope so. The series had a fine satiric bite. It is written in a slangy vernacular that barely shows its age, and it methodically turns all those fine old adventure situations (clichés, even in 1907), neatly upside down. Particularly the cliché of the woman in distress.

2—

The Far East is filled with dragons, they say, lurking invisible but terrible behind the ancient Chinese hills. Among these the Occidental ventures at his own peril. Mr. P. Hock was certainly not the first magazine hero to flee down an Oriental river with quick death at his heels. Nor was he the last, although few heroes combined Hock's terrible luck and distaste for adventure with his penchant for entanglement with complicating women.

Peter the Brazen came close.

Peter Moore, Peter the Brazen, The Brass Man—he had more than his share of nicknames—enjoyed a long series of nearly lethal adventures in and around China, with occasional excursions to Central America, the United States, and assorted Pacific islands. In these places he led an intensely hazardous life and only the happy accident of being a magazine hero protected him from great harm.

His magazine career was in *The Argosy*, that noble publication, where multiple, overlapping serials drew you onward through the years. Most of Peter's adventures were told as serials, since the tangle of Chinese and feminine problems he faced could rarely be worked out in a single issue.

The series had a peculiar history. It first appeared during 1918-1919, then vanished for a decade. Revived in 1930, it continued intermittently into 1935 before shutting down a second time. Since eleven years separate the first and second parts of the series, you might suspect numerous discrepancies between the two. And you would not be disappointed. Discrepancies boil up. Although series events are reasonably chronological, and the internal time flows sweetly onward, Peter's age varies dramatically. Certain adventures seem lost forever. In others, time has gone a little cockeyed.

If this were biography, you would have every right to scowl and grumble. But since this is fiction, you accept what is given and turn another page. Consistency is admirable, of course, but you can enjoy the stories without having every last thread tied neatly off. They were not. But that has no effect on the charm of the series.

The Peter Moore stories reflect (as in a dim, warped mirror) some of the experiences of the author, George Frank Worts, born in Toledo, Ohio, 1892. In his twenties, as a ship's wireless operator, Worts "punched brass" all over the Great Lakes and the Pacific Ocean.

The decision to become a writer of fiction was made for me by fate. In 1914, in Panama, where I spent a week when I was a wireless operator on a little steamer that creaked up and down the Central American coast, I met an author who painted the joys of free-lancing so vividly that I could not resist the call. We were drunk. I was twenty. Since then, I have been trying to catch up with all those joys he mentioned.[2]

After attending Columbia University for a year, he married in 1915—it would be the first of three marriages—and dropped from the university to become motion picture editor for the *Evening Mail*. During 1916-1917, he was associate editor on the *Motion Picture News* and sold his first story to *Argosy*:

> I started writing fiction under the pen name of Loring Brent, because it would have annoyed the owner of the motion picture magazine to learn that I was writing fiction out of hours. He thought I fell asleep at my desk because I was working so hard for him! When my income from fiction exceeded my salary, I quit the job.[3]

After the First World War, the *Collier's* magazine sent him to the Far East to write a series of articles on "China, the Philippines, India, and Malaya." Later, he lived in a small Florida town, where he was postmaster, game warden, and deputy sheriff. From that experience, came a long series of stories about a Florida swamp town named Vingo.

He continued writing for *Argosy*, turning out a steady flow of serials and novelettes. He moved about the country, wrote a few motion picture scenarios, was divorced and remarried. Moving to Hawaii, he became the public relations director on the Kauai Civilian Defense staff in 1941 and the *Collier's Magazine* Hawaiian correspondent during the early years of the Second World War. After the war he moved to Arizona. During the early 1950s, he edited the *Tucson* magazine, and later became a historian at the Reynolds Electrical & Engineering Company. Having invested extensively in real estate, he spent his final years traveling, overseeing his interests. He died in Hawaii, 1968.

While Worts published extensively in the pulps, including *Everybody's*, *Argosy*, and *Argosy All-Story*, he was one of the few writers who made a successful transition to the better-paying slick magazines. He published in *Collier's*, *Red Book*, and the *Saturday Evening Post*, among others. About a dozen books were made from his *Argosy* serials. The first book published, *Peter the Brazen* (1919), severely compressed the original magazine material.[4]

"Peter the Brazen" first appeared as a six-part series in *The Argosy* (October 5 through December 14, 1918). Although each part is complete in itself, all are closely linked by time, character, and a rather nebulous menace that shapes and hardens dramatically toward the end.

Peter Moore, the hero, has all the talents and technical skills of George F. Worts, plus a good deal more. Of hypersensitive hearing, Peter is the major star among ship wireless operators. He could "read a message in the receivers when the ordinary operator could detect only an indistinct scratching sound."

> On his very first trip, he smashed every record of the southern Pacific. When (his ship) was abreast of Acajutla, Salvador, in one of the dead zones, Moore worked, without difficulty, across the mountains and intervening gulf to Key West, Florida.[5]

His reputation rose brilliantly. He became supervisor on a ship monitoring other Pacific operators, but soon transferred to one of the best jobs in his field, aboard the Latonia on the China run.

> That the supersensitiveness of his ears was not waning was soon proved by his receipt of a non-relayed message, afterward verified, from the shore station in Seattle, when the Latonia lay at anchor in Hong Kong. That was a record which has never been broken.

It was understood that Marconi himself wrote Moore a letter of compliment. But Moore showed that letter to no one. That was his nature.[6]

Which would suggest that sweet modesty is his habit. And possibly so. Or possibly what Worts takes for modesty is sort of an inverted pride. Modesty is of soft voice and understatement and Peter Moore is far too sure of himself to bother with such delicate attitudes. Perhaps he would if it occurred to him to doubt himself. But he doesn't. He accepts what he has—his hearing, his physique, his remarkable appeal to women—and proceeds about his business, unselfconscious as a force of nature.

Peter could not see himself as others saw him—could not imagine himself in other's eyes as a dauntless adventurer, who had been shot and hacked and pounded by the pistols, knives, and bare fists of queer men in the mysterious and darkened corners of the uncivilized world. Nor did he realize that his appearance tallied with that picture perfectly.

That he had a splendid figure which he carried with a debonair and reckless stride, that his features were fine and strong, and that his eyes were daringly romantic, were things that he modestly paid no attention to. He had been living with them too long; he did know that they carried a tremendous number of human faults.[7]

Least these traits be too abstract for a series hero, it should be added that he has light, curly hair, dark blue eyes, and his face is tanned and lean; he is a large young man, solidly muscled, although the later *Argosy* covers give the impression of someone rather slightly built and given to gaping in amazement.

All this, plus an extraordinary talent for getting into trouble, is about what you would expect of a magazine hero. In one way, however, Peter varies sharply from the norm established Heaven knows where and Heaven knows by whom for heroes. That is, he is entirely undismayed by women:

If there was an earthly creature Peter was not in fear of, that creature was a beautiful young woman....

He could not be shy with women even if he tried....

He respected them; he admired them; but he could not for the life of him hold them in fear. Strangely enough, his attitude was generally meek, always tender and considerate; but that was his nature. He had a sort of divine conception of woman in the abstract that no disclosures, no matter how harsh, could shatter.

Perhaps it was this inner conception, this acknowledgement of their lovely superiority, which made women find in him something highly desirable. It is to be believed that Peter did not make love to women knowingly; yet one fine young woman of his immediate past has said: 'Peter, you are like brass itself.'[8]

Peter is so unafraid of young women that he becomes dangerously embroiled with a different one, radiantly lovely, in nearly every adventure of the 1918 series. To keep these relationships from becoming permanent requires all Wort's agility. He devises a neat little formula for doing so, slicing off each girl onto the secondary male lead. Even so protected by a thoughtful author, Peter's heart is touched early. The resulting emotional glow continues through the initial six adventures like a burner turned on low, quietly warming the fiction and providing a delicate and lingering suspense.

The harsher continuity is provided by the Gray Dragon.

The Dragon is one of those demoniac international plotters who thrived in the shadow of Fu Manchu. Evil Chinese plotters had long been a staple of the dime novels and various fictions set in Soho and the San Francisco Chinatown. Given high intelligence, a large organization, and the inclination to conquer the world, as in the works of Sax Rohmer and A.P. Shiel, the character type intrigued merrily through the 'Teens. In earlier volumes of this series, we have seen how the lurking Chinese genius became a convention of the mystery adventure and detective magazines, continuing to the present day.[9] In 1918, the convention had not yet become cliché—not entirely—and still offered an interesting way of unifying a series. Suspense was built in, the hero struggling against odds and dangers to the limits of patience.

Much of the Peter Moore series is energized by such conflicts. The Gray Dragon is the first of his Oriental adversaries, a hidden Emperor of Crime, incredibly wealthy and incredibly powerful. His schemes are world-wide; his base is a glowing white palace within a walled city named Len Yang. This place is about fifty miles from Chungking and is surrounded by a plain of red mud.

The red color derives not from blood, which flows casually in Len Yang, but from cinnabar—mercuric sulfide, the ore of mercury. The Gray Dragon operates cinnabar mines. They provide much of his wealth. The mines function in the usual barbaric fashion, manpower and death intensive. In his spare time, The Dragon collects girls. Any race will do, so long as they are beautiful. He will teach them to become subservient.

All over the world slip his agents, locating likely girls and radioing their descriptions to the Dragon. The radio installation at Len Yang is of great power and is operated by the usual opium-crazed Westerner. After the Dragon approves the girl described, she is carried off, helpless and forlorn, the pitiful thing, to become the Dragon's slave. Women have many unique problems; men just don't realize.

And what ails the Dragon, for Lord sakes? Well, he hates beauty. Years before, his wife eloped with someone else, or committed adultery, or something equally unforgivable. That soured the Dragon, who promptly began world-wide kidnapping to punish the female sex, as crazy old men do in these stories.

Peter Moore first bumps into this activity in San Francisco. While in Chinatown, delivering a message for a friend, he sees a lovely Oriental woman glowering down on him from a window. She tosses him a note in Chinese, not noticing a second note tossed out at the same time. With some difficulty, Peter gets these notes translated. The first reads something on the order of "Beware." The second: "Help."

Returning to his ship, the Latonia,[10] about to set sail for Shanghai, Peter observes a desperately secretive group rushing aboard. He recognizes the cruel-faced Chinese woman; she is accompanied by several tough flunkies who haul along a gray-draped woman. Curious. Peter investigates. To his bafflement, he finds no trace of them onboard—no evil woman, no flunkies, no scrap of gray drapery.

The Purser and the Captain refuse to tell him anything. Then clumsy messages in wireless code sputter across his headphones. These messages are close, frantic, unidentified.

Still he can learn nothing.

Inexorably, he was being frustrated, thrust back, by persons of adroit cunning, by powers whose identity maddeningly eluded him. (His) love of the game was gone. This had ceased to be an adventurous lark. It was to become a fight with sons of darkness, against weapons whose sole object seemed to be to guard the retreat of some evil spirit.[11]

From the Chief Engineer of the ship, Peter learns that the *Latonia* is owned by a wealthy Chinese who lives in Len Yang, a place of grisly secrets. There follows mysterious notes, scowling faces at the port hole, savage interviews with the Captain—all the devices used by busy melodrama to maintain suspense at a rolling boil without resorting to physical action.

In the final pages, however, the pot boils over. Peter discovers that the gray figure is a kidnapped girl, being carried off to a life of despair. She had been sending those mysterious signals, using some form of theraputic electrical device not otherwise described. In a violent climax, he saves the girl and deserts the ship to hide himself away in China—at least till all those people he has punched, slugged, insulted, and foiled have cooled down.

This first of six linked novelettes is not entirely typical of what is to come. The Chinese elements are subdued. The contrasts between Oriental and Western cultures, so important later in the series, are not stressed. Much emphasis is placed on Peter Moore's technical skills, later down-played and eventually dropped entirely.

Silent moving picture images crowd the pages. Of these, some are stereotyped images of menace: the glaring face at the porthole, the mysterious message tossed in or out of a window. Other images serve as the prose equivalent of camera close-ups, such as a detailed description of the Captain's drink-ravaged face. The prose is densely packed with strong visual elements, elaborately detailed, against which is played the melodrama of abduction, investigation, and rescue.

Through the adventure move certain character types familiar to the silent screen: The weak male, a secondary character, compromised and fearful, emphasizing Peter Moore's excellence; the innocent girl in deadly danger; the malevolent Chinese beauty, vicious and dangerous; the authority figures whose authority may be flaunted because they have sold their integrity for gold. Familiar images, all. Less familiar, perhaps, in 1918, although as shallow then as now.

All these silent movie echoes are bundled in an atmosphere of thickening menace. Moore is baffled. He paces impatiently. The girl cannot be found. Messages bombard him; they make no sense. The ship rushes inexorably toward China. He is wild with anxiety. The snarling Captain warns him off. Only a few hours remain . . .

We will meet several of these situations and characters again, for much in this initial novelette prefigures the coming content of the series.

The second novelette (October 19, 1918, "The City of Stolen Lives") tells us several things that Worts forgot to mention in the initial adventure. The rescued girl's name, for example, is Aileen Lorimer. (For book publication, she was rechristened Eileen.) Moreover Peter has vowed to hunt down and kill the Gray Dragon because he is such a fiend.

With the second novelette, the series finds its direction and its voice. For all its artful lunging about, the first part was essentially introduction. It brought Peter to China, set him in conflict with the Gray Dragon, and established what might have been a unifying love interest—although Peter's interest in Aileen is so haphazardly handled that it unifies nothing.

Indeed, a rash, suspicious person might conclude that Aileen was merely a pretext for getting Peter to China. Once there, as the story lurched into motion amid a metallic grinding sound, the author discovered that she was inappropriate to the action and summarily dismissed her. We will not see Aileen again until the continuity of the story runs dry and must be revived by shock.

So exits Aileen for a few chapters. She has been taken to the US Counsel, who will send her home. Her role as the beautiful, endangered woman is immediately taken over by Amy Vost, daughter of a missionary to heathen Chungking.[12] Amy is delightful, clever, cute, charming, and loves Peter on sight. All women love Peter on sight, since he is a fictional character and close to his creator's heart. For his part, Peter wants no love affair; he wants only to go to Chungking, the jumping off point for his battle with the Gray Dragon.

If the art of love is to yield your heart to the right person, then no character in this series is artful. They love. But always the wrong person. Amy loves Peter and, in the fine tradition of popular fiction, regards the adoration of Bobby MacLaurin as if he were walking through her living room with muddy feet.

Bobby is one of those genial giants beloved of fiction. One of Peter's former shipmates, a big, powerful fellow, he radiates excess. He is too big, too emotional, adores too much, drinks too much, fights a great deal too much. He confronts adventure as a fire confronts a dry field. He has fallen passionately in love with Amy, tossing his heart before her embarrassed feet. To be near her, he has thrown over his job and become the captain of a tiny steamer sailing the river from Shanghai to Chungking. You will not be surprised to learn that the Gray Dragon owns the boat? You were? Were you really? How refreshing.

Bobby is an enduring fictional type, worn smooth in the dime novels, which had discovered him, roistering and violent, in still earlier romantic adventures. Since he is very big and powerful, the convention requires that the hero knock him down or knock him out or somehow assert physical superiority over him. And the relations of Bobby and Peter deviate not an atom from the convention. Together they have roistered and fought all over Central America, saving each other's lives and squabbling violently in less dangerous moments. Nevertheless, Bobby admires Peter (who knocked him out) and off they all sail up the river toward Chungking.

It is a voyage of considerable emotional tension. Not only is all love unrequited, but the three principals are spied upon by an evil-faced Mongolian, agent to the Gray Dragon. And Peter, poking around the wireless room, discovers an immensely powerful radio coil; while trying the performance of this device, he intercepts a message that reveals the Dragon's traffic in girls. To accentuate this horror, the Mongolian accosts Amy and gets punched out by Peter. In a later encounter, the Mongolian forces his way into Amy's room (it is at least possible that he was seeking Peter, there) and gets killed when he attempts to stab Peter in the passageway.

Thereafter the ship is rammed by a junk and sinks. Peter saves Amy, battling through whirlpools to deposit her on shore—at the feet of her father, who just happened to be standing there. Bobby has vanished and is presumed drowned.

Peter slips away on his mission. When half starved, he meets a wandering mandarin and his entourage, saves the mandarin's life, and, after improbable and exciting adventures, enters Len Yang disguised. There he meets the opium-raddled white man who operates the Dragon's radio transmitter, and learns that Amy has been captured by the Dragon's men and is being brought to the city.

As Peter prepares to rescue her, Bobby reappears. Together they gun down everyone in sight, free Amy, flee Len Yang. Touched by Bobby's devotion, Amy accepts him as her fiance, freeing Peter from the horror of a permanent emotional attachment:

"...Sooner or later, in some reckless moment, he would marry some girl such as Aileen Lorimer. Marriage meant permanency, and Peter Moore loathed the very idea of it. At heart an adventurer, his way was the open road, the rolling sea, the zest and flavor of change, of romance, of new lands—freedom."[13]

Same old argument. It's more fun to rove than to stay home changing diapers and paying off the mortgage. These are, no doubt, delightful and necessary activities, although they don't lend themselves to keeping alive an action series in *The Argosy.*

With Part III ("The Bitter Fountain," November 2, 1918), the story slams off in another direction, exactly as if Worts were improvising the action as he went along. Peter boards a ship for Hong Kong and meets that enigmatic liar, Romola Borria, lovely agent of the Gray Dragon.

Romola claims to be married to a villainous old man. Perhaps she is. But how can you tell with Romola, whose conversation consists of lies wrapped in falsehoods. Even when she speaks the truth, it distorts in her mouth. You feel that honesty would give her blisters.

She meets Peter just after he has pitched one of the Dragon's knifemen overboard. His brisk way of dealing with would-be murderers seems to charm her. Immediately she proposes that he slip away with her to Japan and settle down in a perfumed love nest. There, far, far from her wrinkled husband, they might, if all goes well, even marry. If he had a mind to. Or not if not.

Since *The Argosy* is a 1918 family magazine, Peter flashes out the customary 1918 refusal. Romola withdraws, the ship sails, and a series of harsh events begin.

To summarize a number of chapters of darting in and out of cabins, speculation, attempted seduction, attempted murder, accomplished murder, and other zesty events: Romola filches Peter's pistol, dropping her cameo in his bunk by accident or design. He flames off to her cabin, returns the cameo, reclaims the pistol. She is all soft repentence in a revealing nightgown. Their interview is inconclusive.

As a natural consequence of proximity to a lightly clothed young woman with white skin and scarlet lips, he neglects to check his weapon. It is an unfortunate oversight. No sooner does he enter his cabin, a tiny room with no place to hide, than another Chinese murderer begins shooting at him through the porthole. Peter's gun is empty. But there is less danger here than meets the eye. While Peter is reloading, Romola slips up behind the assassin and stabs him dead.

Several chapters later, parts of this confusion straighten out. Romola is an emissary of the Gray Dragon. She explains that all during Peter's last adventure (Part II), the Dragon amused himself by toying with Peter and his friends. It is his way, the old rascal. Now, however, he has tired of the game. Since Peter has become a nuisance, the Dragon has decreed that if Mr. Moore returns to China, he will die in one hour.

Personally, Romola does care. She feels nothing for Peter. Hates him, in fact. By which we understand that love stirs in her frigid bosom.

Whether it means death or not, Peter goes ashore at Hong Kong. He has received a radiogram from the United States Ambassador there and must report to the Embassy. But no sooner does Peter step on land than a sinister red-faced man pursues him, a boat loaded with killers blasts away at him, a thug rears up huge in an alley.

With gun and fists, Peter battles to the Embassy. There he is told that powerful people want him out of China and he is to leave at once.

Instead he slips away to meet Romola at her apartment. Heavens, no; not for dalliance. She has promised information. What he gets is a gun trap. His left arm broken by a bullet, he barely escapes, taking refuge in the home of a Chinese girl introduced earlier in the story. She loves him, a not uncommon feminine reaction to Peter Moore. Since she loves, her only joy is to serve— and serve she does. Whenever Peter is hard pressed or the plot unusually bumpy, some Oriental woman glowing with love for our hero tends to show up. She is a story device, rather than a developed character, but she is useful. Similar women with assorted exotic names are found in Edgar Rice Burroughs' novels; they slice away Tarzan's bonds, lead John Carter to safety, while their hearts burst with unexpressed love, alas, alas....

To return to Peter: after escaping his enemies, he confronts that sinister red-faced man who has been slinking about for so many chapters. The purpose of Red-Face is to resolve this part of the story; he wishes Peter no harm. Heavens, no. He wants to offer Peter a job on a ship leaving for California.

Romola will reappear later in the series, torn between love of Peter and fear of the Dragon. Her future is unhappy. She will murder her husband and commit suicide. But since these dramatic events happen off stage, we are not sure that anything of the sort happened. With Romola, you are certain of nothing. Everything about her is ambiguous, a loving, faithless, treacherous, reliable woman. An interesting character but thoroughly unsettling to be near.

Romola is by far the most developed personality to enter the series so far. She is, at once, a character driving the action and a symbol reflecting the ambiguity of the Chinese scene. In this Oriental world, nothing is as it seems. A friend's smile may be prelude to a murderous attack. Danger floats invisible in the transparent air. Any door may open to a room squirming with dragons.

This literary paranoia is central to the series. The most obvious events, clear enough and simple enough, tend to shiver suddenly and turn inside out, exposing total strangeness. In China, we are told, nothing is obvious, nothing substantial; reality is a succession of melting images. Plots coil upon plots like layered snakes. No one can be trusted. No event can be accepted without question. Hidden motives manipulate the commonplace. Never are you sure that you have looked deeply enough, that you understand enough. It is an uncomfortable world.

Peter loves it.

The Far East had taken hold of him; its breath was his life, the mysteries of it were his only remaining inspiration. Here he had tasted love for the first time; here he had courted danger and death, backing his courtship with wits that were remarkable when you considered his years, and protecting his adventurings with eyes that were as clear as running water, with a pair of fists that were as quick as the heels of death.[14]

How those writer fellows do carry on.

Worts does not mention Peter's automatic pistol, which he uses with enthusiasm. He takes quite a casual attitude toward killing Chinese and shoots them down as unemotionally as Buffalo Bill picked off another Indian.

The usual dehumanization is in effect here. In order that frequent murder may entertain the customer, the murderee is presented as either a bowelless fiend, richly deserving a well-placed .44 slug, or he is a mere hostile cipher, no more human than ducks bobbing at the rear of a shooting gallery. It is remarkable that so long a series, set solidly in China and rich with the sights and sounds of that country, should be so insensitive to the Chinese as idiosyncratic characters. In only a few instances is an effort made to develop a Chinese character more complex than a rubber stamp, and even these characters seem flat, as if they are moving and talking without benefit of life.

And now to the thrilling continuation of our story.

Since this story is a series of loosely linked novelettes, rather than an integrated novel, there now appears a long, and not very successful, excursion away from China. In "The Dead Spark" (November 16, 1918), Peter returns to California. Promptly he looks up Aileen Lorimer, while visions of a cottage for two disturbs his thinking. But it doesn't happen. At a Valentine Day's party, a professor, elated by the occasion, steals a kiss from her. Peter sees this from a distance. In the finest tradition of hot-headed heroes who leap to conclusions for the purpose of complicating the story, Peter instantly assumes that Aileen loves another. He rushes away, gets drunk, takes ship for Central America, where he is almost killed several times.

Boy has been meeting girl and losing girl for some thousand years of narrative. The theme is popular, has been popular, will be popular. Enthusiastic public acceptance need not conceal that the situation is an exhausted cliche. Was an exhausted cliché even back in 1918. If, however, you can't have a man come through the door with a gun, you can have a romance misfire. Adds suspense to a narrative that shows every sign of not knowing where it is going.

In the book *Peter the Brazen*, the Central American adventures were deleted, without much sense of loss. We pick up the story six months later in "The Golden Paw" (November 30, 1918).

"The Golden Paw," for all its high-tension suspense, is filler only. It extends the series by a part, delaying the necessary reckoning with the Gray Dragon until Part VI. The chief glory of "The Golden Paw" is that it introduces a feminine character type that will dominate the 1930s series. Here, in 1918, the character is not singular but plural: a pair of sisters named Peggy and Helen Whipple.

Charitably, these girls are feather-weights. They are young and lovely, as usual, and infatuated with Peter, per specification. They also combine enthusiasm, inexperience, and brainlessness in lethal proportions. They ask Peter to show them an exciting time in an authentic Chinese setting. He does so. Unfortunately it is a setting provided by Romola Borria. What begins as a gay adventure in a safe house becomes a savage struggle to survive a death trap. Once again, Romola save Peter's life. She will now vanish from the series, save for that rumor of suicide mentioned much later.

Romola vanishes but Aileen returns. In the final pages of "The Golden Paw," we learn that she has graduated from medical school and is coming to China to practice there. She explains the kissing episode. Peter is abashed, and a new world opens for him.

For five parts, Worts has thundered grandly along, pouring out his tale of danger, daring, and death. In the sixth part, it is necessary to weld these casual fragments together. This is more than ordinarily difficult, since each part is a more or less independent action adventure. In "The Gray Dragon" (December 14, 1918), some semblance of unity is created by finally facing that Chinese master of evil and destroying him.

He destroys rather easily, considering that thousands protect and defend him in an impregnable fortress. However, the Dragon has committed a major error: He has kidnapped Aileen again.

Peter joins forces with a young man, Kahn Meng, who is the son of the Dragon's adulterous wife and the jewel of her illicit union. After struggle, intrigue, capture, and a long bloody struggle through the halls of Len Yang, Peter smashes the Dragon's head with a rifle butt. Kahn Meng succeeds to power, swearing to use it to benefit China. And for all appearances, Peter and Aileen are going to marry.

If the adventure has been episodic, it has also been suspenseful enough. The acrid stink of danger wafts through the pages, accentuated by descriptions of streets and houses and rooms as crisp as fresh lettuce:

> Peter was beginning to catch occasional glimpses again of the flaunting blue veil under brass lamps, in the green and yellow light of stained windows. Shadowy faces appeared in doorways and retreated as (the rickshaw) darted past.
>
> Suddenly the rickshaw ahead swerved sharply to the right into an alley that was perfectly dark. Its single illumination was a pale-blue light which burned before a low building....
>
> ...There was a clink of coins. A door opened, letting out a wide shaft of orange light which spattered across the pavement, flattening itself against the grim wall of the building across the way.
>
> Peter caught the bronze glint of wires on the roof under a pale moon.[15]

The exterior scenes are described using images of mystery and menace borrowed from the moving pictures:

Long bright knives of light slithered across the wet payment from the sharp arc lights on the Garden bridge. The ghostly superstructure of a large and silent junk was thrown in silhouette against the yellow glow of a watchman's shanty across the dark canal....

It was a desolate night. The streets were deserted except for an occasional rickshaw with some mysterious, bundled passengers, the footfalls of the coolies sounding with a faint squashing as of drenched sandals, slimy with the heavy sludge of the back-village streets.[16]

The images are intensified not only by the use of sound but also color. The observation is exact:

The odor of costly incense was heavy and sweet, the smoke from a brazier arising in a thin, motionless blue spar which, when it had climbed up through the air for a distance of about four feet, broke into a sort of turquoise fan and this drifted on up to the ceiling in heavy wisps. The incense pot was very old, of black lacquer and brass, greened with blotches of erosion (*sic*).[17]

The descriptive method is precisely the same as practiced by the dime novels in their time, and the adventure paperbacks in our time: the scene is realistically described, dense with detail, a photograph of life. Across the scene, the melodramatic action whoops and prances, its improbability muted by the surrounding detail. The technique is wonderfully useful and is widely employed by those sinister individuals making television films.

For a year after "Peter the Brazen," no further adventures of Peter Moore were published. When the series reappeared, late in 1919, five years of fictional time had lapsed. In the interim, Peter had gone through World War I, been wounded at Verdun, and served with distinction as a lieutenant.

And poor Aileen had suffered the terrible fate reserved for women about to marry a series hero: she was killed when a submarine torpedoed the hospital ship on which she was nursing. (During this period, superfluous characters were regularly stripped from the story by placing them aboard a hospital ship, which Boche then sunk.)

So Aileen vanishes from the story, and Peter, gaunt and ravaged by regret, returns to China in a six-part serial titled "The Golden Cat" (November 22 through December 27, 1919, *The Argosy*). The serial is signed George F. Worts, with the pseudonym Loring Brent appearing in parenthesis.

"The Golden Cat" is more tightly integrated than the loose "Peter the Brazen." With commendable husbandry, the story recycles certain character types and most of the violence of the initial serial.

Peter has returned to China to visit a friend, Jan Sing, and his lovely sister, Shari. Complications begin instantly. By the time Peter reaches China—where he is immediately kidnapped—every character met is lying and betraying with fetching enthusiasm.

Behind it all grins another Chinese master intriguer, lurking and dreadful, whose minions swarm like water fleas: he is the bad evil Fong-Chi-Ah. And here is the lovely young sweetsie, Gloria Dale, said to be Fong's mistress. Gloria is brazen, tender, deceitful, mysterious, and struggles frantically to make up for the absence of Romola Borria.

Gloria shares with Romola characteristics of that female type which reached such popular acclaim during the 1920s—the girl of dubious reputation, whose actions scandalizes the neighborhood, as she drinks, smokes, bobs her hair, and whirls around in an open convertible, singing loudly. The type was familiar in stage melodrama and silent films, but it received its great interpreter in Joan Crawford, who portrayed a series of racy young women flaunting conventional morality. The 1928-1929 Crawford films recaptured the prancing girl who appeared in so many of F. Scott Fitzgerald's short stories—and would appear, warmly matured, in the later Thorne Smith novels.

All these distinguished sources agreed that this young lady only seemed bad; actually she was made of solid gold and stood on Heaven's side, sipping from a hip flask.

As you might suppose, Gloria Dale's reputation isn't much. Not that big, tough Jonathan Driggs cares. He loves her. But she is cool, indifferent....

Around Gloria's neck hangs a seven-hundred year old necklace, ornamented by a golden cat. Into the cat is carved a profile exactly resembling Gloria's own. Inexplicably, the necklace appears in Peter's pocket. Then it vanishes, replaced by a similar necklace in silver, Peter's friends also begin vanishing. A frenzied rushing about commences, seasoned by boat chases, collisions, close combat, gun fire, and scowling faces glaring through the window.

After a major part of the cast is kidnapped, Peter leads a rescue party to Fong's armed city. Following a savage fight, Peter is captured, tortured, driven from the city in disgrace. But not for long. Helped by Jan Sing, Mr. Moore returns to the stronghold and rescues Gloria. She has been kidnapped because her profile resembles that of the ancient Queen Shari—the profile graven upon the golden cat.

Seizing a junk, Peter and company race feverishly toward the Indian border. Behind them rages Fong in a black junk simply crammed with warriors. He overtakes them at the border and the fight is murderous. At last, Fong is taken, although Jan Sing is killed. The golden cat, that sacred talisman of the past, is returned to Jan's father.

By the end of the serial, Gloria has been vindicated and the reader is agog to see how Peter dodges matrimony this trip. But it isn't hard. Certainly he loves Gloria, indeed he does, but Jonathan Driggs loves her more. So Peter steps aside, face twisted by inner pain. No one bothers to ask Gloria her opinion of this admirable self sacrifice. Enough that Peter earns the reader's admiration and, quite incidentally, preserves his bachelorhood for a later serial.

But Worts did not get around to another Peter Moore adventure for eleven years. In the interim, he traveled in the Far East for *Colliers*, struggled with matrimonial problems, and wrote fiction for *Argosy*.

For its part, *The Argosy* combined with *All-Story Weekly* to become *Argosy All-Story Weekly*. Its covers grew bright, colorful, striking. The muted yellows and blues of 1918, which gave the covers the appearance of being printed on dried mustard, gave way to glowing reds and blues. Cover illustrations no longer looked as if the artist had lost interest half through the work. Now covers showed semi-realistic portraits of characters, or charming vignettes of a scene from the new serial. And as the Twenties faded into the Thirties, the cover illustration became increasingly cartoonish, increasingly devoted to picturing that taut moment just before all Hell broke loose.

During the same period, the narrative style of the magazine gradually concentrated. The more leisurely narratives of 1918, lavish with descriptions of scenery, dense with background and character history, fell away. It was as if a wave of acid had flowed across the narrative, etching away adverbs and prepositional phrases, leaving only a polished reef of verbs and short sentences. The short stories and serials, purged of such non-essentials as complex sentences and long paragraphs, raced urgently onward. It was stripped fiction. It shone like brass. Of no great depth and prone to lunge into tight-lipped sentimentality when emotion was called for, it was packed with conflict and action. The characters were vivid as a Picasso sketch, and no more realistic.

Worts was a master of the *Argosy* prose form. Over the years, his own style tightened and simplified. It fit *Argosy* as skin fits a living creature. He published enormous quantities of fiction in the magazine, gliding effortlessly from Peter the Brazen to Singapore Sammy to Gillian Hazeltine to the town in Florida to other non-series stories, and so through accumulating volumes.

Such facility requires payment. In the bright flash of adventure, who noticed that the characters personified single traits. That their experience did not change them. That story time was intensely compressed. That crime and malice drove the story. That the same basic situation repeated and again repeated.

Facile composition imposed such limitations. The reader glancing through a magazine of light fiction may notice nothing. But to read much of Worts is to notice how often Hazeltine is nearly disbarred or suspected of murder. And how frequently Peter Moore bumps painfully against the plots of Oriental Crime Emperors—or becomes involved with irresponsible women. Each Worts' series tends to repeat its own unique situation and characters. Upon these structuring elements, his shining variations are woven.

By the time that the new Peter the Brazen series began in *Argosy*, the adventures had been transformed. Simplified and quickened, they rushed shining across the page. The story atmosphere was still rich with colors, scents, and spectacles of the Orient. Much less of this material is included in the 1930s stories, for not only had the pace quickened but the length of novelettes and serial parts had quietly, and with no editorial commentary, shrunk back. To compare the 1918 stories with those of 1930 is to compare a grape to a raisin.

Still much is left. The action proceeds within a storm of vivid images: white jade bowls, the brazen crash of war drums, black and scarlet junks, thrones of translucent green jade, winding streets and alleys scummed with mud, green columns of smoke rising from breakfast charcoal fires, the harsh sound of river Cantonese, a doorway choked with knives and clubs and staring Chinese faces, sedan chairs lurching along the street, large copper coins, old men with a long bamboo pole between them which sags under the weight of a wicker basket.

The scene sprawls brilliantly, wonderful with foreign marvels. Its vitality springs from Worts' personal observations, but like all observations that get into fiction, the details have been selected and enhanced. Romance lacquers the paragraphs. A high-intensity current sizzles behind the prose. All is intensified.

A smile becomes a leer, a blow a beating, a disquieting thought a pulse of desperate fear.

Such enhancements are standard practice in creating fictional melodramas. They have the tendency to whirl the reader still further from reality. Characters drift quietly toward caricature; situations simplify toward cartoons. The increased narrative speed distorts everything, as speeds approaching that of light are said to distort everything. So the Peter Moore series hurtles along, its narrative pace ever increasing. The mundane world of 1918-1919 melts away. The realistic content of the stories shrinks like bacon in a hot pan. Dazzled and unthinking, we sweep from semi-realistic fiction into a world of fantastic romance as extraordinary as any that H. Rider Haggard or Edgar Rice Burroughs (two primary sources) ever got on paper.

Through the stories glide images that grow increasingly bizarre: a man whose brain has been carved from jade, another man who steals young women's blood, a murdering hypnotizer who collects his victims' skulls, an immense city concealed in a mountain, a lost kingdom of the kind that Tarzan used to discover, a living dragon, all teeth, horribly hissing.

The first Peter Moore story series was concrete, hard-edged, intense with living sounds and shadows. But in the second series, that realistic spareness begins unexpectedly to dissolve, like meaning in a fever dream.

The new series ran for five years, from 1930 to 1935. It consists of thirteen adventures—long and short serials and novelettes. In the course of these, Peter struggles with four continuing villains and contends with a feather-headed girl, Susan O'Gilvie, who provides the love interest, the suspense, and most of the plot situations.

Susan derives from the air-headed Whipple sisters of "The Golden Paw." Susan is trouble. Black-haired, violet-eyed, lovely, she is twenty years old, spoiled, immature, and consumed by the desire for Adventure, Excitement, Thrills.

She is also numbingly wealthy. Her father sold short in the 1929 stock market, doubling his fortune. As a result, Susan has enough personal money to buy a medium-sized city. Although plated by wealth against the world's sting, Susan itches to do something: to travel, to teach, to accomplish.

Her eyes glow. She swirls into action, hazing the world with hundred dollar bills. And, since she is innocent as a new born and has less judgment than a sea squirt, she finds adventure and excitement on every side. As Worts remarks, she was "the romantic type that would look for trouble until she found it."

On graduation from Berkeley, as a Bachelor of Arts, she boards ship for Indo-China and Hanoi. For she has accepted a job. The Sultan of Sakala has invited her to reorganize the educational system of his minute kingdom.

And now her troubles begin—and those of Mr. Moore.

In the first story of the new series, "The Sapphire Smile," February 8, 1930, she is sailing toward Vietnam and abduction in the rich tradition of the gulled girl. Although she doesn't realize it, the Sultan has murdered her father and devised an elaborate plot to seize her person and her wealth. Once more, as in "A Princess of Static," Peter stands between an innocent girl and an Oriental monster. To save her, he locks the bribed sea captain in his room and holes up with Susan in the ship's wireless room to fight off the entire crew.

No sooner has he extracted her from that danger, than she hurls herself joyously into another. In "The Man in the Jade Mask" (April 26, 1930), she meddles in the affairs of a powerful tong, attempting to buy their chief treasure, a solid emerald sceptre from the Ming dynasty. After that, she becomes part owner of a junkfull of opium ("That Cargo of Opium," June 21 and 28, 1930). In "The Hand of Ung," (November 22 and 29, 1930), she creeps into a forbidden temple, hoping to steal a giant ruby, ends fleeing with that most sacred of relics, the mummified hand of the god Ung.

She is frivolous, delightful, reckless. Or, in Peter's sour assessment, she is "too romantic, too excitable, too adventurous." She is barely five feet tall, acts like an innocent school girl with great large tender eyes, and calamity rolls relentlessly behind her. Such a sweet girl, too:

Her voice resembled the sound of pure metal struck upon sharply; clear and rather sweet and, like the rest of her, curiously suggestive of romance.[18]

Peter is drawn to her, infuriated by her. When she buys him a $75,000 jade Buddah as a birthday gift, he explodes: it is the sort of ill-proportioned generosity typical of her. They quarrel violently. Make up. And quarrel again. They agree not to see each other again, and Susan selects a young Englishman with whom she will settle down.

But she finds him boring. Terribly terribly boring. It takes her nearly a week to clear the Englishman from her memory and come rushing after Peter, Darling Peter.

In "Vampire" (April 25, May 2, 1931), she flies into a snit with Peter and claims to be in love with that plotting Sultan from "The Sapphire Smile." As usual, the sky collapses upon her. Not only is the Sultan married, but his wife suffers from an obscure blood disease. She has gone entirely bald and lives from one blood transfusion to another. To keep her alive, the Sultan kidnaps young women and transfuses their blood into his wife's voracious veins.

When Susan marches into his clutches, a chick braving the hawk's talons, the Sultan wants not only her blood but her splendid black hair. This he proposes to transplant to his wife's bare scalp. And in fine "B" moving picture fashion, Susan ends tightly strapped to an operating table, uttering thin noises as the glittering scalpel draws nearer and nearer. In the final seconds, she is saved by Peter and the crew of a U.S. destroyer.

It is all predictable and the effect never fails. Susan indulges herself in rash behavior, inadvertently tumbles over the lip of Hell, ends a microsecond from being drained of blood or hacked to tiny little ugly bits or tumbled off a high tower or devoured alive by a grisly thing. As doom lowers, the story cuts away to Peter, who is having his own troubles.

Resolving all his problems with gunfire or a sturdy blow to the jaw, he lunges into the secret room where Susan howls helplessly. And just in time.

After which Susan repents her rashness and all is well. Susan always repents, until the first paragraph of the next story.

The adventurous girl frequently appeared in those later western dime novels slanted toward a juvenile audience. With every issue of *Wild West Weekly*, Arietta plunged into some new peril, from which Young Wild West must extract her, eyes glinting brilliantly. In a somewhat different medium, Pearl White sought adventure and found calamity, week after week. Susan continued Pearl's glorious example, with her own particular flair for compounding trouble through brainlessness and inattention.

When Lester Dent introduced Doc Savage's thrill-hungry cousin, Patricia Savage, in 1934, he emphasized that she craved excitement as an addict craves his poison—although Patricia was admittedly far more mature and a great deal more efficient than Susan. Under all that radiant beauty, both women hunted adventure with terrifying concentration. As a result, they spent much of their lives being rescued.

The woman in danger is a suspense device that transcends time and fictional form. Some twenty thousand years ago, they told a story, as the campfire snapped and glowed, about a young woman who was told not to walk too close to the glacier. But she tossed her head and did so, anyway. In fact, she climbed on one of the forward bulges and a piece broke off and pinned her in the slush and rocks. She screamed. But nobody heard. It grew dark. Her trapped leg numbed. She shuddered with cold. Then, from the shadows, crept a wolverine. Teeth gleamed in its terrible jaws as it slunk closer...

Any story device that has been around for twenty thousand years should be honored, not dismissed with a sneer—"That's a pulp magazine cliché."

Granted that it is a pulp magazine cliché, just as it was a dime novel cliché, and a ballad cliché, and today a paperback and television cliché. That it was used so frequently in the Peter the Brazen series is a direct consequence of Susan O'Gilvie's character. Given her extreme volatility and ingenuousness, she is predestined to end in terrible danger, requiring saving frequently. It's the heroine's function to whip suspense to the heights. When she is saved, through no fault of her own, a tingling glow warms the male reader's circulatory system. Whether a similar glow touches the feminine blood stream is unknown to this commentator, who is inadequately equipped to unsnarl cosmic complexities.

Susan's personality not only triggers these stories but causes Worts to make certain mild changes in Peter Moore.

From the beginning of the series, Peter is featured as a fearless young man with a talent for getting into trouble. To emphasize that point, the 1930s stories are packed with references to past adventures and the tumult they caused. (None of these adventures were written out for *Argosy* readers.) We are given only a bare reference: how he rescued the lovely girl and won an emerald large as a dove's egg; how he attempted to steal the relic of Ung; how the leader of China's Thieves' Guild detained him for a month in a sort of house arrest; how he helped to drive Zarlo, that hypnotizing fiend, from the Philippines; how he interferred with operations of The Green Circle (China's most powerful tong) and the Blue Scorpion (a secret, silent power greater than Fu Manchu); how he nearly ignited an Asian war; how the authorities directed him to leave the Far East.

And he did leave for five years. Perhaps it was by agreement with The Green Circle; perhaps the French or American authorities cancelled his visa. We are not told why. What is clear that when he again returned to China, he was determined to stay out of trouble, "to put high adventure behind him forever."

That proved difficult to do. And perhaps Worts did not expect us to take that resolution seriously. But what is a poor author to do. It would be injudicious and artistically incorrect to have two major characters banging around in a series, headstrong and impulsive, looking for trouble and finding it. Since Susan is a wonderfully vital character, and since the storyline required that Susan constantly hurl herself into trouble, then Peter's enthusiasm for blood and violence had to be downplayed. Thus his stated disinclination to adventure.

The change is only paper-deep. Peter enjoys as many hair-raising adventures as before. But not because he sought them out, you understand. They were forced on him by Susan's ridiculous behavior. That makes all the difference.

Unfortunately, no friend or acquaintance believes that Peter has sworn off adventure. Oh, no. They know him to be:

...a reckless adventurer and a most dangerous young man. He took all laws unto himself. He was so bold, so audacious that the Chinese coined a name for him—Ren-Beh-Tung, which means The Brass Man. Among Americans and British residents he was known, whimsically, as Peter the Brazen.[19]

That explanation of the nickname was never mentioned in the 1918-1919 stories. The matter need not delay us, unless you get pleasure in watching authors being inconsistent. If such things delight you, the 1930s stories will cause spasms of joy, for inconsistency of minor detail is a major characteristic of the series. It is a consequence of working from memory, not re-reading past work, and assuming that what has been published will evaporate, leaving no residue. Conan Doyle scattered inconsistencies throughout the Sherlock Holmes series, and George Worts is equally casual in recording Peter Moore's exploits.

Neither gentleman is the equal of Norvell Page, whose *Spider* magazine novels attain levels of self-contradiction and inconsistency that suggest bland teasing rather than narrative disorder.

As the second series opens, Peter is employed by the radio research division of General Electric. He has returned to China with instructions from GE to purchase a technological marvel—a device that will suppress radio static. That device has been invented by Fong Toy, a young scientist and near genius.

Peter's search for Fong Toy links the initial six stories. The inventor is as elusive as prosperity. Repeatedly, Peter almost meets him. But not quite. Throughout, the search is complicated by Susan's hair-brained prancings.

The quest nears its end in "Chinese for Racket" (May 30 and June 6, 1931). After months of delay, Peter has an appointment with Fong Toy at one o'clock in the morning. Only a few hours before this time, an acquaintance enters with an astonishing story: his sister was kidnapped in San Francisco. Brought to China, she will be sold this very night to a wealthy Chinese national, unless Peter....

Yes, Peter will help, if reluctantly. And so we proceed from one surprise to another, constantly struggling against that one o'clock deadline. At last Peter faces Fong Toy, examines that marvelous bit of hardware. And the shape of an ambitious swindle becomes clear.

From this point on, the story line gives a little shake, like a horse about to bolt, and becomes a series of struggles against series villains. It becomes Peter's destiny to interfere with three powerful people and get menaced and threatened and chased by armies of screaming minions, hot for his dismemberment. That he lived through even one adventure is proof of miracles.

To begin with, he got crosswise with the Blue Scorpion.

When a young man, the Blue Scorpion tumbled over a cliff and mashed his head. The clever doctor attending him apparently remembered the Oz stories. He operated and gave the Scorpion a jade brain, so that he thinks more wonderfully than all living men. The first thing he thought of was power. Within a decade or so, he was the absolute, if invisible, master of China. He ruled from a marble cave at the bottom of a lake in the Shan Mountains. His henchmen swarmed. His power was total. He, himself, was said to be immortal—as was said of Fu Manchu.

All this is reasonably familiar to those steeped in sensational literature. It is part Sax Rohmer, part H. Rider Haggard, part Edgar Rice Burroughs, and altogether stimulating. The Scorpion—or Mr. Lu as he is familiarly known— is essentially invincible. His weapon is poison:

> ...It is some alkaloid, compounded with the venom of an exceedingly poisonous snake found only in the Tibetan foothills. It is so poisonous...that one drop placed in a stream will kill a man who drinks the water of that stream a mile below....
> ...The victim's body instantly turns a luminous sapphire blue. Its effect is instant and systemic. Yet it particularly singles out the brain. The brain turns to water. A few seconds later, the eyes turn as black, as opaque, as two balls of coal.[20]

That elixir is used sparingly. Before the Scorpion turns you sapphire blue, he sends warning—a tiny pyramid of blue chalk. Receive one of those and either pick your headstone or leave for the States on the next boat.

All this wonderful stuff is introduced in "Cave of the Blue Scorpion" (November 21, 1931). As usual, Susan starts matters off with the wrong investment. She funds an expedition by Prince Took Shan to raid the Scorpion's marble palace and cart off its wealth. To drain the lake, as is his plan, heavy equipment is required. By a remarkable coincidence, Peter is the GE representative for portable power plants and electric pumps.

Before you take two breaths, Peter and Susan are the Prince's prisoners at The Lake of the Flying Dragon. The Prince's men are slaughtering nearby villagers. The lake is being pumped out. Then Susan vanishes, kidnapped by the Blue Scorpion and Peter goes alone into the labyrinth beneath lake and mountain to find her. He does so, after chapters of intense suspense and terror. Eventually the Blue Scorpion permits them to leave. The Prince stays but he is thoroughly dead by then and doesn't care.

"Sting of the Blue Scorpion" (five parts, November 19 through December 17, 1932) and "The Sapphire Death" (six parts, June 10 through July 15, 1933) continue and conclude the story of the Man with the Jade Brain.

In the first serial, Dr. Luigi Strang, an American professor, plans to steal the secret of the Scorpion's poison. Then ambition grows in him like nut grass in a garden. He decides to operate on Susan's brain to make her love him; he decides to kill the Scorpion and take his place. He is full of plans. Unfortunately, his lovely blond wife, Karen, is an agent of the Scorpion. She arranges Susan's kidnapping, sets one of Susan's suitors snarling after Peter with a pistol, and warns the Scorpion of Strang's ambitions.

Two thousand miles away, Peter is directing the construction of a hydro-electric project. Nearby is a Black Pagoda and in this pagoda these twisted threads come together. Strang dies of poison, the suitor of Karen's knife. The voice of the Scorpion, ringing from a sealed room, offers Peter wealth if he will assist in the construction of a ray to annihilate New York City, a worthy objective. The idea is to scare the Americans and take over all that nation's wealth.

Peter refuses, as is only right. Trapped in the flaming pagoda, he escapes with Susan. Finds thousands of sampans converging on the power plant, about to swallow it up for the Scorpion. Obliterates these by opening the dam gates. End round two.

But it has been an exhausting struggle. Peter and Susan, mightily shaken, decide to leave China. Susan is all ready to marry him, but Peter won't hear of it. After all, she is one of the world's most wealthy women and he has nothing. First he must make a million or so, and then....

It may strike you that these frenzied goingson have little to do with the sharp-eared wireless operator of 1918 and his struggles against human devilitry. There is little human in the Blue Scorpion and even less in Zarlo, The Master Magician. Zarlo occupies a single story inserted between "The Sting of the Blue Scorpion" and "The Sapphire Death." In hardly a paragraph of "The Master Magician" (February 25, 1933) is there concern to tell a realistic story. It is continuous, furious action, white-hot. Peter, himself, is transformed to that most marvelous of creatures, an action-story hero. Racing, striking, leaping, carrying, straining, gasping, raging, battling, he pounds through reeling pages, a prince of violence:

In a twisting lunge, he carried the (man) to the floor. For just a moment, the fingers at his throat slipped away. And Peter drove his fists like battering rams into the distorted face. In a space of seconds he struck a dozen tremendous blows before the red-headed man could reach his throat again....

Peter picked up the pistol and staggered to the door, which Susan had closed.

He said hoarsely, 'Come on. It's our last chance!' And flung the door open.

The hall outside was, at a glance, a solid, packed mass of black bodies, black men waiting.

Peter fired into them. A man fell. Another. He aimed deliberately. They fell back, turned to rush him, but they wilted before that deadly fire. Some ran. Peter dropped the pistol when the hammer fell, finally, with a click, and picked up a *parang*. With this, he ran one black man through the throat.[21]

The story, itself, is one long howl of fury. Zarlo, a sorcerer and worker of black magic, is a powerful hypnotist. He steals your will with his searing eyes. Some years before, Peter and four others drove Zarlo from the Phillipines. Fled to Skull Island, south of Borneo, Zarlo has commandeered a castle, turned the owner into a mindless beast, and is now collecting the skulls of the five who defeated him.

Susan has been kidnapped away to Skull Island, bait for Zarlo's trap. Peter follows, plunging into deadly adventures. He is captured. Escapes, making hash of the opposition. Rescues Susan—but not for long; a post-hypnotic suggestion draws her back to the castle.

To save her once more, Peter wages another bloody fight through the castle. Finally he stands face to face with The Beast, the true owner of the castle, mindless and hypnotized to superhuman strength. Peter slugs The Beast so savagely, it/ he turns on Zarlo, crushing him to death and ending a breathless novelette sparkling with energy.

At which point, we return to the final story of the Blue Scorpion series: "The Sapphire Death." It is a peculiar story. Very much so.

Peter has decided to settle matters with the Blue Scorpion, once and for all. This is rather like deciding to settle with Hitler or Stalin. Perhaps the parallel isn't exact, for Hitler and Stalin were, after all, public figures. The Blue Scorpion is a shadow, a hissing voice, a receding dimness.

However intangible the opponent, Peter is determined to end him. It is an echo of former times on the trail of the Gray Dragon.

To have a free hand in his campaign, Peter fakes his own death, after the well-known example of Sherlock Holmes. Like Watson, Susan is not informed that Peter still lives. This is very tough on Susan and you feel sorry for her—realizing, at the same time, that if she were entrusted with The Secret of The Universe, she would tell it in Macy's window at high noon. It only took a couple of months for her to babble out the location of the Scorpion's palace—and she knew that the penalty was an anguished, extended, and atrocious death. Susan was thoroughly terrified of the Scorpion. Yet she talked. By mistake, but nevertheless....

But to continue. No sooner is Peter officially deceased, than he plunges into six months of rigorous physical training. For he has a plan.

He will disguise himself. He will become a member of the Scorpion's inner circle, kill the Scorpion, and destroy the Sapphire Skull, symbol of the Fiend's power.

To do all this, it is necessary that he become High Priest of the Skull.

To become High Priest, it is necessary that he win the Scorpion's yearly gladitorial games. These are held in Vietnam at the Temple of the Coiled Serpent.

How Peter learned so much about the games, the rituals, the selection of the High Priest, and allied information is a consequence of one of those coincidences that occur once every 100,000,000 years. By sheer accident, Peter saved the life of a fierce young Tibetan. This admirable fellow had defected from the position of High Priest, having noted, with some anxiety, that each year's Priest vanished mysteriously toward the end of his term.

Coached by this alert fellow, Peter begins an extended preparation for the games—which are harsh and dangerous. They involve hand-to-hand combat, fire walking, lengthy underwater swimming through a maze tricked out by traps, and related trials in which, if you failed once, you were dead always.

Such merry games mingling physical exertion and death had appeared in fiction long before pulp magazines. The pulps continued that grand tradition. At various times, in various stories, in such various magazines as *Adventure*, *Weird Tales*, *Fantastic Adventures*, and *Blue Book*, some hero would blunder into a lost world; immediately he would be tumbled into an arena, where a tough waited to split him with a sword. Different versions of the situation have appeared in such varied media as an Asterix the Gaul film in the 1980s, a Flash Gordon Sunday comic in the mid-1930s, and a 1928-1929 Tarzan serial in *Blue Book*.

It is as likely that the Scorpion's games were suggested to Worts by the 1932 Olympics at Los Angeles, as by Tarzan's adventure. Only the Recording Angel knows for sure. Enough that the games Peter entered were in the delicious tradition of the Roman Empire: continuous death. One hundred and thirty candidates entered; one survived. Depressing odds.

While the competition for High Priest continued, a second competition was held to select The Sacrificial Lamb. This honor was aspired to only by the most beautiful of women. The winner received the homage of all, after which the Scorpion slit her throat in a touching ceremony.

The Sacrificial Lamb seems an honor no one with sense would seek. For this reason, Susan, appropriately disguised, enters the competition. She intends to avenge Peter's death by killing the Blue Scorpion.

And so the chapters fly, driven by blood and terror. At length, just as in a story, Peter and Susan win their respective competitions and stand breathless before the Scorpion, himself.

After all these pages, he is revealed to us as a powerful, tall man whose face is concealed by a silver mask studded by sapphires. Some calamity has sheared off both hands at the wrists; perhaps it occurred when he tumbled down that cliff. Both stumps are capped by metal, also brilliant with sapphires. Under the black hair at the back of his head gleams a metallic white triangle, indication of desperate surgery long past.

As you know, it is the practice of sinister Chinese terrors to toy with their victims, first allowing them the illusion of success, then snatching that success away, while laughing inhumanly. So the sophisticated reader will feel no surprise to learn that the Scorpion has known all along of Peter and Susan and their participation in his games.

Now confrontation. Contemptuous mockery. The Scorpion attacks, flailing with his arm stumps.

A severely realistic view of the situation at this point would assume that Peter would promptly lose, since he has spent hours undergoing the fury of the ordeal. He should barely be able to stand without help. However, it is universally known that the hero of an action story has limitless physical resources. Usually. In this case, Peter makes a good fight. He attacks savagely, knocking off the Scorpion's gemmed mask and exposing the distorted scar tissue that is his face. But at the end, the Scorpion batters Peter down and the series is about to end as no series has ended before.

At this moment, Susan drives a knife against the metal plate at the back of the Scorpion's head. Down he tumbles, dead. Peter hurls the Sapphire Skull into a pit of flame. The reign of the Blue Scorpion and his three-story series, is over, at last.

The serial ends with the engagement of Peter and Susan. Connoisseurs of popular fiction will instantly assume that Susan dies. But for once that convention is not observed. The lovers are instantly separated, of course, as is only to be expected.

As always in the Peter the Brazen series, the story line takes an unexpected and somewhat uncomfortable turn, as if, just beneath the brightly colored surface of the adventure, another adventure proceeds that we are not permitted to watch. We see the characters do wholly unexpected things and act in ways foreign to their personalities. Particularly Susan. Susan behaves strangely, indeed, nor is it clear to the end of the series precisely what has twisted sideways in her excited mind. It is as if this charming fantasy woman has stepped through a mirror and at once had her warmth converted to frigidity, her enthusiasm to indifference, her uncritical acceptance to studied rejection. You can blame drugs in the first story but not later.

It happens this way.

"The Octopus of Hong Kong" (March 31, 1934) is the first of three sequential stories, separate but closely related. It is the day before the Moore-O'Gilvie marriage and Susan has become cold, arrogant, indifferent, and subtly evil. Improbable as it seems, she has been dosed with a hypnotic drug by that mistress of Oriental Crime called Lotus Burma, the Octopus of Hong Kong—so named because she keeps a giant octopus as a pet, feeding it with her enemies. Wealthy, an opium addict, descended from emperors, Lotus steps onstage amid a thunder of crime. She has stolen two million dollars worth of diamonds, abducted an innocent girl, and drugged Susan into incomprehensible folly.

The abducted girl will be tossed to the octopus for revenge, Revenge! The diamonds and Susan will be delivered to Lotus' half-brother, Hassan Barbarossa, an infernal monster.

Hassan is the hereditary ruler of a pirate swarm operating from a valley hidden away in coastal mountains—The Valley of the Lost. The valley walls are unscalable. Escape is possible only along a waterway that opens into the Gulf of Tongking. Entrance to that waterway is concealed by immense doors that have, for centuries, protected the pirates from discovery.

Hassan, a red-bearded giant of touchy temper, incomparable ego, and eleven wives, is the power behind Lotus. She obeys his directions, fronts for him in the outside world, plots and steals for him. Between assignments, she amuses herself by being desperately evil, as such women are in such stories.

During the events of "The Octopus of Hong Kong," Peter opposes Lotus with sterling heroism. He infiltrates her headquarters, battles her minions, fights her octopus, and saves the endangered girl. Lotus is admirable, a full-scale menace in her own right; she succeeds in retaining the diamonds and, in the best tradition of the dime novels and silent movies, her sinister influence over Susan. It's that purple drug she's been feeding Miss O'Gilvie.

The drug is one of those fabulous elixirs whose medical effect is whatever the author wishes it to be. Popular fiction knows these drugs well. They are usually administered to stimulate a plot whose internal absurdities would otherwise cause it to collapse. One dram of such a drug easily resolves all narrative problems. It can steal away your personality or make you a better one, improve the physique, simulate disease or death, and create necessary plot complications or eliminate them. It is perfectly wonderful.

Under the influence of this drug, Susan cancels her engagement to Peter, trots aboard ship with Lotus, and off they sail to Vietnam and the kingdom of Hassan, where Susan is to become his twelfth wife. Whether she realizes that or not is a moot point. Every so often, the drug wears off and Susan goes to pieces until she is re-medicated:

(Susan's) eyes and cheeks were red and swollen. Her hair was rumpled. Her clothing was disarranged.... She was still sobbing, still blind with tears....

(Lotus Burma) seized Susan by the throat, pushed her head back. And when Susan wriggled away, Lotus Burma grasped a handful of the girl's hair close to the scalp and twisted it. Susan screamed and became limp. She might have fainted.

Lotus Burma unstoppered the phial and pressed the mouth of it between Susan's lips. A drop or two of the incredible purple drug escaped, trickling down the girl's chin.

The woman released her and stepped back. Peter, staring with fascination, saw a subtle change, then a more striking change come over Susan. She no longer wept. Her head came up. Magically, she took on an aspect of haughty dignity. She became regal.[22]

Susan's primary problem is that she is a character in a story which demands that she behave in ways she would not. Through the five parts of the serial, "Kingdom of the Lost" (August 25 through September 22, 1934), she degrades to a caricature of herself. Since her personality was already prancing cartoon, you wouldn't think that possible. But it is. She swaggers, howls, preens, weeps with immense gusto, if little consistency.

Worts blames the purple drug. We blame Worts.

The "Kingdom of the Lost" is no miracle of consistency, either. The action pounds along in a frenzy, accumulating complications with each paragraph.

Terribly shaken by being jilted on his wedding day, Peter decides to recover the stolen diamonds from Lotus Burma. Disguised as a sultan, he boards the ship she is taking back to Vietnam. To confuse matters ever more thoroughly, a representative of the US government is aboard disguised as Peter.

Before the trip is over, piracy and mass murder breaks out. Peter contrives to steal the diamonds from Lotus, is strung up by his thumbs—which does not appear to inconvenience him much—and has a generally sweaty time dodging, tricking, and fighting.

Ultimately they arrive at the Valley of the Lost. There Hassan immediately sentences Lotus to death. No matter that she is his half-sister and has brought a dizzy American woman for his wife. She lost those diamonds and it must be doom. You can understand his feelings. It is a shame to waste so vivid a character as Lotus Burma, but she has no role in the remaining series and can be disposed of dramatically.

And so she is. For in these stories, doom arrives in decorative ways. Lotus is condemned to dance atop a tall tower until her blood bubbles with ecstasy and she flies off into space to puncture herself on that mass of spears far below.

She does. It is most dramatic. Immediately afterward, Peter is cast from the city to die among the clay-eaters along the river bank. Instead he stirs them to rebellion and reenters the city. As murder boils up in the streets, Peter makes a last desperate attempt to save them all. But the man they bribed to help them escape changes his mind. As he bolts to reveal all to Hassan, Susan shoots him dead. Then, to create a diversion that will allow Peter to escape, she rushes to the tower top, dances in view of all, lurches, reels into space, as the spears glint horribly below.

She is dead. She is dead. Lovely Susan is dead!

In white fury, Peter knifes Hassan and leaves him crushed in a bronze door. With his double and the diamonds, Peter sails from the valley. Once outside, he drives the ship solidly against the valley doors, sealing off the area for all time—and, as Peter later lamented, condemning half a million people to die of starvation.

But what is half a million people when we have lost a major series character? Susan dead? Unthinkable.

It is the authentic touch of Edgar Rice Burroughs. How often in his novels does this happen? Tarzan's Jane is believed dead, or Dejah Thoris; or some admirable character offers himself for sacrifice to save his friends and might as well be dead.

That nobody is ever dead is quite beside the point. It is the belief in the character's death which shakes the pages and stains the reader's beard with tears.

As with Burroughs, so with Worts.

Throughout the serial, Susan's behavior has been increasingly inconsistent and bizarre. Now we understand why. It was all in preparation for her redemption by self sacrifice. In order that she be redeemed, she must first fall from grace. And she must fall by personality flaw, not because she was full of purple syrup.

Unfortunately for his plans, when Worts gets this far, he discovers that the worst he can say about Susan is that she is adventurous and lacks foresight:

> Reputed to be the richest young woman in America, if not in the world, Susan O'Gilvie was an insatiable thrill hunter—a girl with a craving, a hunter for adventurous excitement that nothing could appease. Time after time, since she had been in Asia, she had plunged herself into dangerous predicaments, and had frantically called upon Peter Moore to help...she had—always with the most innocent of intentions—drawn him into one dangerous Oriental complication after another.[23]

But this is describing a person by a single passion, as they used to do by personalizing one quality as a character: Lord Greed, Mr. Sly, Miss Simple. Since one-quality characters have all the interest of a comic valentine, it is now necessary to whip up some derogatory remarks about Susan in order that she may rise above them.

Which explains this sudden burst of character assassination as Susan preens before a mirror:

> ...Susan was fully aware how beautiful she was. She was proud of her loveliness, of her slim, exquisite body, of her small, beautiful hands and feet. She was an aristocrat....
>
> But Susan was as selfish as she was lovely. She loved Peter Moore as she had never believed she could ever love a man. She adored him. But she had no intention, after their marriage, of letting Peter spoil her life. There would be no children. There would be no settling down, no comfortable security—and respectability.
>
> Why should they settle down? With the whole world at their disposal—a world teeming with exciting and dangerous adventure for the asking. And her wealth—her wonderful

millions—a magic carpet on which they would fly here and there and into the most fascinating and dangerous thrills.[24]

Within two pages of this moment, she has been forced to shoot a turn-coat dead, and has decided to give her life for the others. No particular reason, except that it will make a strong dramatic climax.

> She was not afraid now. Her eyes were shining as they had never shone before. Her face was transfigured. It glowed as with an inner light. For perhaps the first time in her life, Susan—spoiled, selfish, willful, greedy Susan—was proud of something beside her exquisite beauty.[25]

It's depressing to be told that she is spoiled, selfish, willful, and greedy, since all along she has been presented only as a light-headed darling. A little willful, perhaps. But those other adjectives! Where did they come from? We have never noticed that Susan was spoiled, selfish, and greedy to this point. Worts completely forgot to let us know. And now, when we must have this information, in order to marvel at Susan's redemption, he is forced to load all his adjectives into a single sentence and blast us with them, all at once, as if he were firing a muzzle-loading cannon.

But there's no point to sitting here snarling. Psychological realism is no part of this story. If the narrative technique seems, at best, unsophisticated, its purpose is to bring the story to an intense emotional climax. Effect is everything. If effect required that narrative probability be sacrificed (as in Burroughs) or character distorted (as in Worts), you sacrificed and distorted with zeal. The reader never remembered. Or, if he did, he didn't care.

You would think it impossible that such a literary trick as a leading character's presumed death could be used more than once. Burroughs, however, used it unsparingly throughout the Tarzan and the John Carter series. The trick was promptly adopted by the single-character magazines, the hottest fad of the 1933 news stands. Soon the presumed death of Doc Savage, The Phantom Detective, Richard Wentworth. Operator 5 was lamented monthly. Not that the hero died or even got scratched much. But his friends and enemies continued to believe it so, issue after issue, long after readers grinned at the device.

In the Peter Moore series, the reader is not asked to grieve long for Susan. She returns promptly to life in the novelette "Over the Dragon Wall" (April 6, 1935), published six months after the conclusion of "Kingdom of the Lost." "Dragon Wall" would be the final story of the series.

According to the Worts, "Over the Dragon Wall" is a Chinese image for either the act of dying or the ascent to new earthly happiness. The novelette opens in misery: Peter's misery. "Moore, with his gaunt eyes (*sic*) and tragic, embittered mouth, looked haggard, old." To forget his load of grief, he accepts a job to seek out a dragon, rumored to be found in a hill temple of Sandrakar, Indo-China, up near Tibet. If there is such a thing as a dragon, he will attempt to capture it for a circus.

Rumor says that it is an admirable dragon twenty feet long and having three eyes. Of a rich, deep green, it gulps men whole, and also becomes white-hot twice a year.

As Peter heads toward Sandrakar, so does Susan. She does not know where she is going and she does not know who she is. Amnesia, you see.

Amnesia is a plot device afflicting Burroughs heroes; minor pulp fiction characters whose true identities are discovered at story's end; and characters in soap operas, whose condition extends the story line well nigh forever. When encountered in the psychiatrist's office, it is a serious problem, being a condition whereby a personality evades intolerable reality by extinguishing itself. In popular fiction it is an interesting condition caused by being scared or thumped on the head, and the sufferer can be cured by re-thumping the head or re-scaring them, after suitable adventures.

Susan's amnesia started right after she was saved from death. As she toppled over the edge of the tower, her robe was gripped from behind. The angle from which Peter watched prevented him seeing her rescue. Soon she is in the custody of Lak Lon, a sly plotter, who smuggles her out of the unescapable valley through a secret cleft. He plans to take her to Tashwar and present her as a gift to his sultan.

Before she becomes royalty's toy, they arrive in Sandrakar. There the ruler slaughters Lak Lon, who has served his purpose, and tosses Susan to the dragon.

Some time passes.

Peter arrives in Sandrakar and *he* gets tossed to the dragon. To his surprise, the dragon is as large and green as rumor said. But it is also gentle, sweet, and a vegetarian. The famous third eye is an emerald set in its head.

The dragon is tended by a priestess, also gentle and sweet. He is stunned to find that she is Susan. "He had never seen (her) so subdued, so meek, so gentle. She had been so gay, so exuberant, so mischievous." Since she has amnesia, she can give no account of herself. However, old habits of the heart die hard; in a matter of pages, she has fallen in love with him again.

The rest of the story is undemanding light adventure. They almost escape, are trapped, trick the wicked by painting themselves and the dragon with phosphorescent paint, in the manner of the Baskerville hound. In a brisk climax, the dragon snaps up the villain of the piece. Peter and Susan escape, meet a caravan heading back to civilization. So all problems are effortlessly solved.

Susan's amnesia still needs fixing. To do so, Peter fakes an apparition of the Blue Scorpion that scares Susan back to herself.

They are married in Angkor.

The dragon is delivered to the circus.

Susan is as bouncy as ever.

And the series ends.

3—

The Far East is filled with dragons, they say, lurking invisible among the ancient hills. Over those old lands hangs the smell of blood. There have been too many people, too much passion, too much death, far too much history. All those things create dragons.

George Worts saw the Far East and whatever it was that disturbed him about it got into his prose. Darkness peered around the ends of his paragraphs, and now and then, behind the simple cadences of his sentences, you can hear a distant, uneasy whispering, as if something rather frightening is muttering to itself, off in the darkness.

Something troubled him about women. Something bothered him about long-term relationships or becoming emotionally involved or staying that way. Other men have sweated under similar pressures. Worts transformed his into action fiction.

That public exposure of private dragons revealed less than you might think.

You can sense him grappling with them down in the basement of his fiction. It is the way he selects events and defines his characters. His Singapore Sammy, you realize, is a fine fighting leader; but he is also a man emotionally sealed off, as if a slice of interstellar space were enclosed in a human skin. Peter the Brazen, you recognize, regards emotional commitment as dangerous. How deftly does Peter dodge about, grasping his immaculate bachelorhood. And how immature are the women in his life. So infantile, so spoiled, willful, and greedy.

Only the meek little supporting women of the series can love. And they love Peter. And it is hopeless.

These are dragons, indeed, of some kind. What they mean, Lord knows. We know by their repetition in his work that they mean something. Beyond that, we know nothing. Even the present author, towering intelligence as he is, will go no further.

Worts' version of the Far East action story began as melodramatic romance flushed with realism and ended as high-action fantasy. His Orient was a composite of what he had seen and what he had read in Sax Rohmer, Edgar Rice Burroughs, and such action writers as Gordon Young. As the Chinese Crime Emperor is reflected in Peter the Brazen, so the hardboiled fighting skipper looms over the Singapore Sammy series.

For about five years—to 1935—Worts' China was the main version to be found in *Argosy*. Only W. Wirt's Jimmie Cordie series provided an alternative: that series offered a series of para-military adventures by a band of irregulars who fought Chinese war lords and such sinister folk.

For all his continuous presence in *Argosy*, Worts does not seem to have been an important influence on others. His characters, images, and devices were conventions of the time. Essentially he invented little, although he applied, with wonderful vigor, the materials of his precursors. His most vivid figure is the adventure-mad young woman; but even she, as we have noted, was borrowed from moving pictures.

Makes no difference. His prose crackled with vitality. Scenes shot past, hot with tension. They sparkled brightly. They dragged you on, intent, to the final period. It is wonderful work, crisp and fresh.

And no wonder. Worts had crossed the water to touch the Orient, himself. He did. It showed.

While Peter Moore followed adventure's banner through Far Eastern dangers, other notable figures tried their luck in lands even more remote and less civilized. Along great slow rivers, beneath tropical canopy, through humidity and menace, other adventurers tramped the treacherous soil of Africa.

It is to the ferocities of the Dark Continent that we now turn.

Chapter 3
Out of Africa

China is ancient and has an extended history, but that history is human, a record of shining successions folding one into the other back through time. It is otherwise with Africa.

Africa is an elder god and lives detached from human time, most of its history untainted by the curious behavior of man in his various ancestral forms. Though we can trace man far back in time, Africa's history is longer, larger, richer, grimmer, and more beautiful. Mankind is one of many shadows drifting across its enormity. For Africa is not just a place of specialized vegetation and animals, but a place that stretches back through time like an immense corridor, resonating with the past, little of it touched by human concerns.

That is the point of so much fiction about Africa and African adventure. The usual story tells how a member of our culture faced Africa, that dark and deadly place, and opened such secrets as he was able, and acquitted himself finely or not in the face of the ancient, the primitive, and the terrible. This form of the African story, then, is an adventure moving along two levels.

On the first level, an individual travels across physical Africa, marveling at its contours and evading its frequent dangers. On the second level, the individual confronting Africa also confronts himself. He finds his soul floating among the thorn trees; it is his face that glowers beneath the savage's paint.

Which sounds rather tedious and psychological. Heaven forbid that we should become tedious and psychological in discussing magazine fiction about Africa. Just listen to that lion roar. Just look at that lost city, and that perfectly splendid priestess without any clothes on. And what was it you said about psychology?

2—

H(enry) Rider Haggard (1856-1925) was a young man of no particular promise, at all. Despairing that the boy, then nineteen, would amount to anything, his father arranged an appointment for him on the staff of a family friend, Sir Henry Bulmer, who was preparing to take up the duties of Lieutenant Governor to the South African state of Natal. So Rider Haggard came to Africa, still in his teens and with the rather vague duties of a social aide-de-camp.

Things African fascinated Haggard. He plunged into the languages, the history of the region, the history of the Zulus, whose kingdom the area had once been, and he got a strong, first-hand sniff at the political complexities tainting the air.

In that time and place, men still lived who had fought during the brutal Zulu Wars, forty years before. Communities of Zulus still lived throughout Natal, although no longer unified into a warlike kingdom. Rider Haggard went among them, learning their language, hearing their stories. In 1877, he began his extended writing career with the publication, in the *Gentleman's Magazine*, of an account of a Zulu war dance.

If the Zulu menace seemed past, the Boer menace was soon to fume up. Sixty years earlier, Dutch farmers, known as Boers, rejected British rule, left the Cape Colony, and marched to a region north of Natal that became known as the Transvaal. That became Dutch independent territory, carved, of course, from the land of the natives. That also caused continuing dissension between the Boers and the tribes. Shortly after Haggard arrived in Natal, so much disturbance had boiled up in the Transvaal, that the English government appointed a commissioner to investigate the cause of all the unrest. Amid rumors that the British were preparing to annex the Transvaal, Sir Theophilus Shepstone, the government's special commissioner, began a tour of the area, taking with him Rider Haggard.[1] For some months, they moved through old Africa, hunting, exploring, camping, meeting a variety of personalities and races, many of whom would appear in Haggard's subsequent work.

In 1879, at the age of 26, Haggard returned to England and took up the study of law. He also wrote two novels, which suggests that his law studies were not pursued with undivided zeal.

With his third novel, *King Solomon's Mines* (1885), he found both his subject and his public. The *Mines* was written in six weeks, the result of a bet with his brother that Rider could write something as good as *Treasure Island*. In this novel, Allan Quatermain, the great white hunter, is introduced, and fiction was enriched by a new character. Unlike most Great White Hunters of other fiction, Allan Quatermain is small, unpretentious, past middle age, so quietly modest that no one suspects the depth and intensity of his cynicism. A deadly shot, he knows intuitively the exact point where the bullet will meet the target. As a professional outdoorsman, he is most comfortable among the bushes and snakes. Formal clothing strangles him. Society—and the ladies of society—frankly terrifies him. Through fourteen novels and four short stories, Haggard followed the fortunes of Quatermain, one of the most interesting of all adventure heroes— particularly since the second novel about him, *Allan Quatermain*, set at the end of his career and describes his final battle and death. Not many heroes die and then continue through another dozen books.

In the United States, Quatermain's adventures were reprinted in *The Popular Magazine*, the *New Story Magazine*, and in *Hursts's American Weekly*, in various hardback editions, authorized and otherwise. Later they got into the silent movies and have continued through the years, reprinted, rephotographed to the present day. *King Solomon's Mines* has proved to be one of the enduring books of the century and, together with *She* (in which Quatermain does not appear) and *Allan Quatermain*, strongly influenced the content and direction of African adventure fiction.

Stories of lost races, treasure behind distant mountains, battle against savages, strange encounters far from civilization, remote cities, unknown and astounding— all these matters had appeared in fiction before, as far back as the epics of Homer.

The subject matter was not new, but Haggard brought to it such authenticity of detail that his wonders stood on the page like concrete walls. The people of the story may have been larger than life, or endowed with such supernatural powers as to be demi-gods, but they lived in print, indisputably real.

Which made many of them uncomfortable acquaintances, for they included a homicidal Zulu king, a lovely woman who had lived since ancient Egypt, a withered African witch doctor of high intelligence and clearly supernatural skills, a dispossessed king who was also one of literature's great fighting men. Vividly portrayed, strongly developed, these people have presence. They cast shadows.

And they appeared in stories of roaring violence, where melodrama vied with improbability. But little the reader cared. While the story was underway, it seemed perfectly real. Haggard could give the most lurid material the edged reality of a television news tape. As you might suppose, there were those who looked for other things in fiction and did not care for Haggard's work. Henry James did not care for Haggard's work, complaining of its unrelenting and continuous violence:

> Such perpetual killing and such perpetual ugliness!.... They seem to me works in which our race and our age make a very vile figure....[2]

The English literary establishment also regarded Haggard with a critical eye. It is quite true that his adventure novels are full of death and blood and by the end of the story, so many corpses have piled up that you could write the names of the remaining characters on your thumb nail.

But given the characters and story situation such slaughters appear inevitable. It's true, of course, that the Victorians took a less lenient view of mass killing than we now do, except when it was necessary to maintain the Empire. Which demonstrates how far they were from achieving the heights of civilization we enjoy today.

3—

The form Haggard devised for his African adventure novels was copied, imitated, redone in greater or less detail, with his characters and scenes liberally drawn upon. Whoever wished to write an African adventure novel, or, for that matter, an adventure novel placed in South America, Tibet, or the South Pole, borrowed freely from Haggard. He was popular. His novels sold well. He was clearly doing something right: so follow his lead.

And follow his lead they did. Dozens of writers marched the trail Haggard had opened. All around rose lost cities, forgotten races and, for those enjoying furious, violent action, there was "perpetual killing."

To sketch the main action lines in such an adventure novel, let's begin with a small group of explorers going forth to investigate the rumor of wonders. Leaving civilization, they embark to Africa, gather capable lieutenants and a supporting group which will function much as a war party, and forth they trek into the unknown.

It is a difficult march. The explorers are beset by savage beasts and ferocious men. The stern beauty of Africa rises about them, endlessly beguiling, continuously lethal. The party steadily dwindles, scoured by hardship, accident, and death, chapter after desperate chapter.

Now an even more terrible transition faces them, for they must pass from the travel-and-search part of the story to the adventure-in-lost-land. That transition is one of dramatic danger—they are captured by savages and conveyed to horrifying caverns; a river sweeps them helplessly through the roots of a mountain; disaster obliterates all but a few of the characters, who prepare to die.

They do not, of course. The heart of the adventure remains to be experienced. Once past the danger, at the end of the transition, lies the lost city, the forgotten race, the ancient culture possessing miraculous knowledge—although, most often, the culture has gone vicious in its isolation. The appearance of the explorers polarizes factions within the city, factions which have long struggled for dominance. After some chapters of intrigue and bloodshed, civil war erupts. We now arrive at such a climax as distressed Henry James.

Afterwards, as the blood cools and the bodies stiffen, the explorers take stock of their wounds and prepare to leave for their own country, pursued or not, with or without riches, with or without love—for love is often found among these violent chapters.

This brief summary barely suggests the richness of the story form. Suffering, danger, violence, heroism, love, social criticism, travel, humor, character portrayal—all were accommodated in the fiction. Even when the adventure is immersed in nearly opaque metaphysical jargon, as is *Ayshea (The Return of She)*, the narrative movement still whisks the reader onward, eyes wide, heart wondering.

The reader is no more delighted than the adventurers. These stride across the page, cross the veldt, scale the mountains, see strange shadows in strange territories.

Strange to them. Familiar to the inhabitants who view the newcomers with astonishment or amusement or with a bristle of spears. And why not? You spend your life in a remote village, eating yams and sacrificing virgins. Then the incomprehensible pale-skin foreigners arrive.

These babble of vast, impossible villages and distant, impossible rulers. Obviously they are afflicted with devils. And even if they are not, they are so different that they should be killed. See the disgusting color of their skins. See their nasty thin mouths. Smell their acrid stink.

What is it that these monsters babble? Of lost kingdoms and lost races? A maggot gnaws their brain. Lost? Not us. We have been here all this time.

It all depends on your viewpoint. To the savage, the white explorers are menaces, bringing a heavy dose of cultural shock. To the explorers, the savages are, often as not, brutal sub-humans who may be shot and robbed, as necessary, to keep the narrative excitement at high levels.

Since the pulps were excitement oriented, many of the writers who produced stories of African adventure after Haggard hardly bothered to justify white violence against the natives. In the Tarzan series, the initial stories, which are fairly typical of the period, represent the natives as depraved sub-humans, ignorant, treacherous, vicious. Violence against such creatures didn't have to be justified.

Later Burroughs modified that crude viewpoint, although the people of his lost civilizations were always inclined to use strangers as targets.

Similar stereotypes appear in the works of Robert E. Howard, who borrowed such Haggard characters as the clever witch doctor, and such Haggard images (filtered through Burroughs) as the frowning walls of the lost city, and corridors twisting weirdly beneath the mountain, and the lovely young woman all ablaze with magic, and such struggles, battles, and slaughters as would bitterly distress Henry James.

All this material rose first in the mountains of H. Rider Haggard, was borrowed by the dime novels, entered the pulp magazines through *The Golden Argosy* and *The Popular Magazine*, moved into *Adventure* and *Short Stories*, later could be found in *Blue Book* and *Jungle Stories* (first and second series), *Top Notch*, *Fantastic Adventures*, and other wonderful titles recounting innumerable explorations for lost cities and forgotten treasures, and all those battles along the way.

Along these well-tramped paths passed Tarzan, Semi-Dual, Solomon Kane, and Doc Savage. Also Nick Carter, KiGor, and Sheena. All looked back, consciously or not, to the glowing imagination of Haggard, drawing wonder from the extraordinary content of Africa.

Haggard's way was not the only way to write of African adventure. While he was profoundly influential, Edgar Rice Burrough's variations upon various Haggard devices, locales, and character types may have been even more so. But there were still other approaches.

Edgar Wallace discovered one of these.

Wallace's African series is found under the generic title of Sanders of the River. It began in 1909, making Sanders the senior of Tarzan. Sanders' adventures, like those of Tarzan, filled multiple volumes, got into the moving pictures, made the hero internationally known, and, in England, at least, can still be found in print, with a new edition of one or more books floating up every year or so.

You wonder what on earth there is in the series to preserve it so. But Wallace was a most ingratiating writer and his special vision of Africa—and the white man's burden—spread through the pulps like ink through water.

4—

Tiny villages of grass huts scattered on hard-beaten earth slanting to the river's edge. Beyond slides the river, calm or in frenzy, depending on the season, tossing up sand bars today, erasing them tomorrow, vastly powerful, vastly wide, rising from the mountains far off behind the borders of the Ochori people, curving down through the sweltering country, heavy with jungle, where two million natives live subject to their wives and husbands, their chiefs, and Mr. Commissioner Sanders, representative of the Foreign Office of Great Britain.

It is Sanders' responsibility to maintain the peace of the territory. In doing so, he must deliver justice, punish the wicked, and protect the people of the river from swindlers, slave traders, liquor peddlers, and each other. He also collects taxes, or remits them, on occasion. And he is obligated to write an unending succession of reports. This he finds grinding, dreary work.

To assist his labors, the mighty British Empire, thundering along its course of scarlet-eyed Imperialism, has provided Sanders with one or two little gun boats, and the services of one hundred or so Houssas—native troops, the 9th Regiment. Commanding these troops is Captain Patrick George Hamilton; assisting him, rather ineffectively, is Lieutenant Francis Augustus Tibbetts, better known as Bones.

Later in the series this tiny cadre will be augmented by Miss Patricia Hamilton, the Captain's sister, who does wonderful things for morale and occasionally gets severely endangered, as is the right of any woman appearing in an adventure series.

These rather limited resources are supplemented by a dovecote of pigeons to carry Sanders' messages throughout the territories. And he is further aided by an army of spies who range through the river country, serving as the antenna and the eyes of Sandi (the River's name for Sanders).

One thing of critical importance remains. That is the loyal assistance Sanders receives from Bosambo, chief of the Ochori tribe. The name Bosambo undoubtedly grates on modern ears, which are endlessly delicate and sensitive, but it is taken from a real place name (the Bosambo River) and we must accept it, cheerfully or not. Bosambo, himself, is sketched brilliantly, a vivid, outsized character so powerful that he nearly steals the series—as he steals nearly everything else.

With this motley collection of assets, Sanders administers his enormous territory. This is situated, if Mr. Edgar Wallace is to be believed, at Latitude 2 degrees North, Longitude 46 degrees West.[3] That places the area in the North Atlantic, about two hundred miles off the coast of Brazil. Mr. Wallace is evidently gaming with us.

What Wallace was thinking about seems to have been a mixture of various British territories—Nigeria (West Africa) and Uganda and Nyasaland (East Africa). In telling his story, he scrambled these artfully together:

> The river need not be specifically the Congo, since his hero must be an Englishman, and an empire-builder if possible...; no, an unspecified native territory in West Africa was best—impossible to identify on any map, yet containing all the romantic dangers of the Congo country.... He would have a residency (for the territorial commissioner) in his fictitious territory...on the coast, at the mouth of the mysterious river which flowed through crocodile-infested swamps and illimitable forest.[4]

Like the physical location of the series, the characters are lightly based on reality. Very lightly. Sanders seems to have been suggested by Sir Harry Hamilton Johnston, who served as District Commissioner in the Uganda area, was a member of the Royal Geological Society, and wrote both fiction and non-fiction.[5] The adventures he had while Commissioner, and the success with which he administrated his territories, entered folklore, English, and African. From these stories, Wallace conjured up the figure of Mr. Commissioner Sanders:

...a man of medium height...a big white helmet shading a face tanned to the color of teak. His face was thin and clean-shaven, his eyes unwavering, his every movement conveying the impression of alert vitality.[6]

That description makes Sanders sound like any other white man who has hung around Africa for a while. However, you judge a man by his decisions and his actions, and in the views you get of him in unflattering moments. Thus:

Heroes should be tall and handsome, with flashing eyes; Sanders was not so tall, was yellow of face (from fever and quinine), moreover had gray hair. Heroes should also be of gentle address, full of soft phrases, for such tender women as come over their horizons; Sanders was a dispassionate man who swore on the slightest provocation and had no use for women any way....

He was a maker of kings in the early days. He helped break a few, so it was in obedience to the laws of compensation that he took his part in reconstructive work.[7]

In the Upper River districts, he is called "by a long and sonorous name, which may be euphemistically translated as 'The Man Who Has a Faithless Wife.' " (This is one of Bosambo's more subtle jokes, for it meant that Sanders was 'wedded to his people.') But there is also a grimmer side to Sanders, and this is celebrated by a second and darker name—"The-Little-Butcher-Bird-Who-Flies-By-Night." Under this name he is honored and feared, and in this name he punishes coldly, mercilessly, and at once.

He does not usually punish. His chief function is to keep the peace. When he sits in judgement it is to resolve disputes that the tribes and their kings could not peacefully resolve themselves. When it is necessary to judge, he comes with his gun-boat and his soldiers, hears cases and gives judgement. In a few cases, he will punish by whipping or by sending the offender to The Village of Irons, the regional equivalent of Sing-Sing.

But occasionally, the offense is grave: Murder of a missionary, fomenting an uprising, invasion of another tribe's area, or simply indiscriminate and promiscuous killing. For these offenses, Sanders hangs.

He hangs men more readily in the pages of fiction than was ever done in reality. But then fiction forever covers itself with bright feathers and paints. "Oh, man," Sanders says, "you have lived too long." Immediately afterward, there is an opening for a new chief or witch-doctor, these being trades particularly susceptible to death by hanging.

'I tell you these stories of Sanders of the River,' Wallace writes, 'that you may grasp the type of man he was and learn something of the work he had to do. If he was quick to punish, he acted in accordance with the spirit of the people he governed, for they had no memory; and yesterday, with its faults and errors, and its teachings, was a very long time ago, and a man resents an unjust punishment for a crime he has forgotten.'[8]

These are amusing tales, charming and pleasant and light. But blood and terror lie close to their surfaces and ferocity hunts behind the smiling paragraphs.

Wallace is rather imprecise as to the number of nations under Sander's control. One time he mentions sixteen; later, twenty-three. Whatever the precise number, each was

...isolated and separated from the other by custom and language....

In the good old times before the English came there were many wars, tribe against tribe, people against people. There were battles, murders, raidings, and wholesale crucifixions, but the British changed all that. There was peace in the land.[9]

So to speak. The series records endless numbers of battles, murders, raids, abductions, robberies, and attacks. All these occurred under English rule, which would appear to make any statement about "peace in the land" rather optimistic; the point is that the English presence limited the duration of the violence. The majority of the stories are concerned with the telling of events that could have flared to major slaughters but which were restrained, one way or the other.

The story "Bosambo of Monrovia" (from *Sanders of the River*) is a fair sample of this—and also has the dual advantage of introducing Bosambo and demonstrating Sanders' easy flexibility in dealing with potentially appalling problems.

Not to shock you unduly but Bosambo is an escaped thief and murderer. At the beginning of his recorded career, he organized the stealing of a buoy and bell from a river channel. One of his three wives informed the authorities, and his wonderful exploit dimmed to a ten-year sentence. Soon after, he killed a guard and escaped. All this happened in the Republic of Liberia at and around the town of Monrovia.

Even at this time, in his relative youth, Bosambo was a tall, powerfully built man, of massive chest and shoulders. Having been a student at mission school, he had acquired some English and owned a bound copy of *The Lives of the Saints*, with which he overawed the less educated. He was ingenious, original, sharp witted, far more of a realist than those around him; and if he was also given to taking advantage of the least opportunity to increase his personal wealth, remember that he was a fugitive and a stranger in a far country that, by force of character, and perhaps a discreet poisoning, he had made his own.

That country was the land of the Ochori, some eight hundred miles from the irate authorities of Monrovia. The Ochori were a pacific people, mild and gentle, not to say spineless, weak, and fearful. The least powerful of their neighbors trampled them ruthlessly. But the Ochori were as timid as they were defenseless, an unfortunate condition that persisted until Bosambo came trotting through the jungle and revealed himself to them.

Soon after, their king died, rather mysteriously. Bosambo generously offered himself as king, and since he was so powerfully assertive, he assumed the throne. Immediately he began practical classes in theft. All his subjects were required to attend. And learn.

Soon after, their enemies, the Akasava, found to their bewilderment that they were losing goats, salt, and other transportable property. They paddled down river to lay their problem before Sanders.

Who had recently heard of the peculiar games Bosambo was teaching his people.

Who had received a notice of a convict, escaped from Monrovia, believed heading toward English territory.

Who promptly sailed to Ochori country to interview Bosambo.

As mentioned earlier, Sanders was a most pragmatic man. And these problems he handled in a most pragmatic way. No blazing avenger, he, blasting down the evil convict and restoring to the worthy Akasava their vanished possessions. Not at all.

To have done so would have been to explode war between the two tribes—and the ferocious Akasava would have bathed Africa in Ochori blood.

Nor did the convict seem peculiarly evil. Instead, he appeared thoroughly competent, perhaps able to give self-respect to the Ochori and perhaps stabilizing that part of the world a bit more.

So Sanders gives the Law to Bosambo: stop the stealing, *but*, in interest of peace, quietly retain what was stolen. And nothing will be said about any escaped convict in the region. Particularly if taxes are remitted properly and a stable government maintained.

After which Sanders goes downstream. Although he doesn't realize it, his field glasses remain with Bosambo, who advises his people that they were a gift from Sandi—his loving father.

From time to time, Bosambo varies that wonderful story. In "The Wood of Devils," he reports that Sandi married his brother's wife's sister and is therefore related to him. In the same breath, he also claims that he has met the Great White King who lives beyond the big water. Shaken his hand, too. Bosambo's imagination is nearly as limitless as the credulity of his listeners. Or so it seems.

5—

To read the stories, you would assume that Edgar Wallace was merely indulging an imagination that hurled out characters and situations as vivid as sparks from a burning rainbow.

Curiously enough the series is peppered with fact. For Wallace did not invent it altogether out of his imagination but out of things seen and heard while he was in Africa.

He was in and out of Africa a number of times—as a medical orderly with the British Army, as a war correspondent during the Boer War (1899-1901), as editor of a microscopic newspaper in Johannesburg, as an investigative reporter of atrocities at Congo rubber plantations. Each time, his imagination assimilated material which eventually burst forth as the Sanders of the River series.

This is a major difference between Wallace and most of the popular adventure writers to follow him. Unlike them, and like Haggard, Wallace had seen Africa at first hand, heard the stories, traveled in strange places, met, however briefly, a few of the natives and heard their language and tried his hand at speaking it. His experience was direct. When he describes the look of mist on the River at morning, he had seen it. He knew how the vegetation overhung the water and the look and sound of little villages of grass huts sweltering in that huge tropical light. He knew the look of the villagers and how the sun shone on them and the sound of their voices as they laughed. Direct experience. It illuminated his prose from within, as a stained glass lamp blazes around its inner bulbs. If his fiction were often melodramatic, simplified, guided by formula, that inner illumination softened all faults.

In 1909, Edgar Wallace was in London and at a deadly low career point. His self-published book, *The Four Just Men*, in which the modern justice figure first appeared, had plunged him into debt.[10] He had embroiled his newspaper, the *Daily Mail*, in two lawsuits, and, as a result, had been quietly fired. No newspaper was interested in a reporter who generated libel actions. Money problems ground him; failure chuckled at his ear.

At this gloomy time, he met Mrs. Isabel Thorne, fiction editor for Shurey's Publications. During an extended conversation, Wallace mentioned some of the things he had seen in Africa and repeated a few of the stories he had heard of Sir Harry Johnston. Mrs. Thorne recognized possibilities. She asked Wallace to write some African stories for the *Weekly Tale-Teller*. These began appearing in 1909. Almost at once, Sanders and Bosambo came on stage, and one of the most popular series of the time began flowing through the *Weekly Tale-Teller* and later magazines and, still later, into books.

The Sanders stories reached the United States early and there they traveled a curious path. Initially, they were published in the slick magazines. These included *McClures* (1910), the 1911 *Metropolitan* (a very large thin magazine most usually ornamented by a cover painting of a beautiful woman), and the 1911-1912 *Harper's Weekly*, a tabloid-sized magazine that contained half fiction, half news and editorial material. A few stories also appeared in the *American Magazine* (1912-1913) and *Colliers* (1915-1916).

By then *Adventure* magazine had published half a dozen stories, thinly scattered through 1913 and 1919, as well as a few in *Blue Book* and *All-Story Weekly*. Since the pulps paid considerably less than the slicks, they were not primary markets. Not till later, in 1915, did a substantial number of Sanders stories appear in Street & Smith's *New Story Magazine*.[11] Much later, in 1926, *Short Stories* offered a small selection of Sanders adventures and, in 1930, the *Golden Book*, which is hardly to be classified as a pulp, reprinted five stories.

Reprinting in the pulps continued, sporadically, however, to the end of the 1940s with appearances in *Jungle Stories* and *Action Stories*.

Reprints to one side, the series ran from 1909 to 1921. It includes about 150 stories and a novel, *Sandi the King-Maker*, that was first serialized in *The Windsor Magazine* (December 1920 through November 1921).[12] The characters of the series appeared as walk-ons in *The River of Stars* and the comic novel, *Bones in London*. In addition, three further books of Sanders' adventures were written by mystery author Francis Gerard: *The Return of Sanders of the River* (1938), *The Law of the River* (1939), and *The Justice of Sanders* (1951).[13]

Initially the stories were published in a loose sort of sequence. Soon enough the chronology became tangled, stories from late in Sanders' career mingling with earlier adventures. Nor did the books of collected short stories correct the confusion, since these were usually issued as published in the magazines, rather than with a pedantic strictness of chronology.[14]

Not that it makes all that much difference. The passage of series time is mainly marked by the appearance of this character or that. The adventures stream onward. In the River Territories, time seems faceless. Murders, uprisings, fish dinners, trips up the river and down—all melt together, a blurred abstraction in which no single incident stands clear.

What we remember are the characters of the series as they arrive, one by one. Sanders, first, and then Bosambo, both appearing in *Sanders of the River*. In the collection, *Bosambo of the River* (1914), Hamilton is named as a Captain of the Houssas, but he remains a name only, wholly undeveloped until the 1915 *Bones*. In that collection, Sanders returns to England for a six-month leave. That opens the way for Hamilton to flare to life. And into the series blunders that remarkable character, Lieutenant Francis Augustus Tibbetts, familiarly called "Bones."

...cheerful as the devil—a straight stick of a youth, with hair brushed back from his forehead, a sun-peeled nose, a wonderful collection of baggage, and all the gossip of London.

'I'm afraid you'll find I'm rather an ass, sir,' he said, saluting stiffly. 'I've only just arrived on the Coast an' I'm simply bubbling over with energy, but I'm rather short in the brain department.'[15]

That is the first and last time Bones (as Hamilton immediately names him) is in the least diffident. Far from it. He in infuriating, childish, over-confident, inept, ridiculous, and lucky. But he is not diffident. We see immediately that Wallace had little idea how the character would grow. That introductory description rings false in most details when we compare it with the later Bones. But knowledge of how a character will change is given to few authors; the rest must struggle along with those extraordinary and secret processes of literary evolution as best they may.

Bones was introduced to the series because Hamilton was not flamboyant enough. Bones is exaggeration, caricature, and cartoon. In speech, he is the stereotype of the monocled dim wit who drifts vacantly through the fiction of the time:

Bones: 'You're a jolly old rotter, Bosambo. I could punish you awfully for telling wicked stories. I'm disgusted with you, I am indeed.'[16]

Through the stories he ineptly blunders, a semi-literate ninny played for laughs. Who squanders his salary on correspondence courses. Who writes fanciful letters to England describing his heroic adventures. Who is barely able to distinguish between fancy and reality, and entirely unable to read the hearts of men.

But....

...who is, incredibly enough, quick in action, cool and clever in emergencies, able to handle small military actions, and competent enough for Sanders to trust him with missions representing England.

From this you would assume that Bones is inconsistently drawn—and you would be right. But consistency has nothing to do with a character's appeal. Bones is a long-nosed, round-eyed, fish-mouthed ninny who blunders into hair-raising situations and blunders out of them again. The most simple action he complicates. Constantly bungling, he still succeeds, often as not. By luck. For he is incredibly, unbelievably lucky.

Even the least reader could feel superior to this inane fumbler and smile tolerantly when he lucked out an assignment. You never mind when Bones succeeds by accident. That is part of the joke.

Bones may have been suggested by the larger-than-life figure of Marquis Henri Testaferrata, a Maltese nobleman who served in the British Colonial Service during the early 1900s. A practical joker and amateur naturalist, he was retired from service because of eccentric behavior. His relatives later made it clear that the character of Bones was entirely different from that of the Marquis.[17]

That would seem obvious. Bones is a vivid recasting of that familiar character, the wise fool, a cliché honored by antiquity. The presence of Bones introduces the saving grace of farce into a series of stories rather heavily weighted toward the macabre and the violent.

As mentioned before, writers tend to make the most of African violence, and Wallace's stories are filled with battle, murder, and sudden death. Unlike other writers, his tone is casual, light, nearly dismissive; however brutal the events described, the tone is nearly always gently understated:

—(Sanders) sent word to the chief that the revival of the bad old custom of blinding would be following by the introduction of the bad new custom of hanging.[18]

—(Chief Karat's) messenger returned and met (Bones') party on the road. What was his attitude towards the intruders it is impossible to say. He may have been insolent, secure in the feeling that he was representing his master's attitude towards white men; he may have offered fight in the illusion that the six warriors he took with him were sufficient.... It is certain that he never returned."[19]

—The N'Gombi people had a weakness for forbidden fruit; they raided and burnt and pillaged, but in the main the treasure which they carried away with them took the shape of eligible women."[20]

—"There had been a man murdered on the Little River and none knew whose hand it was that struck him down.
"His body, curiously carved, came floating down stream one sunny morning, and agents brought the news to Sanders. A life more or less is nothing in a land where people die by whole villages, but these men with their fantastic slashings worried Sanders terribly."[21]

You can describe only so much blood and horror. Genial understatement gets the point across as effectively, if less graphically: the suggested horror is more awful than the horror described.

Into the midst of this frequently grim scene strolls Miss Patricia Agatha Hamilton, "of a certain Celtic type, above the medium height, with the freedom of carriage and gait which is the peculiar possession of her country-women. Her face was a true oval, and her complexion of that kind which tans readily but does not freckle."[22]

Pat first appears in "Bones, Sanders, and One Another" published in *Colliers* (May 16, 1916). The story ambles gently from this point to that and Pat, hardly described, appears in the final pages, a victim of Bones'....

But we are getting ahead of ourselves.

First we visit M'lama, a widow woman reputed to be a witch. Then abruptly, the scene snaps to Sanders who has just learned that Patricia Hamilton is coming to visit her brother. To investigate the rumor of M'lama's miracles, Sanders sends Bones upriver. There, Lt. Tibbetts is forced to arrest M'lama. When she is imprisoned on the boat, she promptly tears off all her clothing. Bones applies to a nearby Jesuit settlement for clothing and is given a white skirt and blouse donated by a London congregation. These, M'lama puts on with every evidence of satisfaction.

As the boat approaches the Residency, M'lama leaps from the deck to shore and vanishes into the brush. Remembering that she is in the habit of tearing off her clothing, Bones grabs a bed cover and takes off after her.

Moments later he sees a flash of white, hurls the cover over it, and hauls his wiggling captive back to the boat. Since the joke is obvious and you are astute, you will have guessed that Bones has captured Miss Pat. And so he has. She forgives him, but he is scoured by shame, which lasts well into the following story.

Which is "Bones Changes His Religion" (*Colliers*, June 3, 1916). In this, Bones takes Pat on a little joyride upstream and they end tied hand and foot, about to be branded by a crazy chief who has created a new religion and appointed himself high priest and primary god. He pronounces himself sacred and deathless.

Bones negotiates to save Pat from the branding iron. Just as the glowing metal singes his shirt:

> ...a voice hailed the high-priest of the newest of cults.
> Bucongo turned with a grimace of fear and cringed backward before the leveled Colt of Mr. Commissioner Sanders.
> 'Tell me now,' said Sanders in his even tone, 'can such a man as you die?'
> 'Lord,' said Bucongo huskily, 'I think I can die.'
> 'We shall see,' said Sanders.[23]

Afterward, Pat learns that Bones had persuaded the chief to brand him twice in order that Pat not be branded at all, and the story ends in glow of sentiment and heroism that is quite admirable.

Sentiment, heroism, and humor are what you remember of these stories. They are told in a jaunty style, dealing casually with dark subjects, the humorous situations become rather obvious after all these years, and the rescues rather too often occurring on the final page. The stories proper often consist of two separate parts that you would swear could never be joined together. They flow along independently, la la la, until, abruptly, the narrative shudders like a politician hearing the word *ethics*, and behold, the two lines have merged, the climax glares, a scarlet spot, and it is over. Slick, tricky, a little self conscious, and very very neat.

"The Crime of Sanders," (*Adventure*, February 1913): Derik Arthur Jordon, an unemployed London clerk seeking frantically to support his wife and children, attempts trading in Africa as a last resort.

Sanders grants him a trading license and a few words of advice:

Avoid the N'Gombi, who are thieves and the bush people who are chronically homicidal. The Isisi will buy salt with rubber—there is plenty of rubber in the back country. The Ochori will buy cloth with gum—by the way, Bosambo, the chief, speaks English and will try to swindle you. Goodbye and good luck.[24]

And, dismissing Jordon, Sanders returns to a report of three mysterious men, far up the river. Spies advise that nothing is known of these men, who live alone, wifeless, inoffensive, growing a few crops. Until they suddenly vanish.

Obviously the three-men line and the Jordon line are somehow going to intersect. Here's how Wallace works it.

One year passes. Jordon has been unsuccessful. His family starves in London, living on tea and hope. Just one more try, he tells Sanders, then he'll give it up and return to England.

As he leaves, drooping dramatically, Sanders learns that one of the three missing men has returned. Visiting him later, Sanders learns that he is a Zulu named M'Karoka. That's about all he learns. As he leaves, Sanders sees Jordon paddling glumly upstream.

Jordon does a trifle of trading with M'Karoka and spends the night at his camp. In the middle of the night he wakes to a loud disturbance, sees M'Karoka fighting a stranger, who bolts, leaving the Zulu dying.

Jordon shoots the killer, returns to help M'Karoka. Who, with his final breath, tells where a packet of uncut diamonds is concealed.

These Jordon joyously carries down river. Finally, he tells Sanders, he'll be able to rescue his family from poverty and keep them properly.

He leaves rejoicing.

And Sanders, who has just received official warning to watch for three men smuggling diamonds from South Africa—arrest men, confiscate diamonds—ignores his duty, lets Jordon and diamonds go.

"Arachi the Borrower" (*Adventure*, August 1913): A glib native con man, Arachi, lives well by mooching from his fellows. One day he steps over the line into slave trading, dealing with Abdul Hazin, who promises to make him rich.

Hoping to become chief of the Ochori, Arachi plans to entice Bosambo into Abdul's clutches. In little matters like this, it is nearly impossible to fool Bosambo. He passes word to Sanders and permits himself to be captured. As a result, Sanders catches Abdul in the act. Thinking that he has been betrayed by Arachi, Abdul kills him. It is another of these stories that begins lightly as a Spring day and ends splashed with gore.

"The Fetish Stick" (*Adventure*, 1st April 1918): To warn the Akasava not to kill the chief's crippled son, M'Fosa, Sanders causes them to erect an enormous pole, thick and high; on this pole—his fetish stick, Sanders says—he will hang any man who injures the boy.

Who grows up protected by the pole. But he grows up murderous. When Sanders leaves for a six-month vacation, M'Fosa feels that the law no longer exists. He prepares to celebrate a huge feast, then cut down the pole and commence a refreshing career of murder and war—beginning with Bosambo and every white man within reach.

He invites Bosambo to come to the feast (without spearmen) but receives polite regrets. However, Bones does come, as representative of the government, and is promptly taken, tied to the pole, and scowled at by hostiles. But before M'Fosa can knife him, something unexpected occurs, something more than faintly supernatural. Sanders, who is in England and at a party, suddenly sees the figure of M'Fosa in a corner of the room; just as unexpectedly, M'Fosa is confronted by the snarling image of Sanders.

Before M'Fosa recovers from the shock, Bosambo and his spearmen arrive in another of the series' remarkable last-second rescues, and they clean up on the wicked. All this is highly satisfactory. The story has been repeatedly reprinted.

As has "Nine Terrible Men" (*Golden Book*, February 1930):

The Nine Terrible Men live secretly in an inaccessible place, emerging only to take what they will and kill if they wish. Sanders' spies look for them and fail. Sanders beats the forest for them and fails.

One day, missionary Ruth Glandynne makes a convert of that treacherous fellow, Fembeni. Sanders, knowing the man, doubts the depth of his conversion. That seriously annoys Ruth, who has so far been able to convert only this one man. (Before Patricia Hamilton came along, Ruth was the series' white woman, and was endangered and saved as is usual with female characters in that role. There was always the possibility that Sanders might fall in love with her. Well, he did, more than halfway; but then Patricia came along, you see....)

Since Fembeni has elected to become a Christian, there is a trifling problem about what to do with three of his four wives and associated children.

When Sanders stops to talk with one of the wives, she accidentally reveals knowledge of the Terrible Men. Immediately clutching this lead, Sanders calls his troops. But too late. Fembeni has taken Ruth hostage and fled to the swamps. As the horrified woman is dragged away, she is accidentally splashed with cheap perfume. That scent later leads Sanders to the concealed camp of the Terrible Men. Shortly afterward, there are a whole lot of deaths, none of them regretted.

"The Northern Men" (*Colliers*, December 2, 1916) is another often reprinted story. The Northern men are the people of North Ochori country. They barely tolerate Bosambo's rule and one day, they reject it entirely—immediately after Bosambo directs the death of an important Northern chief who got sassy.

War erupts. Warriors in all their painted thousands sail south along the river to attack Bosambo. At this exact moment, unfortunately, the Zaire—Sanders' little gunboat—chugs into their midst.

The Zaire is potting around on the river to give Patricia a farewell jaunt. After a year in Africa, she is preparing to return to England. But as blood-mad savages surround the boat, it seems that the only home she will ever see is the Heavenly one in the sky. The North Ochori are in a mood to slaughter them all: Sanders, Bones, Hamilton, Patricia, the entire cast.

Captured and waiting to be killed, Sanders manages to convey to Patricia that he loves her. It is one of the most inarticulate love scenes in fiction. Sanders contrives a few grimaces and nervous noises, and after Patricia has properly interpreted these, he puts his arm around her. It is love and they are to die together.

The sentiment is large, coarse, obvious stuff, and yet emotion glows from the page. You absolutely, positively know that they are going to be saved by someone bursting in from the outside. You realize Wallace is working your emotions for all he's worth. But there is no force on earth sufficient to stop you from reading the final paragraphs of that story. Perhaps it is sentimental, formula melodrama, predictable as a clock's tick, but it grips like a hawk's foot.

Yes, Bosambo and his tribe do burst in at the final second, after some distraction by Bones. The insurrection dissolves in general slaughter. It is a famous and celebrated story.   Patricia and Sanders get engaged, later marry. He retires from African service on a pension, they move to Twickenham in England.

As for Bones, he inherits money, resigns his commission, and becomes a businessman in London. (That's what *Bones in London* is all about: his adventures among crooks and shysters, and how Sanders gets swindled and Bones helps him out, and how Bones finds love: all this.)

Finally Hamilton leaves West Africa and joins Bones in business. There matters rest until *Sandi the King-Maker*, that interesting book first published as a 1920-1921 serial.

The Colonial Office calls upon Sanders and his associates to return to Africa and settle the problem, once and for all, of The Great King, Lord of the Land of Rimi-Rimi. Dwelling in nearly inaccessible territory, in what had once been a Germany colony (the time is after World War I), The Great King is prepared to attack the Ochori. He has already slaughtered several missionaries and a British representative, and is burning gifts, a signal of impeding war.

Reluctantly Sanders, Hamilton, and Bones return to Africa, travel upstream, with great difficulty, to The Great King's domain. There they rescue Bosambo and obliterate The Great King—who, scowling fiercely, hurls into the fire Sanders' gift, a brightly painted aerial bomb.

With this, the story gets underway. It is not quite a novel and not quite a collection of short stories, but a fascinating mixture of both. Two problems hold this slightly unstable structure together: who will rule in place of the Great King and what was the fate of the missionaries, the Fergusons, father and daughter?

The Great King had always been a special problem. No European power had been able to discipline him or his people, shielded as they were by mountains and jungle. The people are more strange than anyone might realize, for they are, in fact, distantly connected to a small group of Romans who strayed into this land, erected their monuments, expounded their culture, then died, leaving only echoes behind.

This familiar Lost Race theme is remarked on for a few pages but hardly developed. It rises. It falls away. And off the story rushes, aflame with new ideas, pushing this way and that like a modern woman seeking meaning in her life.

Sanders has small success finding a replacement king. Those he selects have a way of ending up dead, either speared, stabbed, or hanged. For a few moments, Bones is selected as ruler, after a deadly encounter. Then suddenly the problem is solved as Sanders calls Bosambo to the throne—and, as you might suppose, Bosambo accepts the offer with characteristic relish.

From Chapter V on, the Devil Woman of Limbi becomes a major force in the story. The Old Woman—Devil Woman—has been alive on the order of 120 years, collects virgins to kill them, and intrudes herself into the power struggles of the kingdom. Her minions slip through the brush by night to paint double red crosses on the foreheads of the elect—soon to be carried away and hacked to pieces at her sacred cave in the mountain.

Sanders, himself, ends up with red crosses on the forehead. Then it is learned that Diana Ferguson, daughter of the murdered missionary, is still alive in the hands of savages. After this, Hamilton is abducted and Sanders and Bones witness the waving of a bloody sword that marks his death.

Following which civil war breaks out.

Slaughter, massive even by Haggard standards, walks the pages.

As Sanders' shattered troops waver, as waves of howling savages rush upon them, as guns flame and men scream and blood gushes out and it is all hopeless, hopeless, in these terrible final seconds, Bosambo's wife appears, leading thousands of spears, to crush evil permanently. Not only that but Hamilton materializes from nowhere, alive, unbloody, telling an astounding tale. And in the final chapter, the ultimate secrets of the Old Devil Woman are revealed. And mighty strange secrets they are, too.

To sum it all up, Bosambo gets a kingdom; Hamilton gets a wife; Sanders and Bones get to return to England alive, having stabilized the wasps' nest. And that, chronologically, completes the Sanders of the River series.

6—

Fiction though they were, only lightly tainted by fact, the stories of the series were wonderfully appealing, stylish—and imitated. Their vision of black Africa was reflected in steaming chunks through the pages of *Jungle Stories*— when these were not recycling Tarzan movies in other form. *Adventure, Argosy, Blue Book, Top Notch, Wide World Adventure, Action Stories*—these and other titles shaped their jungles to resemble those clustering along the River, described their natives like those filling Sanders' territories, spiced their stories with humorously played chiefs with the manner, if not the style, of Bosambo and featured strong white men, vaguely resembling Sanders, who ardently loved peace and would heap the dead in layers to get it.

Seabury Quinn seemed much taken by the Sanders series. His very very British character, Hiji, appeared in *Short Stories* (1947) as the English representative of law in Africa, using situations and occasionally phrases direct from the River series. (Hiji would also appear in *Weird Tales* as a companion to Jules de Grandin; in those stories, Hiji's personality underwent another change and he became more Lord Roxton—of Doyle's *Lost World*—than Sanders.)

Variation followed upon variation in the splendid tradition of the pulp magazines, where variation upon a theme was as usual as in a jazz chorus. One of the more interesting variations was played by L. Patrick Greene in the pages of *Adventure* and *Short Stories*. His character, The Major, began as an artful scamp who evolved to full hero status. In other ways, the Major was a most peculiar fellow. He appeared very much like Bertie Wooster—or Lt. Bones, himself. But in Africa, and African fiction, as you well know, almost anything can happen.

7—

At the outset, let's have no mistake about it: L. Patrick Greene, author of the Major series, may have read the Sanders series. But he had no need to borrow Bones as a model. Not at all. The exterior model for the Major had been in existence for more than seventy years. It was the great root stock from which both Bones and Bertie Wooster were drawn—and also Johnston McCulley's detective extraordinary, Terry Trimble, whose personality and adventures were so brilliantly examined in *The Solvers*, the preceding volume of this series.

To summarize briefly, Trimble was the embodiment of the brainless fop, a languid, affected lounger, whose vapid exterior and listless ways concealed a mind of dazzling quickness. He thirsted for action, Trimble did, and found it. And since he had a magnificent physique, he handled himself well in the face of robbers, master criminals, mad scientists and similar hostiles.

Like most of McCulley's other characters, Terry Trimble was afflicted with garrulous factiousness whenever he found it necessary to bluff an opponent. Bluffing was often required because McCulley characters never carried loaded guns. And so:

Stay right where you are. Don't move a muscle. As you can see this is a heavy calibre automatic I am pointing at your head. And note my finger. It is strained tight around the trigger. I regret that this is a hair trigger. It goes off so easily—and such shocking things happen when it does. Please make no sudden movements, for that might startle me and cause my finger to contract. That would be most distressing for both of us.

Thus, Mr. McCulley's chattering hero. And so, by slow degrees we return to Greene's character, the Major, who is, at this very instant, pointing a heavy pistol at a sweating blackguard:

The Major: 'Don't make me angry—because anger contracts the muscles and that would be very unpleasant for you. This revolver has a light touch and the slightest contraction of the finger would—well, I would hate to be hanged for killing a swine like you.'[25]

The man who sounds so fierce hardly appears to know one end of a gun from the other. He is a big, young, clean-shaven fellow, whose black hair, already streaked with gray and thinning at the temples, is combed back into a pompadour. He is dressed like a dude in dazzling white, his clothing crisp, clean, his brown boots glaring with polish. In his eye glints a monocle—he carries a stock of them. He speaks in a mannered drawl, salting his remarks with "Old chap," "Old thing," "beastly," "my word," " 'pon my soul." On his round face is an expression that suggests someone has stolen his brain.

All this is the stock in trade of Aubrey St. John Major, known in Africa simply as the Major. The fancy exterior and idiotic expression are to encourage you to underestimate him. Those that do are soon filled with regret, for he is a shrewd operator, indeed.

When the Major first strolls into the 1919 *Adventure*, he is one of those charming criminal heroes who refreshed the pulps for so many decades. To be accurate, the Major is an Illicit Diamond Buyer (an I.D.B.).

That doesn't sound like much of a crime. In South Africa, however, the de Beers Syndicate controls all diamond mining rights. Only licensed miners and traders can handle diamonds or sell them. If an I.D.B. purchases diamonds from someone and has not secured a permit, he is, therefore, a criminal dealing with a criminal. That applies whether the diamond was found along the road or in someone's pocket.

No sooner is the Major branded a criminal than Greene begins to qualify his guilt, using that most familiar of techniques: The Law is Wrong; The Major is Morally Right:

> The miners knew of the Major by repute. Knew that beneath the clothing of a fop was a red-blooded man; a man whose strength was always on the side of the under dog no matter how great the odds might be against him. They knew that he was, in the eyes of the law, a notorious criminal; but they also understood that his crime—that of illicit diamond-buying—was his protest against certain unjust laws protecting the diamond-mining monopoly. And their sympathies were all with him.[26]

Not only the miners, but the police regard him with unmixed admiration. If they caught him with illegal diamonds, they would haul him in, certainly. Until that unfortunate time, the police regard him with pride. He is such a sportsman, such a "damned good sort." The Major is royal game, treated with respect. Even when he gulls the police, which is often, they excuse his naughty behavior, knowing that he is a man of principle, ever defending the weak, ever standing strong for justice.

Like other series heroes from the Just Men to the Spider, the Major tends to trample over certain laws. His help is unorthodox, not to say frequently lethal to a number of unwashed people.

> He might, but for his quixotic generosity, have been an immensely wealthy man. Even so, he was rich enough to travel in princely style; rich enough, had he wished, to live luxuriously in any of the world's big capitals. But Africa had marked him for her own. Money meant nothing to him; civilization still less. He lived dangerously— and remained young and still an idealist.[27]

He is not always as wealthy as that quotation states. "Lines of Cleavage," (*Adventure*, First February 1921), begins with the Major broke and disgusted.

> This other game [illegal diamond buying]—there's nothing in it. I've made money, lots of it, and lost it all. Yes, Jim, we're going to be honest and we're going home.[28]

He talks like a man with a hangover. Soon enough, his determination to be honest and go back to England melts in the complexities of the story. First it is necessary to save the son of a powerful chief from frame-up and death. In gratitude, the chief gives him a huge, uncut diamond. This the Major splits in half along its large fault. He heads for town with the diamond pieces. But before he finds a place to sit down, two women catch his attention. Both are being blackmailed by Kafir Smith, who is threatening to disclose to English society the sordid fact that they were once bar maids.

The Major, recognizing Smith as a wanted criminal, promptly blackmails him into returning one woman's money, the second woman's impulsive letters. He plants one half of that diamond in the mine of the boy friend of Barmaid 2, so that they can return in triumph and financial security to England.

By this time, several bad guys have clumped together and framed the Major by planting illicit diamonds in his tent. The police pounce, catching his servant and close personal friend, Jim the Hottentot. A trick frees Jim and off they glide into the wilds—having left the other diamond half with the Chief of Police. He thinks it's a big chunk of glass.

It is early in the series but already we note what will become such repeated events and situations as:

—Jim in trouble and saved.

—The Major impulsively giving away all he possesses.

—The Major facing the threat of arrest; also, the fake arrest for reasons of secrecy.

—The nasty villain of unclean habits who believes he has the Major trapped, only to find out otherwise.

—The Major is trapped but since he acts like such an idiot, no one takes him seriously until....

—Someone unwholesome is stirring up the natives.

—Illegal diamonds are planted on The Major and the police tipped off.

—The Major (or Jim) is probably dead and Jim (or the Major) vows revenge.

It's a tough life out there in Africa with nobody you can trust but your faithful Hottentot. Action, danger, a good deal of personal suffering, very little rest. If, however, you are an abnormally strong Englishman, lithe and lean, who can ride, shoot, and read the back country like a road map, then it would be nearly criminal to leave your series and return to England. *Adventure* and *Short Stories* would miss you terribly as would all those faithful readers from 1919 to the mid-1950s. As would Jim.

Jim is a wonder. A black secondary hero in a series rarely happened—Jericho Druke of *The Shadow* magazine and the Newtons of *The Avenger* are notable exceptions. Back in ancient times, the dime novels occasionally included a black character, dredging up every possible stereotype and cliché, and in virtually every case offering a caricature that seemed to have tumbled from the minstrel stage onto the printed page.

During the early years of the pulps, English writers provided almost all the prominent black characters. Many of H. Rider Haggard's novels present strongly developed blacks, from Zulu kings and witch doctors to that astonishing fighting man, Umslopogaas. (Although his name seems ridiculous, he is vividly drawn and one of fiction's great warriors.)

Jim, of the Major series, is hardly of that stature. Squat, ungainly, broad of shoulder, heavily muscled, and with a crescent-shaped scar on his right shoulder, he is a child of nature, touchingly simplified for popular fiction:

All his senses were highly developed. His sight was keen as an eagle's; his hearing abnormally acute; his powers of endurance little short of miraculous. He had besides, a sixth sense of direction, and an uncanny instinct which warned him of impending danger.[29]

Nothing particularly intellectual here. What is remarkable about Jim are the extremes he combines: he is superstitious and realistically level-headed, capable of self restraint but also given to getting hopelessly drunk or gorging himself to sickness; he is terrified of rifles but learns to shoot; he is out-going and honest and, at the same time, a gifted liar in the Major's service.

He comes through this tissue of contradictions rather well, an interesting and effective character whose influence on the series is nearly as great as that of the Major.

This ill-assorted pair, the fop and the savage, float blithely around Africa, from the Cape to the Congo:

...they had made the waterless waste of the Kalahari their play ground and had trekked through the steaming swamplands which bar the way to the coast of Portuguese territory; they had scaled the peaks of the Mountains of the Moon, had shot white water rapids in clumsy, native dugouts and had blazed trails through the Congo jungle. At such times, savage men and beasts had added to the peril of their treks; hunger, thirst and the fever which saps a man's courage as well as his strength had often been with them.[30]

By which you know that the Major is an outdoorsman, used to taking care of himself in a big savage country filled with big savage animals, snakes, natives, and scummy white men. Unlike most outdoorsmen from Leather Stocking to Young Wild West, the Major sees no reason why he should sleep on a pile of rocks in the rain or eat stewed thorns and bark. If it is at all possible, he travels with a 16-mule team pulling a fancy wagon simply packed with amenities.

When the Major travels, he is dressed in gleaming white clothing, unsullied by sweat. His creases are sharp. His hands are unsoiled. His hair is cut.

When the Major camps, he does so inside a good-sized tent, where sits a comfortable bed elaborately swirled in mosquito netting. Light carpets give the illusion of a floor.

When the Major eats, he does so from china. The food, all prepared by Jim the Hottentot, is not merely adequate but excellent, superlative, admirable.

When the Major sleeps, he does so in silk pajamas. He is as much an ornament to society when he rests as when he is out there trekking with those sweaty fellows.

To keep his camp in shape, set up the tent, cook the meals, tend the sixteen mules, cut the Major's hair and tend the Major's clothing, load and unload, day after glorious day, the Major has Jim. Understand, Jim doesn't seem to be paid. He does all this because he delights in trekking with his "Baas." He admires the Major's slick ways and classy behavior, and the way he strides about Africa like a minor king, seeking out difficulties and disposing of them with a flick of his nicely scrubbed fingers.

Jim counts himself lucky to hang around with such a superior fellow. And if it is any trouble for him to perform the work of a dozen and a half native carriers, he never once mentions it. He's a fine fellow, Jim is.

8—

This remarkable pair was the creation of L(ewis) Patrick Greene (1891-?), formerly Louis Montague Greene. Born in England, he went to Africa when he was eighteen as a Rhodesian civil servant. He remained in Africa for about four years. In an autobiographical sketch published in *Adventure* ("The Camp-Fire," February 3, 1918), Greene talked fondly of those years. "Dealing almost entirely with natives, I learned to speak their language and came to admire them. They taught me many things that were good for a youngster to know." Invalided back to England because of sunstroke and a severe back injury, he came to the United States in 1913. During the next several years, he was a "timekeeper in a New York construction company, life insurance agent, sold stock for a 'shady' broker—though I did not know it at the time." For several years, he worked in Boston, Massachusetts, with a society for the care of children. He married and became an American citizen.

In 1918, *Adventure* published the first of a long string of Greene's stories: "The Snakes of Zari" (February 3). From 1919 to the early 1950s, Greene poured out fiction about the Major and Jim for both *Adventure* and *Short Stories*. At least five collections of novelettes were published in England between 1924 and 1938. His torrent of prose pinched off after 1939, while he served in the Royal Air Force. After the war, Greene returned to writing and the Major returned to the pages of *Short Stories*.

Over thirty years, Greene created an enormous body of work of remarkable consistency; the characters show minor changes toward the end of the run. But only minor changes. Jim becomes a little uglier; and the Major alters from a charming rogue to a near saint. That happens early, however. Greene's high regard for his character already glows through the 1921 stories.

As, for instance, "Tools" (*Adventure*, First August 1921).

In this story, the police arrest the Major for murder. But not really. It is only a pretense, because the Chief of Police wants the Major's help and has been unable to catch his ear. Or that's the reason given.

Well, the wicked Portuguese Colonial Service has schemed to get power over Mangwato, a tough native chief with a land full of gold and diamonds, and a heart full of dislike for white men. He trusts the Major, however.

Which is just as well. For the Portuguese are about to entrap Mangwato's son, Shimba. After the Major spoils that plan, the Portuguese blackmail two English crooks into kidnapping Shimba and blackmailing Mangwato into allowing his land to become part of Portuguese territory.

Toward the end of the story, things look awful. The crooks have the Major handcuffed, Shimba in their power off in the jungle, and Mangwato melting before their demands.

Then, in an instant, everything is reversed. The Major has sent a task force to free Shimba. They do. He returns, roaring for vengeance and displaying a lot of assagai in the vicinity of the criminals' throats. Through the courtesy of the Major, they are jailed, rather than buried.

The action is episodic, brisk, and contains enough incident for a novel. As is his habit, the Major plays rather a passive role. He fixes the attention of the criminals and they fail to see that a task force is slipping up behind for the purpose of batting them over the head.

"Tools" seems to be the last Major story published in *Adventure*. The series now switches to *Short Stories*, the initial story, "Royal Game," appearing in the November 10, 1921 issue.

Royal Game refers to the Major, himself—for he is as highly regarded by the police as Al Capone was by the Chicago politicians. In this story, a pair of tricky Portuguese and a Sergeant of the Mounted Police team up to catch the Major with a pocket full of illegal diamonds.

And he has such a pocketful, since he has just lifted them from a detective who tried to use them as a snare. Fortunately the plots of these wicked men immediately go sour, as the Major deftly makes fools of them all.

He does not keep the diamonds, however. That would be dishonest and no hero in *Short Stories* is going to be dishonest, whether a crook or not. He returns the diamonds in such a way that they cannot be traced back to him: the diamonds, loaded into a shotgun, are accidentally fired into a haunch of kudu. Finding that this solves his problem, the Major delivers haunch and diamonds to the Sergeant.

"With One Stone" (September 25, 1924) features a Cape Town crime boss who is stirring up the natives. By inciting them to war, he will take all the police heat off his operations. And the Major, perhaps the only man in Africa who could stop him, is wandering around the landscape blind, or the next thing to it. A spitting cobra has envenomed his eyes.

As permanent darkness closes inexorably in, as the Major gropes across the sunlit yard, as Jim watches in horror, a gang of tough thugs swagger forward, leering and coarse-mouthed, to make sport of this good man, helpless and alone.

Afterwards they are sorry, and so is the crime boss. The blindness (to ease your concern) is cured by a Boer housefrau.

In 1934 begins a loosely connected series of stories which continue to mid-1935. To rescue illegally imprisoned natives, the Major leads an armed force into Portuguese territory. Several Portuguese end up dead. As a result, the authorities offer a 1000-pound reward for the Major, dead or alive.

In "Flight" (March 25, 1934), he decides to surrender to the authorities, in order to publicize the Portuguese crimes. His own followers think this is a witless thing to do. So they tie him up nicely, and, as they head for the safety of the border, take turns impersonating him—to the confusion and disgust of the authorities, who keep arresting the wrong man.

After this, the scene shifts to the Congo. In "Squeeze" (August 10, 1934), a crazy missionary holds a portion of the Congo in a reign of terror. The Major is captured before he can crush this menace. Tied to a post, he is about to be slashed to ribbons. But Jim has finally overcome his fear of firearms and, at the final second with his final cartridge, applies the final solution.

Perhaps it's the heat of the Congo, but the Major seems to have run into quantities of crazies there, each doing his lunatic thing, "By Rule of Drum" (September 10, 1934, reprinted April 1954), tells of an insane fellow named Weiss. He has stolen a magic drum and with it plans to unite Africa under his rule, for all tribes listen when the magic drum speaks.

Weiss lives in an oasis at the center of acres of interwoven thorn bush. To this impenetrable place, he conducts the Major and Jim, who are acting their familiar parts, as usual: Jim is the contemptuous native guide sneering at the fool white man; the Major is "a man who was hopelessly inefficient and brainless...so obviously a dude."

The end is a nightmare flight through the thorns in the deep of night. The menace to African peace ends violently when a herd of charging elephant, diverted into the brush, flatten all plans of conquest and Weiss, himself. "The Miracle" (April 10, 1935) tells of a near-disastrous encounter with red-haired "missing links" in a Congo swamp.

Still another plot to rouse the natives against the white man's rule is met in "The Lake of the Dead" (June 25, 1935, reprinted April 1953). A German trader and a British secret service operative are of some assistance in locating the lake. But it is up to the Major and Jim to penetrate the Cave of Bats and search out the secret way to that tiny ledge of rock rising at the center of the lake. There a fierce priestess cries rebellion and slaughter until the Major forces her to recant and disperse the waiting tribes. She dies, soon after, by her own hand.

You would hardly expect the Major to gun her down. Men—particularly the leading men of a series—simply did not shoot women, no matter how richly they deserved shooting. As a matter of record, the Major rarely shot anyone. Snakes, lions, kudu, an occasional elephant fell before his gun, but rarely a human, male or female, black or white.

Such delicacy was characteristic of his period, for lethal heroes were not yet as warmly celebrated as in 1931. It is true that if the hero roamed the western plains, like Hopalong Cassidy, or sailed the scarlet waters of the South Seas, as did Hurricane Williams, he was permitted a loose hand in slaughtering his fellow man. But strangely enough in mystery fiction, where you would expect heroes of a violent sort, only Don Everhard meant business with a gun.

The African story seems an odd place for such civilized qualms. As we have seen earlier, neither Haggard, Burroughs, or Wallace hesitated to splash their hero with gore. Quatermain and Sanders are too pragmatic to avoid giving death when necessary, and Tarzan was fierce by nature and red in tooth and nail.

The Major is not. His character and his interests may seem to be in the wilds, but he remains firmly within the upper-class culture of England. In that culture, acquiring illegal diamonds may, perhaps, be excused, but—Agatha Christie to the contrary—murder is quite another matter.

Unlike Quatermain, the Major doesn't forego civilization, but carries it along with him, neatly boxed. Along the way, he might take a moment to right wrongs and see justice done—or, if we must further clarify such crystalline idealism, to assure that the high sentiments of his culture are expressed by works, even in the bush, even in the pages of a popular magazine.

"The 'Oyster's' Pearl" (March 10, 1936) nicely illustrates the Major's dexterity in accomplishing wonders while avoiding homicide. After many months, the Portuguese authorities have withdrawn their charges against him. Leaving the Congo, he returns to Cape Town by tramp steamer. Once more he plays the monocled fool, leading on Sam Lane, a crooked type met aboard the ship.

Sam doesn't have much luck cheating the Major at cards. So he decides to kidnap him and clean out that Dude's bank account. Aided by Flash Savage, a tough crime boss who runs the gangs of Cape Town, Sam lures the Major off into the wilds. For some pages, the Major torments the city-bred tough with practical jokes that strongly suggest they have been drawn from the pages of boys' books. Finally, he pretends to blunder onto a pipe of diamonds. Sam and Flash fight for the spoils. Sam is murdered; Flash is arrested by the police and his gang broken up. And the Major glides away, serene and wholly immaculate.

The conclusions of other adventures are tributes to the Major's devious planning, rather than his quick draw. Often he blackmails the villain into retribution ("Cleavage") or arranges for the police to arrest the wretch after the Major has wrecked his plans ("Tools," "With One Stone").

Or he will play the innocent popinjay for a whole story, turning the tables on those seeking to victimize him in the final pages. Then, after stripping them of their diamonds, he sets them adrift of the veldt, with a few supplies and a sense of outrage ("A Hottentot's God," "The Quickness of the Hand," "Kaffir Orange").

Many stories end with death, but in few instances does the Major deliver it. On occasion, a frenzied elephant herd tramples the villain ("By Rule of Drum," "The Biggest Game"). At other times, other hands—Jim shoots the madman about to sacrifice the Major ("Squeeze"); enemy agents destroy their own tool ("Blank Charge"); an old woman knifes the tough native about to do the Major in ("A Major Masquerade").

Those readers long accustomed to superhuman feats by the series lead will be astonished to learn that the Major, for all his steel muscles and supple grace, frequently gets the worst of his many hand-to-hand encounters. During the events of "A Major Sacrifice," he is shot, clubbed, helpless, the assagai at his throat. Friends arrive at the last microsecond to save him. In "Blank Charge," he is knocked cold during the terminal struggle. And in "Masquerade," he is entirely outclassed by a ferocious native who could have given Tarzan problems.

That the Major does not always, in every circumstance, excel physically, simply means that the series points in directions other than slug and shoot. In this series, the hero as trickster stands out. Although the scene is Africa, the Major has more in common with Jeff Peters than with Tarzan. In this world, duplicity is all.

9—

The magazine which published these prancing adventures, *Short Stories*, had a long and imposing history, which began in 1890, amid a thunder of good intentions. The publisher, F. M. Somers, was also editor and publisher of *Current Literature*, a publication of crushing respectability. As originally planned, *Short Stories* was to be an over-sized quality magazine, printed on book paper and offering the public the finest of fiction drawn from all ages and most cultures: "Twenty-five stories for twenty-five cents."

The pages of the magazine were filled with a rich selection of reprinted fiction by such modern masters as Zola, Brete Hart, Turgenev, Kipling, and Anna Katherine Greene. The magazine was sold in 1904 and, after several years of uncertain direction, management was taken over by Doubleday, Page, and

Company, which in 1910, transformed *Short Stories* to a quality pulp paper magazine.

In its new pulp format, *Short Stories* offered action adventures by such writers as Clarence Mulford, J. Allan Dunn, Henry Herbert Knibbs, William Macleod Raine, W. C. Tuttle, and H. Bedford-Jones. There was a strong emphasis on western stories, with jungle and Canadian wilderness stories following behind. Brisk narrative lines plunged across crisply evoked landscapes; and the characters, drawn firmly and with color, if with no particular depth, behaved like human beings and often spoke like them, too.

For the greater part of its life, *Short Stories* was one of that impressive group of all-fiction magazines, including *Adventure*, *Argosy* and *Argosy All-Story Weekly*, *Blue Book*, and *The Popular Magazine*, which for some forty years constituted the mainstream of popular adventure fiction. These were the giants. In them developed the narrative techniques, subject matter, and characters that continue to energize our contemporary adventure fiction. And they generated, as well, an extraordinary cadre of artists, writers, and editorial personnel, some of whom remained active until the late 1980s.

By 1921, *Short Stories* was so successful that its issuance was increased to twice a month. The editor of this admirable magazine, Harry E. Maule, served from 1911 until 1936. His Associate Editor, Dorothy McIlwraith, then settled in as editor until the mid-1950s. (McIlwraith also edited *Weird Tales* during its final years.)

An extended editorial term, such as enjoyed by Maule and McIlwraith on *Short Stories*, or Frank Blackwell on *Detective Story Magazine*, suggests both stability and success. In truth, the magazine experienced few revolutions of format and content. Change there was as the years wore away. But compared to the convulsions which racked other magazines like recurrent attacks of the black death, *Short Stories* seemed almost static.

The most significant change came in 1931, during the brief editorship of R. de S. Horn (who, with associate Editor Frederick Clayton, temporarily interrupted the long Maule service). At that time, the magazine's format was thoroughly overhauled.

Short Stories had shamelessly modeled itself upon *Adventure*, borrowing page composition, illustration style, and departments in which readers and writers exchanged views and, occasionally, blows.

In 1931, the contents page was expanded from a minute rectangle centered on the first page, to a full page and, soon after, to a double-page spread. At the same time, the rather cool cover illustrations were replaced by colorful views of violent men gritting their teeth and displaying huge, poorly illustrated pistols. Inside the magazine, large drawings accompanied most of the stories and the type size increased. These benign changes were accompanied by a progressive cheapening of the paper, likely not noticed at the time, but quite apparent at this late period, when sulphite embrittlement has left the pages crisp as overcooked bacon.

The revised magazine continued to be priced at twenty-five cents, regardless of the Depression. Slightly more urban crime stories appeared. But the familiar westerns, jungle stories, and, particularly, the James B. Hendryx Klondike series, continued twice a month. Late in 1937, Doubleday sold the magazine; the new owner, Short Stories, Inc., introduced few changes, other than a continued coarsening of the cover art. The magazine seemed stable. But it was an illusionary stability, for on every side, the Twentieth Century roared toward the second major war in twenty-five years.

After the war, the pulp magazine business seemed like a man with a wasting disease. The war had caused a chronic shortage of experienced personnel, magnified costs, and severely damaged the publication distribution systems which had served for so long; the former readership, wooed by inexpensive paperbacks and the deadly charms of that new enchanter, television, no longer seemed willing to return to caped justice figures and hardboiled mystery-action stories. The combination of problems was deadly. *Short Stories* returned to monthly issuance in 1949. By the early 1950s, the magazine, like an old man returned to childhood, once more filled its pages with reprints.

In 1957, M. D. Gregory presided as editor over the final issues. By that date, *Short Stories* had become an uninspired pocket-sized magazine, with an unillustrated cover. But by 1957, the whole idea of sitting down and reading a magazine containing nothing but fiction seemed bizarre. The studied disbelief in the magazine and its likelihood of attracting potential buyers clearly shows in the shoddy production values of those final years.

To the last, however, stories by W. C. Tuttle and L. Patrick Greene continued to appear: the great ship was sinking but the band continued to play all those fine old tunes.

10—

Early in 1936, the Major became involved in another plot to incite a native revolt and drive out the whites. Between "Crooked Barrels" (April 25, 1936), the first story of the group, and "Blank Charge" (February 10, 1937), the final story, the premise wavered unsteadily along, like a bit of paper caught in cross winds. The plot against white rule became a plot against British rule; the instigator was a sinister secret group, was a sinister secret white man, was a red-headed native genius in disguise, was a foreign power manipulating native outrage.

The Major begins by jeering at the menace. In doing so, he takes a few good-natured pokes at assorted icons of African fiction:

The Major: 'No, gentlemen, despite the lively imaginations of certain fiction writers, there is nothing to unite the tribes. They would rather fight each other than the white man. Besides, they know that that is safer. No. There is no sacred symbol, no mysterious Deliverer. The sacred fire of Quarre Quate has gone out and can not be relit. There is no beautiful woman, white, black, or halfcaste, to lead them. There are no hidden valleys harboring an unknown race; no priestess of some strange cult, endowed with supernatural powers....'[31]

This is admirable, particularly since Greene has used most of these subjects in previous Major stories. No one notices an ironic interlude in a pulp action story, however, and the adventure flutters onward.

Four wealthy men, the living power behind the South African government, have called in the Major to consult with him concerning omnious rumblings throughout the continent. Somehow, the tribes have been receiving arms and ammunition. A vast organization seems to be at work, and the Major and Jim trek into the wilderness to sniff out the operation.

They are not entirely alone. The four powerful men have placed at the Major's disposal a large undercover network. Members recognize each other by displaying a golden compass and reciting a ritual which could easily have been composed by Penrod or Poppy Ott:

Secret Agent 1: 'You have a compass. A man never need be lost if he has a compass.'
Secret Agent 2: 'With such a charm, a man never need be lost. The needle will always show him the way home.'

The Major considers all this signing and countersigning ridiculous. He constantly forgets to display the compass and can rarely remember what he is to say when he does display it. He has fundamental doubts about the safety of such a system. Sooner or later, it will be compromised, he feels—and he is right.

But at the beginning, the ritual is infrequently of some slight help. "Crooked Barrels" describes how one deposit of arms is discovered and destroyed. This exploit is immediately followed by "Kaffir Orange" (May 25, 1936), which seems to have been published out of sequence and describes events occurring immediately after the Major and Jim have returned from the Congo.

In "A Major Masquerade" (July 10, 1936), the Major disguises himself as a worthless white man, despised by all. Insinuating himself into another nest of rebellion, he manages to stop it. Not alone. He is helped by an old woman, a store keeper, some dynamite, and a giant boulder.

The mastermind behind all this trouble is a red-headed halfbreed named Pavan. He lives in Durban, disguises himself as a white man, and sends his agents everywhere.

Almost trapped by the Major and the police, Pavan kills his associates in a fit of temper and vanishes. During the events of "Blank Charge" (February 10, 1937), he decides to trap the Major, using the ritual of the compass, which he has learned by foul means.

Undeceived, the Major plays along. He wishes to talk with Pavan and warn him of a double-cross by the foreign nation providing all those guns and ammunition. Pavan feels that he can master the situation but he reckons without the need of a pulp action story to compress time and probability: the next day, the foreigners appear to take over the rebellion. Pavan is mortally wounded.

The Major leads a last ditch struggle against the foreigners and their troops. Just as our hero is struck down in his tracks, as all is lost, and the series seems about to end in a dirge, over the hill pour reinforcements for the side of Truth and Justice, and the series ends gloriously.

If the ending is the usual Greene boiler-plate, the character of Pavan is drawn with more complexity than usual. The Major regards him as a patriot, sincere and honorable, even if opposed to British rule. He is certainly more intelligent and decent than his associates, who resemble stable sweepings.

"The Biggest Game" (April 10, 1937) might as well be called "The Midas Touch." In this, the Major has refused a peerage (for his work in crushing the rebellion). To reward him, in spite of himself, the four powerful men arrange that wherever he goes in Africa, he will be charged nothing for supplies or equipment. All is free. That delightful state of affairs rapidly becomes intolerable to self reliant fellows like the Major and Jim. But then the story veers from these ethical complexities to tell how a tricky poacher nearly ran amok in a game reserve. The end he comes to is satisfactorily bad.

The January 25, 1939 novel, "Major Sacrifice," recycles some earlier materials and contains a whiff of Haggard, a more intense whiff of Burroughs. The Major sets off to find Sarah Gray's lost husband, missing ten years. That sounds conventional, but it is not. The husband is missing because he can't stand her: he ran off to become the chief of a lost tribe in Happy Valley. She is a grim, greedy plotter of the Deadly Female variety. She wants the Major to get her husband's signature on a piece of paper, then kill him. Out of curiosity, the Major agrees to track down Gray. And kill him? She thinks so, a small error the Major has led her into. But after he has departed, she learns that this dandy with the monocle isn't as crooked as he pretended. Ice-eyed, she sends a pair of killers after him—and the unfortunate Mr. Gray.

It's a pretty set of problems that the Major must handle: he must discover why Sarah Gray wants the paper signed, dodge killers behind every bush, put down a rebellion of young men in Happy Valley, and find a way to preserve Gray's happy life as leader in that place. He manages to do all this in about forty-five pages.

After 1939, the series vanished from *Short Stories* for about seven years, Greene being involved with more serious matters than fiction. He returned in the October 10, 1947 issue with the first of a few new novels which, if they weren't quite as long as *War and Peace*, averaged around thirty pages.

"A Major Double Cross" (October 10, 1947) and "The Quickness of the Hand" (November 10, 1947) are loosely sequential. Evil white men plot and plan and underestimate the Major, with unfortunate consequences to themselves. In "Quickness," the corrupt whites have become the Major's prisoners. They manage to overawe a tribe of natives with sleight of hand prestidigitations, but the Major counters with parlor magic of his own and some dazzling rights to the jaw.

Differences there are between the post-war stories and those published in the Thirties. But not many differences. The exhuberence of the early stories smooths to a polished surface; the Illegal Diamond Buyer of 1920, whose good deeds brought him a healthy profit, became, during the 1930s, the selfless Savior of the British African Empire. For the remainder of his published life, the Major remained a charming eccentric, competent, sometimes prickly, often endangered, never finally defeated, and simply blazing with altruism.

Part of the series' charm is the deliberate contrast he provides to the other African series. The Major is always a shining bit of civilization dropped into the wilds and coping brilliantly, thank you. He is unruffled, is cool and clean, is mindful of good manners and restrained social behavior. No leopard-skin shorts and raw meat for him. He is satisfactorily competent, even though he presents to the world a face that is a self-created caricature, whimsical and lightly mocking. That is the basic joke of the series: competence in masquerade astounds a series of unsavory people.

It is perhaps this restraint that kept the series alive for so many years. Unlike Hurricane Williams, the Major is no semi-mythical figure. He bleeds, hungers, gets the fever, becomes confused, loses fights, and is repeatedly saved by Jim, the most faithful companion in contemporary literature.

All this seems quite real. The improbabilities and melodrama are nicely understated. The battles ending so many stories may be as bloody as the climatic scene from a Haggard novel, but the narrative leading up to these explosions is matter of fact, reasonably calm, filled with human concerns. Filled, also, with etched pictures of Africa, these, in their vividness, evoking a powerful feeling of place:

It was blazing hot. Not a cloud broke the fierce yellow-green light of the noonday sky; the sun had ceased to have form. It seemed to have melted under its internal heat and spread like a molten, brazen flood above the thirst-parched land. Heat waves danced grotesquely above the veld; distant hills changed shape constantly. Now they seemed near, now they vanished completely from the trekkers' blurred vision. Now they seemed substantial and unchangeable, now they shivered like a glutinous mass which threatened to dissolve into nothingness or, by some strange illusion of vision, they seemed to lose all contact with the earth and float in air, towering over the veld....[32]

...they found themselves in the heart of a wild, desolate region of barren hills where nothing lived—where nothing could live! The peaks made fantastic patterns against the blue of the sky and here and there, looking like streaks of molten silver, water cascaded from unbelievable heights above to the dark somber depths below.[33]

The eastern clouds were no longer gray but tinged with ever deepening colors—crimson, purples, lavender and gold commingling. A white ground mist spread over the veldt rising to the height of five or six feet and the hills seemed to be islands in a silver sea. And then, quite suddenly, the sun shot above the horizon and there was no more color in the sky—save a big disc of molten gold in an electric blue sky. It was no longer cold. The mist lifted, disintegrated into wraith-like wisps, trailing like lingering, reluctant fingers up the jagged side of the hills, finally vanishing.[34]

For a time the banks of the river were lined with mangroves. Then the mangroves gave way to palms and the palms, in turn, to giant arum with their green sheaths and purple-splashed cream flowers. Further back from the river's edge grew mimosa and trees bearing white flowers which shone like pearls amidst their dark leaves. Here and there were beaches of white sand on which—their presence destroyed the beauty of the scene— crocodiles sunned themselves.

At one point an enormous python, holding a still fluttering white plumaged bird in its mouth, swam across the river, passing just in front of the Major's canoe.[35]

It is a special delight of the adventure story that it gives us these concentrated glimpses of other places. For an instant, distance is pierced. Ragged mountains rise up, the python and its struggling prey cross the river, sheets of vines sprawl upward, an eland bounds in the sunlight.

Carefully selected pictures, these, sudden images that embed themselves in the imagination. You may forget the villain's name, the hero's accomplishments, the exact nature of the violence ending a story. But some of the glimpses of other places burn into the memory, remaining so living and brilliant it seems strange you can't remember experiencing them.

Each reader has his own set of pictures: perhaps of that tongue of rock shuddering over the abyss, deep within She's cavern; or the strange smells and sounds rising from Hong Kong Harbor, as you stand at the ship's railing with Peter the Brazen. Or the yelling shock of a hundred war canoes converging upon the Zaire at the upper reaches of Edgar Wallace's river.

Whatever the picture, it remains vivid long after the content of the story has dropped away, as the apple seed remains after the pulp has gone. The adventure story gives immediate joy, thrusting and shifting to its conclusion. But it provides another, more lingering pleasure: it invests memory with scenes of place and event that remain crisp and delightfully alive, long after the story has melted away.

That isn't exactly what the author intended, perhaps, but in the chancy world of fiction to be remembered in any way is a kind of triumph.

We have stayed long enough among the lost races and diamonds of Africa. To the west beckons another, equally omnious continent, densely jungled, filled with beasts and ferocious men and dangers, glorious dangers. As Quatermain, Sanders, and the Major grappled with the complications of their lives, other men faced equally deadly problems in South America. To that extraordinary place, we now turn.

Chapter 4
The Pathless Trail

1—

To South America, seeking his fortune, came Mr. Geoffery Heronhaye. Through highland and jungle, he sought gold, sought orchids, sought any reputable way to build his future fortune. All the while, his heart remained securely in New York City.

For in a New York City studio, the extraordinary Miss Gabrielle van Rooven, whose presence glows serenely through this series like some scented secret sun, creates an unending series of paintings. And Geoff must have these, every one. Or as many as he can afford. No sooner does he extract small sums from the terrors of South America, than he forwards a check to New York for the purchase of still another van Rooven masterpiece.

As a result, van Roovens are scarce and command ever-increasing prices. But little Geoff cares for these economic consequences: he is doing it for her!

So much for the spring that winds this twelve-part series, published in *The Popular Magazine* from October 1906 through September 1907, under the title "The Fortunes of Geoff." The stories were written by K. and Hesketh Prichard.

Aside from his monomania about Miss van Rooven and her artwork, Geoff is a perfectly splendid man who should have been modeling shirts instead of groping through lethal backwoods. He is "grave, handsome, imperturbable, and quite unaware of the attention his good looks won him from" women. He is also big, strong, and quick witted.

With all these virtues lavished on the hero, you would assume that the stories would have none. But not so. The stories give off an authentic reek of danger. Geoff must come to terms with edgy Indians; he must carry a message through sprawling battle lines where both sides distrust him: he must enter a town being ripped apart by rampaging rebels.

The dangers are large. No matter how strong and handsome Geoff is, he is only one man. Like any sensible person, he dodges direct confrontation. For what is one man against armies? He bluffs. He uses light disguises. He takes advantage of every opportunity.

For all his skill and care, matters occasionally go deadly wrong. In "The Insurgent General" (July 1907), he is captured by rebels and strung up by the neck and only the sudden arrival of government forces prevents the termination of his series.

More usually Geoff avoids such unpromising situations. Early in "The Pass of the Mexican" (June 1907), he discovers that he is being led into the clutches of a famous highwayman—a rebel officer turned bandit. Agilely enough, Geoff traps the trapper. As it turns out, the highwayman is a high-minded patriot.

He has taken up this unorthodox profession as a way to finance the rebel cause. His altruistic plans come to nothing when his men decide to steal the concealed spoils.

The officer dies a suicide, refusing to reveal where the loot is hidden. Thoroughly dramatic. But Geoff has learned the secret and spirits it all away. The story doesn't say that most of the treasure goes to New York to buy paintings, but you are permitted to suspect what you will.

The high-minded highwayman, like others in this series, suffers from Spanish Honor—the peculiar belief that a man's word binds him absolutely, whether it is convenient or not; that a life is a small thing to lay down for a principle; that personal integrity must be kept unstained. All these are quaint, romantic, obsolete ideas that have no validity today, since we and our elected officials have grown sophisticated and able to discard such ethical rubbish.

Geoff keeps bumping into Spanish Honor. At one point, he is all ready to save a general who has been tricked into a death cell by liars. But the general refuses to leave. He has given his parole that he will not attempt to escape. This presents Geoff with a nasty problem. He has promised the general's wife that he will attempt to save this prickly officer. But death is preferable to dishonor, at least in 1907 fiction.

Eventually Geoff slugs the general unconscious and carries him off. Which is all right with the general, who hoped that Geoff would have wit enough to see that way out the dilemma.

This insistence on honor gives the series an amusing, old-fashioned flavor. The action whirs along over a skin of social turmoil, with quick death by arrow, gun, or knife hovering close to the paragraphs. Geoff, who is touched by Spanish Honor, himself, is hard pressed to stay alive, much less make his fortune. Which he does at last.

But it was certainly getting rich the hard way.

2—

Early magazine fiction rarely honored the lands below the Rio Grande by showing them as they were. The view from North America was that of a far-sighted man who could read a newspaper across the room but couldn't count the number of fingers on his hand. Africa and China could be seen clearly. But Mexico, Central America, South America—all those lands extending immensely southward into the freezing ocean at the bottom of the world—appear as a blur. Or rather as a series of well-worn clichés, giving the same effect as a blur. It is as if some wicked magician had transformed the Southern countries to backdrops for a stupendous traveling carnival. Some backdrops are labeled Jungle, Lost Mountain Range, or Temple of Gold; others, Rebel Encampment, Smoky Cantina, Dangerous Native Village, or Port Full of Banana Ships. Before these backdrops move such standard figures of romance as Deadly Natives, Indolent Peons, Exquisite Señoritas, Overdressed Generals, Comic Opera Armies.

These exotic places and papier-maché figures set off splendid Anglo-Saxon heroes, virile, energetic, lethal, who adventure with such confidence. How bravely they plunge into jungles crawling with snakes and murderous Indians. How cheerfully they face bandits, rebels, corrupt government officials. At any moment, they may be captured and tortured or stood before an adobe wall to see if they are bullet-proof. At any moment, something dire may happen. Something unreasonable and more than a little sweaty.

For south of the Rio Grande it is all chaos, a howling mixture of savagery and incompetence, depending on whether you visit the jungle or the city.

(You wonder if there was a corresponding slant to the magazine fiction published in those far countries: do they tell, for example, of a dashing young Brazilian who adventures north of the Rio Grande, battling fierce natives and corrupt officials?)

As is usual with the adventure story, the backgrounds are drawn with precision, the characters are thinly realistic, and the situations melodramatic in the extreme. In the Billy June series, which appeared in *Adventure* during 1916, the realistic backgrounds dominate the story. They reek of danger, savagery, casual violence. By contrast, the twists of the story line seem as artificial as green eyeshadow.

There seems an excellent reason for this. If the author, Wilbur Hall, is to be believed, the stories are solidly based in fact:

For the Billy June stories, I am endebted (*sic*) to Mr. Cecil Haig (a young engineer) who knows his Mexico and his South America as well as any American of my acquaintance—as well, I believe, as any man anywhere, and who has supplied the local color and the characters, and most of the stories themselves....[1]

As a result, we may suppose, the Billy June series has the hard ring of authenticity, except on those occasions when the plot writhes around and bites itself on the hip.

Billy June is a trouble shooter. He is "the man who has had more adventures in South America and has more friends in the continent, and who can do more toward straightening out any sort of mess—political or business or international—than any other individual south of the Zone. Deliberate, calm, slow, patient, tireless, Billy June simply won't be hurried. But start him on a search for a lost exploring party, or a missing official document, or a man who has disappeared, or give him a commission to treat with a tribe of Indians, or ask him to settle a strike, or instruct him to go into the interior and deliver a message where white men are looked on as devils and killed at sight, and Billy June will very deliberately consider the job, accept it if it suits him, and be swallowed up around the dark corners of South America.

"And when he comes back, which will be in his own good time, Billy June will have fulfilled his mission and delivered the goods."[2]

The paragraphs, enchanted by the roll and rumble of non-stop sentences, drone monotonously in the cadence of a forgotten past. The adventures described bounce aggressively along. In the first story of the series, "Billy June and the Private Document" (February 1916), the problem is relatively simple: That rotten crooked Walter Donar has got himself engaged to that adorable delight, Esther Martines de Silveira. Walter has marched off into the interior jungles to shoot her a *tigre* skin and vanished.

Billy June takes the job of locating Walter. In his private heart, he also intends to find some way of breaking the engagement. His opinion of Walter is not high.

The trail leads up the Tocantins River toward the Serra de Oro region. Here live mean Indians who are given to stripping the skin off a prisoner's feet, then giving him a five-minute start through the jungle before they light out after him with spears. Immediately these Indians tie up Billy June's boatman and make fierce faces at our hero.

Billy June: 'I never found any good to come of lying off and making signs to Indians, not in South America, anyhow. If they want to do you bodily disfigurement, they'll probably do it, and if they don't, you might as well go up and find that out. That's the way I estimate it.

'So I walked into this bunch and knocked a couple of them forty feet into the *matto* and untied my boatman. That did them good. They growled a little and talked murder and arson for my benefit, and then we had a confab.'[3]

From the Indians, he learns that Walter has stumbled into Indian territory, stolen lumps of gold from their private gold field, tickled their women meaningfully, and ended up in a hut, closely guarded. Billy June manages to talk him out of having his feet skinned. But it's close.

In his wallet, Walter is carrying a very fancy document—the Private Document of the title. Billy waves this document at the chief, telling him that Walter represents the government in Rio and has been sent to reassure the Indians that their gold fields are theirs alone. Which is nice.

Having delivered that message, the white men walk swiftly away. Once safe, Billy June tells Walter to withdraw from the wedding.

Remarkably enough, Walter does.

That's because Billy June has read that private document, which is a marriage license issued to Walter and a woman other than Esther Martines de Silveira.

It is never explained why any man, even if dazed by romance, is waltzing around the jungle carrying his marriage license. It is never explained because it can't be explained. Nonetheless that is the whole point of the story—the irony, the stripper in the cake, the astonishment at the final line. The story requires Walter to carry that license.

Which also suggests that the story, as told to us, is bosh. Perhaps Mr. Cecil Haig told Mr. Wilbur Hall of a document that looked so official it was used to overawe the Indians. From that anecdote, Mr. Hall constructed this self-conscious story filled with self-conscious complications. Perhaps.

Although the story depends upon an infamous cheat, the adventure, itself, has a fine, high, realistic feel. The descriptions are just right. The South American scene has presence. The Indians put cold at the pit of your stomach. The climate of the jungle is suitably intolerable. It's a shame to saddle these strengths with such a sickly story plot.

"The Private Document" is a framed story—that is, it is told by Billy June to a group of friends. This device permits some rudimentary characterization of Billy June. He drawls and teases and lounges, professing to be sluggish and lazy, claiming that he thinks slowly and needs time to collect his thoughts:

"Don't hurry me, now."

"Don't crowd me. Don't rush me."

"Just you let me take my time."

For fifteen years, Billy June has been trouble-shooting in South America. As he explains it: "Dropped off in Rio in the November of '99 because I and old Captain Nels Sorenson—he went down with the clipper *Mary May* off Cape Horn ten years ago—couldn't get along as to my having part of one watch, at least, to sleep in.

"And since then I've knocked around a good deal and found that about every man in South America, and his brother, is trying to get rich. Most of them figure it out to be done in, say, a year or two."[4]

He talks as if he had met Geoff.

The series begins using a framed story, but before long the frame has been dropped and the story is narrated in the first person by a friend and admirer of Billy June.

In "Billy June and the Amazon River Scandal" (November 1916), narrator Eddie Doag wants to marry the ethereal Carmen de Barrosa. Her father thinks otherwise. To get Eddie out of the dumps, Billy June talks him into applying for a job on a new railroad being built in Brazil.

Eddie speedily discovers that the railroad is a fake. The promoter is bleeding the government, squeezing the help, and is ready to duck out with bags of cash. By fraud and trickery, this rascal has also laid hands on $60,000 in government funds which Senhor Oswaldo Jose de Barrosa is now accused of embezzling.

An emergency call goes out for Billy June. Before BJ arrives, violence explodes. The railroad workers riot; an engineer is shot dead. During the roaring confusion, the promoter vanishes with everybody's money.

At this instant, Billy June lounges on stage, drawling, slow, but forceful. Very forceful. He promptly lays hands on one of the crooks to squeeze out some information, and we are treated to one of those little moments when the past seems exceptionally close, after all.

> *Crook*: 'Don't you hit me.... I've got some rights.'
> *Billy June*: 'Oh, yes, you've got some, but not the kind we'll recognize.'[5]

Presently the missing promoter is detected in his hiding place. The money is recovered, Senhor de Barrosa's name is cleared, and Eddie becomes a certified suitor.

In the December 1916 "Billy June and Padre Paolo's Revolution," Eddie has not yet married her. He is too busy traveling to one of Brazil's northern states with Billy June. Up there, a crooked governor is looting with both hands and the aggressive Padre Paolo is said to be leading a revolt. Rio wants to know if the padre will support the government.

There follows some highly dangerous work. The streets are full of the governor's secret service. Every individual is treacherous. The governor is a murderous liar.

Billy June ends up jailed for most of the story. It is Eddie's responsibility to seek out the Padre, satisfy the government's questions about that good man, then save Billy June from death by firing squad.

He does. But the story is just gathering momentum. In an ending of breathless violence, Billy June forces the governor to resign, only to be shot through the chest as they escape. Doesn't kill him, though. Next morning the rebels confront the regular army and it's all over. Virtue wins wonderfully.

The governor, by the way, flees the country with piles of loot. Talk about realism.

While the clack of gears in the Billy June series is sometimes deafening, a latent ferocity simmers realistically under the mechanical demands of the plot. We recognize that ferocity without difficulty. We have been living with it for generations: that casual tendency of the human species to murder its own in the most off-handed way, as if crumpling up a tissue.

The Indians of this series may be gullible and the soldiers and secret service operatives inefficient. But they are also lethal. They will do harm. They will give death, every one of them. And the potential for casual slaughter gives this series its own curious flavor. The danger is always here. Even while the plot machinery grates and grinds, impending death waits like a fanged thing barely under the surface of the black water.

It is altogether unsettling. You wonder how Billy June stood fifteen years of it.

3—

According to Arthur Olney Friel, people not only enjoyed the sensation of death just around the corner, but they went marching out into the Amazonian jungle to seek ever more intense sensations of danger.

Arthur Friel (1885-1959), newspaperman and free-lance writer, published nine serials and numerous novelettes and short stories in the 1920s-1930s *Adventure* magazine. He also wrote articles for other publications and a book concerning his personal explorations in South America.

While not all Friel's fiction was about South America, at the heart of his work lies the Guayana Wilderness, drained by the Orinoco River and its innumerable tributaries. Back then, this wilderness was nearly unknown. Even today, much of it remains untouched jungle, thick with vine and edged leaf. Insects swarm and through the tangle move curious South American animals. Along the river, the sun has cruel weight. The air is a thick, hot towel, for this country is less than ten degrees north of the Equator.

In the forest prowls a variety of death. Subtle death by insect bite. Death by poison fang or jaguar claw. Death by sting or horn. Or by poisoned blade or dart—for the Indians guard these territories jealously. Of these, some are ritual cannibals, eating their enemies' hands and feet. Others snick off heads. Others kill only when suspicious—but they trust few men.

In these brutal areas, there is fortune and the rumor of fortune. Fortune enough to draw white adventures, pulled by the mystery resident behind the next bend in the river. These adventurers are men inflamed by the need to plant their feet on uncharted plains and see mountains without a name jab against the sky. Curiosity drives them. They come to test themselves against nature's ferocity. The prospect of being extremely uncomfortable for very long periods bothers them not at all.

Friel wrote a series of connected serials about three such explorers. The first of these stories, "The Pathless Trail," was published in *Adventure* as a four-part serial (October 10, 20, 30, and November 10, 1921). Issued as a book in 1922, it was reprinted as a paperback in 1969.

"The Pathless Trail" is one of those pleasing gems you find sprinkled through the pages of *Adventure*. Since this particular gem was sprinkled some seventy years ago, it shows certain prejudices and conventions that have not aged gracefully.

But even allowing for time's erosion, the story rushes wonderfully along. Suspense heats the pages. Danger and violent action burst out with agreeable frequency. And the occasional coincidence, thrown in to lubricate the bearings of the plot, does not distress you much. The pages fume with the excitement of travel in dangerous places, the first requirement of an adventure story.

Before the series is over, we will taste much excitement with the three adventurers: McKay, Knowlton, and Ryan.

Since "The Pathless Trail" was published about three years after World War I, waves from that struggle still ran high. The story glints with memories of the war. All three adventurers are ex-combat soldiers: Roderick McKay, former captain, is tall and lean, with grey eyes, black hair, and, after weeks in the wilderness, a black beard. He speaks with the voice of command. But not often. Among the three, command is little needed. McKay is sensible and knows men; he can also be pig-headed whenever required by plot.

Meredith Knowlton, called "Merry" later in the series, is a former lieutenant, a slender, blond man. During the series he takes more than his share of knocks, once nearly dying. But it takes more than fever, blows on the head, and assorted wounds to do in a lead character in an on-going series.

Tim Ryan, ex-sergeant, is a stocky, impulsive Irishman, red-headed and red-faced. He is not nearly as ostentatiously Irish as was the wonderful Terence O'Rourke. Compared to McKay and Knowlton, Ryan tends to be a little more physical, is a little more prone to action, a little slower in thought. You have met similar Irishmen in a hundred books and five hundred moving pictures. But possibly the character type was not so much a cliché then as now.

These three men have traveled up the Orinoco in search of the lost millionaire, David Dawson Rand. Who does not know that he is a millionaire. Family deaths have settled a large estate on him. But he has vanished into the jungle. Rumor reports that he has gone native, that he is with the Red Bones, cannibalistic Indians living beyond the horizon. If the three adventurers can locate Rand, his estate will pay them a hefty reward.

What they locate is trouble. Immediately.

First they meet an evil German named Schwandorf—at this time, all Germans were villains. Schwandorf learns of their mission and determines that he will collect Rand and the reward. Since the three plan to paddle far up-river to a village where Rand has been seen, Schwandorf offers to secure a crew for them. As you may have guessed, the crew is a choice collection of thugs, paid by the German to slaughter the adventurers.

The plan flops. When the crew finally attacks, it gets mowed down in a brutal fight. Standing with the three against the crew is Jose Martinez, a Peruvian outlaw, a hard, embittered man of bad reputation.

Eventually Martinez will become the most interesting character of the series. Of Castilian descent, he became an outlaw after quarreling with an official over a girl. The girl went to a convent, and Jose took to the wilderness, the Peruvian army howling at his back.

In time, Jose, will become a king of white Indians. But at this early date, he is still only a hawk-faced knife artist, and man of honor. McKay and the others accept him for his abilities, not his reputation. He becomes their close companion and the fourth major character of the series.

From this point, the story is straight-ahead adventure. After they reach the Mayoruna village up-stream, the travelers are received with great distrust. Someone has been stealing native women. That someone is thought to be a white man with a black beard—like McKay's.

After this is straightened out, they discover that Rand is not in the village. He's off in the wilderness with the cannibalistic Red Bones.

They travel to the village of the Red Bones. There they get captured by as mean a bunch of killers as ever got on a page of fiction. They are fastened in a hut overnight, with the promise of an ugly tomorrow. In another hut, the stolen women wail.

McKay plans a night escape. Before they slip away, a crazy man comes creeping through the shadows; they slug him with a rifle butt.

It is Rand, of all people. Rand was shot in the head (by a German) about five years before and lost his memory, went native, was regarded by the Indians as a holy lunatic.

The adventurers scoop up Rand, gather together the women, steal canoes enough for the crowd, and off they go, hotly pursued by the Red Bones. After hair-raising adventures, they reach the Mayoruna village.

There McKay takes charge. Anticipating an attack by the Red Bones, he tells the chief and villagers to dig a series of protective trenches (a typical aftershock from World War I). Soon the Red Bones attack in howling masses, led by Schwandorf. After a furious battle, the Red Bones are obliterated. Schwandorf, snivelling and cowering in defeat, is casually dispatched by Martinez and his long, sharp machete. And Rand recovers his memory, cured by that blow with the rifle butt back at the village.

So much for "The Pathless Trail."[6]

All this story summary is for a purpose. "The Pathless Trail" established the structure and selection of events for the series. It is the blueprint for all the subsequent serials. As for instance:

—the narrative is motivated by a search: for a lost man, for riches, for a legend.

—the search requires extended travel through a wickedly hostile country.

—the country is vividly described, with detailed descriptions of the flora and fauna. Specific details are given of native customs, weapons, and beliefs.

—women usually play no major role in the story, although in "The King of No Man's Land" and "Mountains of Mystery," a woman strongly motivates the action.

—at some point in the story, there will appear an important madman.

—at least once, often twice during a story, McKay and company will perform an act of respect. That is, they will treat a man fairly, or save him, or honor him for his abilities, thus winning a powerful ally. In "The Pathless Trail," McKay treats Martinez as a honorable man; later he saves the life of the chief's son, who has been wounded by a poisoned arrow. In "Mountains of Mystery," McKay manages to ignite a feeling of personal worth in a man rotten with self disgust.

—at least one of the adventurers gets severely damaged during the action.

—chapters habitually end with hints of menace, suspense, and the promise of danger.

—the search for whatever it is they are searching for is complicated by the greed of the villain. His plots forever hover just overhead, compounding the dangers of the journey.

—two or three violent fire fights break out during each adventure. The final battle is a full-fledged war, a mass slaughter on both sides, hundreds of yowling savages flinging themselves at a few men with guns.

Most of these elements are used in the splendid serial, "Tiger River," (four parts, July 20, 30, and August 10, 20, 1922, *Adventure*). Issued as a book in 1923, it was republished as a paperback in 1971.

In "Tiger River," the three adventurers join with Jose and Rand to search for gold in the Langanati Mountains beyond the Tigre River. That river rises in the mountains of Ecuador and runs south-east through northern Peru to the Maranon, which, in turn, feeds into the Amazon. For the next two serials, the scene of action will focus on the North Peru/Ecuador area.

And what is Rand doing out here in the wilderness? Unfortunately he didn't receive that legacy. Instead it went to a relative who was not as dead as had been thought.

Which may explain why the entire cast is paddling north-west up the river, pursued, as usual, by a plotter's malice. Somewhere in the wilderness ahead is gold. Possibly. But gold is, after all, only an excuse. Excitement is their true goal:

Rainbow chasers all, hardy, venturesome, fearless, they were of that breed which plunges straight into the jaws of death if within those jaws lies a prize worth the daring.[7]

They need daring. They have a nightmare encounter with a pair of jaguars during a storm. Next they are captured by Indians and escape having their throats cut only by painting themselves to resemble smallpox victims. Fleeing, they are hunted by Jivaros. These they trap and gun down, saving a party of white Indians from massacre.

Now McKay and Jose disagree. Since each is too bull-headed to back down, the party splits. Jose leaves with the Indians. McKay and the crew continue up the river toward other marvels.

Marvels indeed! Including green men silently prowling after them. A bell booming from trackless jungle. A forgotten colony of Spanish Indians living at the center of an over-grown volcano that pulses with earthquake.

Down inside the cone, a fat-faced Circe operates a gold mine. Her laborers are men with drug-dulled minds, victims of her inhospitable potions. She has captured Jose and the Indians. Now she attempts to add McKay and the others to her collection.

But Jose leads a rebellion and McKay refuses to be doped. The Circe's schemes come to nothing and she ends up dead. Very quickly. She is hardly a menace before she is a corpse.

After this stimulating episode, gangs and hordes and swarms of Jiveros attack. The slaughter, as violent as the Battle of the Alamo, is terminated by an earthquake. The wicked woman's cache of gold is revealed, so all the shooting and sweating has been worthwhile.

The adventurers return downstream with the gold. Jose remains behind as King of the Indians.

His problems drive the following serial, "The King of No Man's Land" (four parts, March 20, 30, and April 10, 20, 1924). Rand has got lost again and so has his memory. Apparently he has become king of a Jivero tribe.

The adventurers set out to find him. Instead, they discover an enigmatic Spanish girl, Nuné, who lives with headhunters. As luck, necessity, or plot requirements have it, they also meet Jose Martinez, who is leading a war band of white Indians out among the trees.

Jose has created a small kingdom in a strip of land claimed by both Peru and Ecuador. With the kingship, he has acquired a king's problems. Peru threatens war. The Jivaros have actually begun war—and one of their four main tribes, the Huambizas, has become a dangerous threat to Jose's kingdom. So the stage is set for desperate deeds, captures, flaming guns, just as in the works of Rider Haggard.

Leaving only a sketchy force to protect his central city, Jose marches his forces to war. With him go the explorers and Nuné. Six days down the river, after slaughtering a Jivaro village, they learn that the Huambizas have passed them. Under the command of Rand, these Jivaros are moving to attack Martinez's city.

Back up the river they race wildly. At the city, they intercept the Huambizas. There follows an inferno of killing. McKay, Knowlton, and Ryan help shatter the Jivaro attack, killing one or two million each. And at the climax, they also capture Rand, immediately after he has captured Jose.

In the final chapters, everyone persistently misunderstands everyone else. That adds suspense and conflict to a story which has accidentally climaxed before the end of the book. After the tangle is unraveled, we learn that Rand attacked because he thought Jose had stolen Nuné. After learning otherwise, he agrees to become Jose's partner in rule. Seems that Rand's Huambizas kingdom has collapsed, most of his people having been killed attacking this place and that. Rand never wishes to return to civilization, which is vile, shallow, and so forth. All his wealth, he gives to the three explorers. For himself, he is content with his share of the Hoseran kingdom—the spelling derives from Jose-Rand.[8]

At the conclusion of this serial, the three explorers indicate pretty clearly that they intend to return to civilization and never shoot another native again.

Doesn't happen. In "Mountains of Mystery" (four-part serial, January 30, February 10, 20, 28, 1925), we find them at the headwaters of the Orinoco in Venezuela. The search, this time, is for a lost white race hidden some place behind all those leaves.

The search for a race of white Indians was dear to Friel's heart. Fascinated by legends and tales of this race, Friel had traveled to South American in 1922. With considerable difficulty he paddled up the Orinoco and its tributary, the Vintuari, into the Guayana wilderness. In that area lived the Maquiritare Indians, white skinned by reason of white or Spanish blood.

Friel did locate the remains of the tribe—two of them, the only survivors. After which he returned to civilization, paddling "a thousand miles on flood-swollen rivers through a country upset with revolutionary fighting and banditry." Later he described his experiences in the non-fiction travel book, *The River of Seven Stars* (1924).

"Mountains of Mystery" is filled with exact, closely-observed detail. The plot, however, gives a single long weird cry and flings away into fantastic melodrama.

Seems that way off in the mountains of central Venezuela, there lives a tiny tribe of Indians. They are dying out because of in-breeding. Their leader, the sorcerer of the Talking Mountain, is attempting to correct this situation by capturing nice healthy men—white men, if possible—for breeding stock. Those captured are given a drink which changes their skin color to a muddy black. That keeps them from running back to civilization. It doesn't affect the color of their children, however. Some of the captives, like the American, "Black White," get to brooding about their transformation and go mad.

In White's case that is dangerous, for he is a big, powerful fellow, a living fighting machine and horribly dangerous in his craziness.

Our adventurers are led through jungle and across plateau by mysterious benefactors, until they reach the sorcerer's cave in Talking Mountain. Once there, they are uncermoniously dumped into a muddy pit from which there seems no escape. Either they drink the skin-blackening potion or they can die of exposure and thirst.

Instead, they get out. White beats the sorcerer to death against the walls of his cave.

At this point, right on schedule, begins the grand battle with which Friel customarily closes these festivities. This one is approximately as violent as the end of the world. After the jungle has been depopulated, the adventurers collect a bag filled with rough emeralds and head back downstream. Hot after them comes White, muttering and snarling to himself, hot to kill them all before they tell what happened to his skin color.

On the final page, however, he overhears them speaking warmly of his fighting abilities and agreeing not to reveal his condition. Their respect warms the fragments of his sanity. Leaving them unmurdered, he slops away, jabbering to himself, a figure drawn in ice and blood, not at all amusing.

The writer of these strenuous adventurers, Arthur O. Friel, was born in Detroit, 1885. Graduating from Yale in 1909, he became a reporter for the *Concord Monitor* (in New Hampshire). He would be a newspaperman for most of his life. From 1911 to 1920 (with a year out for military service), he worked for the Associated Press, and later for the *Manchester Union-Leader*. In 1919 he began to write freelance fiction, his work appearing in *Adventure* to the end of the 1930s. Most of it reflected his trip up the Orinoco in 1922.

In 1942 he became the War Editor of the *Concord Monitor-Patriot*. Later he wrote editorials and columns for the *Union-Leader* and served as the associate editor of the New Hampshire *Sunday News*. He died January 27, 1959.

Friel was one of two or three dozen men who made the *Adventure* magazine a thing of wonder. These writers turned out action fiction that was a distinct cut above the usual magazine fare, a few of them contributing steadily for more than thirty years. About his fiction, Friel remarked:

I let the story tell itself. Straightaway as a whole. Ending not clearly in mind. Revise comparatively little. Sometimes I rewrite a section but usually not....

In writing, I don't lay out my story and get it all nicely framed up before starting to write. I start with a general idea which comes to me from God-knows-where, and soon I'm marching along with my characters without any very clear idea of where we're all going to wind up. We get into swamps and cut our way through the brush and clamber up on a hill and maybe find something on the other side; one thing leads to another, and eventually we make a good finish....

...I have tried, on a number of occasions in the past, to make my characters and events fit a more-or-less definite idea of mine as to what they were to do, but it didn't work; they just took matters into their own hands and did all kinds of things I never meant them to do, and all I could do was trail along; and, darn 'em, they made a far better yarn of it than I'd ever made if I'd clubbed them into submission...."[9]

Nearly as prolific as Tuttle, Greene, Young, Spears, and Sudrez (to name a few of the magazine's giants), Friel published many short stories and nine novels between 1919 and 1931. Most of the novels first appeared as serials in *Adventure*. During the 1930s, the novels shrank to novelettes, usually published as two-part serials. None of these appeared in book form. His later fiction is lighter in tone, less concentrated than the work of the 1920s, and less touched by those fantastic elements which link his early writing to H. Rider Haggard's African novels.

To the end, his fiction glittered with observed detail. Concerning one of his serials ("The Fate of Anton LeBaron"). Friel wrote in "The Camp-Fire" department of the November 15, 1931, *Adventure*:

The characters, habitations, and habits of the Indians have not been altered in this story. They are real, even if their names are not. So are other conditions along my river with the disguised name...as some of you real back-bush rangers can testify.[10]

This foundation of precisely described reality supports Friel's more imaginative flights. Even the most fanciful elements of The Pathless Trail series seem somehow possible. They are dreams with granite roots. Chapter after chapter, the details of the scene always seem right. Vistas open, revealing terror and beauty and bloody marvel. As danger coats the heart with cold. As the insect-tormented adventurers struggle along a muddy path.

Until abruptly the foliage falls away. Ahead the Andes lift enormous against the far sky, pale stone clawing at the sun.

The pathless trail is difficult and demands much. If it leads to wonder, we are already half persuaded. We accept, without complaint, Friel's dangers, his repetitious plots, his inclination toward cliché, his amazing climaxes, strange with coincidence.

These are trifling matters. The intensity of the adventure sweeps us along, wonder-struck and nearly believing, caught up in the fellowship of the trail.

4—

When Geoff marched through 1906 South America, ever alert for gold, Nick Carter still appeared in his own dime novel and only a few representatives of that vulgar new phenomena, the pulp magazine, adorned the news stands.

By 1921, the year of "The Pathless Trail," the dime novel was a rarity and the pulp magazine had become a major vehicle for popular fiction. Popular magazine fiction, itself, ever sensitive to the reader's pleasure, had grown increasingly hard-edged, increasingly violent.

Not that violence was unknown to earlier fiction. Since your attention has remained unflagging through these delightful chapters, you will recall that Rider Haggard's novels feature mass slaughters of a quality comparable to the best that the Western Front could offer. Similar events tended to erupt in both the Sanders and the Major series.

That the victims were natives rather than Europeans undoubtedly reduced the impact of such mass killings. The natives didn't really mind dying, since they lived in straw huts and went barefooted and otherwise lacked cultural advantages. Moreover, the natives died in irrational outbursts which were opposed and ultimately contained by Anglo-Saxon heroes. If a native indulged himself in irrational outbursts, it served him right that clean-cut white men gunned him down. What on earth did he expect?

The random violence of modern war, that began seeping into prose around 1918, was qualitatively different from battles with irate natives. The prose so tainted accepted wholesale death with chilly indifference. The heroic struggle against overwhelming odds became less a personal matter than a technical problem. The Haggard heroes fought for principle; Jimmie Cordie and his boys because they were paid professionals who took pride in their work. The brute savagery of the Hurricane Williams series with its desperation and self-hatred amid the wreckage of civilization, springs from the Western Front as surely as Jimmie Cordie's machine guns or Friel's terminal fire fights. Violence had been dehumanized.

Certainly other factors influenced the tone of pulp fiction. After the war, a few months rejoicing gave way to joblessness, Prohibition, tight money, and jazz music, symptoms of those apocalyptic times, which burst upon society like demons bursting from evil eggs. These matters all influenced popular magazine fiction, stirring darkly behind the exciting pages. But chiefly, the change reflected the large-scale violence which had entered the pulps, never to be exorcised as long as the magazines were published.

These harsh transformations hardly show in the magazine fiction of 1916. In that year, Nick Carter edited the *Detective Story Magazine*—so we were assured—and if war hammered dreadfully in Europe, the dismaying sounds of death were far away. The Munsey publication house churned out ever more copies of *All-Story Weekly* and *The Argosy*. *Adventure* still offered readers a cover illustration of a pretty girl, rather than a pirate or rampaging gunman, as would be the case in a few years. And the story of adventure was not invariably salted by multiple deaths. Extraordinary as it may seem, some adventure series depended primarily on the interplay of character. To one such series, we now turn.

Illustrations

ADVENTURE *for November*

Volume I   1910   Number 1

Yellow Men and Gold. A Serial Story. I . .   Gouverneur Morris, ...   3
A Tale of Treasure-Seeking in the South Pacific

First of All—The News. A Story . . .   E. J. Rath . . . . — .   15

Sergeant McCarty and the Black Hand Red.
     A Story . . . .   P. C. Macfarlane   22

On the Way to La Gloria., A Story . . .   Edward S. Moffat   34

A Battle Won. A Story . . . . .   Donal Hamilton Haines . . .   39

When I was King of Botel-Tabago. An Article .   Walter J. Kingsley   48

The Red Ring. A Story . . . . .   William Le Queux   52

Carmelita Sofia McCann. A Story . . .   Clarice Vallette McCauley . .   59
A Soldier of Fortune in Petticoats

Man Friday. A Story . . . . .   Owen Oliver   71

Can a Man be True? A Serial Story. I . .   Winifred Graham   77
A Tale of Romance and Intrigue in the Balkans

A Collision in Elysium. A Story . . .   John A. Heffernan   96

Exiles of the Outlands. An Article . . .   E. Alexander Powell, F.R.G.S. . .   103
Tales of the Men That Can't Come Back

And a Child Led Them. A Story . . .   Harry Allyn   113

The Woman in Fifty-Three. A Story . .   MacGregor Bond   119

The Mystery of the Twenty Sacks of Coal. A Story   Albert Kinross   127

The Apotheosis of Fencedown Slade. A Story .   Nevil G. Henshaw   137

Pearls. A Story . . . .   H. F. Prevost Battersby . . .   143

Lion Hunts in East Africa. An Article . .   Alfred Jordan   150

The Crook and the Doctor. A Complete Novelette   John I. Cochrane, M.D. . . .   154
. A Tale of Adventure in the Underworld

Cover from a painting by M. Leone Bracker
Headings and Decorations by Charles B. Falls

Issued monthly.   Yearly subscription, $1.50 in advance.   Single copy, fifteen cents
Foreign postage, $1.00 additional.   Canadian postage, 30 cents.
Copyright, 1910, by The Ridgway Company in the United States and Great Britain
Published by THE RIDGWAY COMPANY, Spring & Macdougal Sts., New York City
5, Henrietta St., Covent Garden, London, W. C., England
Entered for entry as Second-Class Matter at the Post-office, at New York, N. Y.

1. *Adventure* (November 1910). The Table of Contents for the initial issue of this
extraordinary magazine.

2. *The Popular Magazine* (March 1905). H. Rider Haggard's adventure novels mixed realism, fantasy, violence, lost civilizations, and wonders beyond the horizon. A swarm of writers exploited his vision.

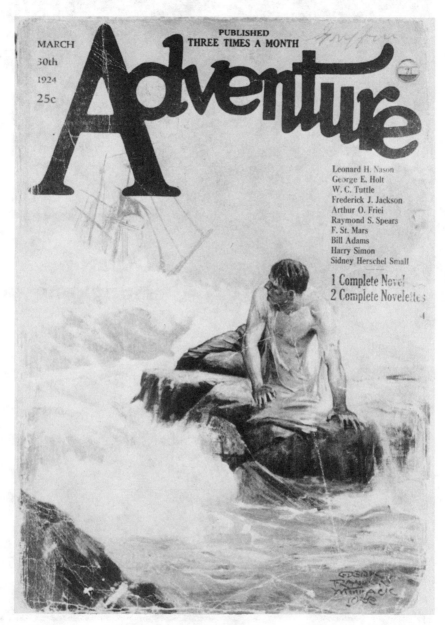

3. *Adventure* (March 30, 1924). Published three times a month, the magazine stressed action rising from character from 1910 to 1971.

4. *Argosy* (March 31, 1934). Peter the Brazen appeared in two separate series, about ten years apart, that dazzled the reader with cyclonic action and Oriental scenes.

5. *Short Stories* (March 25, 1923). The popular Major, an Illicit Diamond Buyer in South Africa, transformed from a crook to a hero over the course of his series.

6. *All-Story Weekly* (February 1, 1919). The Suffragette movement sent thrills of competent, intelligent women through popular fiction. Including Janie Frete, shown here gunning a devilfish, who was the equal of any man, and a feminine jewel, besides.

7. *Adventure* (July 15, 1935). Hashknife Hartley and Sleepy Stevens, range detectives extraordinary, appeared in *Adventure, Argosy,* and *Short Stories* for more than thirty years.

8. *Young's Magazine* (July 1922). Oldest of all the girl-exploitation magazines, *Young's* merged with *Breezy Stories* in the 1930s, suggestive to the last.

9. *Snappy Stories* (Second September 1924 issue). Interior illustration for "Confessions of a Gold Digger," showing a rich old fellow about to foot the bill.

10. *Big Story Magazine* (March 1929). Flaming novels of flaming youth, jazzing the nights away.

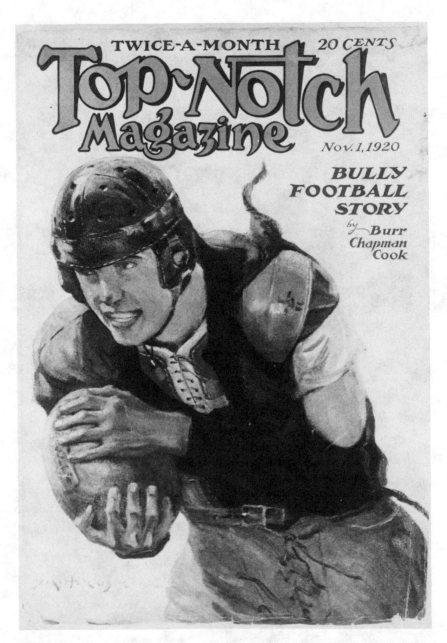

11. Sports stories surrounded the lead athlete with scarlet veils of melodrama through which showed details of the crucial game.

12. Popular fiction used the bum for crude menace or crude comedy, rather than as a symptom of social pathology.

Chapter 5
Adventuress

An "Adventuress," we regret to say, is frequently a woman on the prowl for fun and profit, like those naughty ladies who made memorable the 1930s pages of *Scarlet Adventuress* and *Modern Adventuress*—or like Vivian Legrand (The Lady from Hell), who accomplished so many interesting things in the mid-1930s *Detective Fiction Weekly*.

Rapacious adventuresses were not confined to the 1930s. Way back in the 1920s, assorted gold diggers conducted their exciting profession in *Snappy Stories*. Before then, Blue Jean Billy, that buxom girl pirate, robbed the wicked rich in the 1918 pages of *Detective Story Magazine*.

These heroines conform to the formal definition of "adventuress"—"a woman who seeks wealth and social position by unscrupulous means."

Granted that other series featured women who enjoyed scrupulous adventures while seeking truth and justice. Miss Marple did. So did Madame Storey and Mother Hansen. The wonderful Sheena, in leopard skin, fought evil men in sweaty shirts through the pages of her own magazine.[1] And the fearless Barbe Pivet shot down the wicked right and left in *Air Stories*. All these were adventuresses—meaning women who had adventures. Not *adventuresses*. Is the difference clear? Is there any need to go into further clinical detail?

Way back in 1916, a real, true adventuress cropped up in the careful pages of *All-Story Weekly*. Her name was Janie Frete and, at first, she nearly fit the worst definition, more or less. Not that there was any sexual irregularity associated with Janie. Good Heavens, no! She appeared in *All-Story* and, in 1916, sexual activity meant visiting the cabbage patch to see if the babies were ripe.

Janie was the heroine of six magazine serials published between 1916 and 1920, and a moving picture filmed in the early 1920s. She was a wonder, Janie was. Her description varies a little through the years, but she seems to have been young, tall, and slender, with bright-red cheeks, untouched by rouge, a square little chin, brilliant blue eyes, and wavy brown hair. "Though not exactly petite, she was not a large person. She carried herself with her head up and just the smallest kind of a swagger-twirl to her shoulders."

She also had the mind of a world-class money-making machine.

"Women," remarked author Raymond Spears, "watched her covertly and turned to try and puzzle out where she obtained her 'style'." Surely it was not from her clothing, which was simple, plain, and unadorned, hardly relieved by jewelry. At her most formal, she wore only a coral clasp, a single string of pearls, and "simple rings." At her least formal, she wore a hickory shirt and masculine pants with hiking boots. For Janie was essentially an outdoor girl. She spent much time in forests and on lakes, toughing it out in tough country.

If women have their doubts about Janie, men do not. About 96% of all the men she meets are in love with her. All around the world, they sit thinking about her, adoring her, sending her little gifts. When possible, they teach her useful things—such as how to open a safe by listening to the tumblers with a stethoscope. They also send her warmly inscribed photographs, and remember her with legacies and checks and such things as might catch her attention.

"Men were very amusing to Janie. They were such simpletons! The brightest of them always shriveled up under her attentions when she so minded. The brighter the man, the more the shrivel."

You needn't take that remark seriously. That's only Ray Spears straining to present his heroine as something equivalent to a natural force. He is not content to allow her exceptional qualities to speak for themselves. He must always be polishing the image, creating a figure larger than life, regarded as wonderfully clever by all men, and wonderfully capable, and wonderfully desirable. Such fantasy work would amuse Janie wonderfully.

Janie Frete: "It's real convenient that men are so stupid, too."

But you must forgive her these little digs. All day long, men come knocking at her door. They wish to adore her. Or serve her. Or marry her. If they can't woo her with checks and charm, then they attempt to frame her, blackmail her, whisk her protesting away to marriage.

These tactics never quite work and she is never quite compromised. Or at least no more compromised than any 1916 woman seen wearing pants.

Janie is fairly tolerant of all this foolishness. She "enjoyed forgiving men. It made them look so grateful and humble." Besides, a man woozy with admiration can be manipulated by a clever woman who is working out her own plans. After all, she didn't ask him to come rapping on her door, did she?

You might deduce from this that author Raymond S(miley) Spears was rather in love with Janie, himself. It's possible. Spears was born in Ohio, 1876. Like his father, he worked as a reporter on the *New York Sun*, writing news of the outdoors. From 1896-1900, he worked on the *Sun* and the *New York Herald*. During this period, he began submitting material to the Munsey magazines. Later he was on various magazine staffs, including *Forest and Stream* and *West Magazine*.

In 1900, Spears took the first of a series of extended camping trips, for he was an avid outdoorsman, hunting, fishing, hiking, and then writing articles about his experiences. During the next fifteen years, he traveled extensively. He boated down the Tennessee and Mississippi Rivers, traveled the Great Lakes and Chesapeake Bay, rode a motorcycle through the Dakota Bad Lands, and drove an automobile cross country to California and back—no easy feat in those days of ghastly roads, unreliable tires, and a hair-raising lack of service facilities.[2] There was every reason in the world why Spears became one of the "Ask Adventure" experts of *Adventure* magazine, answering readers' questions about outdoors activities.

Drawing on his excursions, he wrote eight travel books, including *Camping on the Great River* (1912), *A Trip on the Great Lakes* (1913), and *Camping, Woodcraft and Wildcraft* (1924). He also turned out a stream of articles for *The Outing Magazine, Harpers, Colliers,* and *Scientific American*. At the same time, he published fiction in *Scribners* and in such pulp magazines as *All-Story*,

Adventure, Munseys, and *The Popular Magazine.* Four novels were published, none of them about Janie Frete. Later he contributed to the *Saturday Evening Post, Golden Book, Nature,* and the *Reader's Digest.* Eventually he moved to California, where two of his stories became motion pictures. He died in 1950, seventy-four years old.

Spears' personal experiences flowed directly into the Janie serials. She, too, travels the Mississippi, sails Lake Superior, and crosses the Nevada desert. The descriptions of landscapes, weather, and light is firmly exact, if richly embellished with adjectives, for this writer had been there.

> . . .he lifted his eyes to look ahead to where the Waning Glories (mountains) raised their myriad peaks and knobs and heads. . . . They were still far away; they were laved at the foot by mirage lakes and false, atmospheric waves; they were, at last, dusted and sun-dogged with haloes of gold and flaming waves of blinding skylights, as the sun set steadily down to them, and in a blaze of burned orange glow, sank behind the range, whose shadows turned rich purple, and whose far eminences were sky-blue in their ethereal heights; there smote the walker's face a chill breath that turned his dry-sweat to a raw bleak, shivering cold."[3]

Set against these vividly drawn backgrounds are a series of rather melodramatic stories in which good and evil are not all that hard to distinguish. Janie, herself, begins as a Bent Heroine. Her personal record is blotched, and, in the first story, she's not particularly careful to wear a shining white hat. Sometimes you can hardly distinguish her from the crooks.

"The Trail of the Otter Pelts" (four-part serial, *All-Story Weekly,* January 29 through February 19, 1916) was, according to the Editor of the magazine, a collaboration between Spears and his wife, C. Eleanor.

The story tells how a band of fur poachers, operating on the Canadian side of the St. Lawrence, corrupt the regional game overseer (warden) and proceed to snatch a fortune in illegal pelts. A fine young investigator is set on their track. But Janie Frete arrives before him.

Janie is a heroine of dark past. She penetrates the gang, twists it around her finger, and eventually makes off with the profits. The wicked get lambasted good and the young investigator finds love. All of which is as it should be.

You would assume that such subject matter would guarantee non-stop action. But you would be wrong. Instead, the secondary heroine (daughter of the lead criminal and beloved of the young investigator) gets lost, gets found; then she runs off only to get found again. For a few pages, a drunken Indian radiates menace, until Janie maroons him on a lonely island. The investigating hero locates some stolen furs. After that, the weather turns bad and they all go indoors to sit and reflect on the snow and destiny and eat moose steaks and wonder what each other is thinking.

All these words eat up the pages. When some action finally creaks up, at fairly extended intervals, matters move crisply for a few paragraphs. Then the action passes and the prose relaxes back into a dreamy murmur.

Between the exciting moments, while you are waiting for something to happen, Spears amuses you with demonstrations of applied woodcraft, scenic views of the St. Lawrence and the Canadian North Shore. And he dumps in enough details of the fur business to leave the impression that you are learning something:

> *Janie*: There's a difference between furs caught in the lake and furs caught in the timber. Sand-bottom lakes and clear water give better fur than mud bottoms and dark water.[4]

One characteristic of this series is that general information is offered like teaspoons of rare wine. The next serial, "The Green Sachem," flits lightly across the pearl business. The later "Janie Frete Intrudes" is sprinkled with miscellaneous information on the dyeing of silk; and "A Shortage of Perfumes" has various things to say about the perfume business. You feel that you have been invited into secret places to watch the wheels spin.

In spite of all these inspiring facts, the narrative does have a tendency to drag. Now and then, a scene heats with potential drama. But Spears carefully subdues it, so the customer won't be frightened—or wakened up, either.

Thus, in "Otter Pelts," the fur thieves cluster into a boat cabin for a crime conference. Fingering illegally-taken pelts, they whisper meaningfully.

Into this gathering of evil trips Janie. She takes a seat, tells them in detail what they're doing, summarizes what they're planning, then drags out a few concealed pelts for critical commentary.

Any well organized gang would have biffed her on the head and had her overboard in thirty seconds, well wrapped in anchor chain. But not in a Raymond Spears' serial. What these grim criminals do is gawk and marvel and shuffle their feet and grin with embarrassment. All because Janie is so forceful. So cute. So smart.

"How in blazes did *you* get onto that?" a criminal cries.

"Oh, a woman has ways," Janie replies, just as if she is certain no one was going to wind her in anchor chain.

Well, it's a charming story and Janie is very interesting. Indeed she is.

We might as well face the fact, right now, that our delightful heroine is a jail-bird. It is the familiar pitiful story of a fond young girl entrapped. When she was very inexperienced, that glib slicker, St. Lawrence Jack, tangled her in a diamond-smuggling scheme. She was to carry the diamonds from Kingston across the lake to Cape Vincent on the American shore.

But something leaked. St. Lawrence Jack bolted, leaving Janie to face the Law and a year in the Kingston penitentiary. When she got out, she was taken into the home of a Mrs. Parkway, who became her surrogate mother and eased her back into life. (All these people reappear in the fifth serial, "Janie Pays a Debt of Honor" (1919).)

As the sophisticated reader has already noticed, great chunks of information about Janie's early life are omitted. Her parents don't seem to be mentioned; her age on being jailed is certainly not. All we are told, in Spears' artless way, is that she was a lonely child, greatly troubled. Apparently she is an orphan fallen into bad company, as happened to the Lone Wolf (1914). Unlike the Lone Wolf, she doesn't plunge into a life of crime, but merely hovers uncertainly at the edge for a few years—as in "Otter Pelts"—before setting up in business as an adventuress for hire.

Her home base is a neat little house on Two Canoe Island in the St. Lawrence River. She can be hired on commission, rather like Travis McGee. "She knows her worth but does not exaggerate it. But if she does not succeed, she refuses either commission or time, except if one engages her by the week." Even so, her services come high; she charges $100 to $300 a week, plus commissions.

Her work requires much traveling. "She had been in Florida, and had crossed Cuba once upon a time; she had, of course, been through the Panama Canal, and central and southern California were familiar enough." In addition to traveling through these far lands and over those bright seas, she has been in Mexico, Central America, and the islands of the West Indies.

During these travels, she has picked up all manner of skills. She can operate ice boats, power launches, and navigate a houseboat. She can operate an automobile, a typewriter, or a horse, read a contract, unwire the parts of an interlocked trust, cook for a work gang, perform chemical analyses. She also handles, with blithe superiority, a rifle or a heavy pistol.

All these are the normal skills required by an adventurer of either sex, who has a series to prance around in. As is the case with all series characters, Janie's abilities arrive by accretion. Each serial demands different skills, additional knowledge. Whatever is needed, the author bestows with generous hand, thus keeping the story flowing and Janie in control.

By blessing Janie so thoroughly, Spears inadvertently links her with other larger-than-life heroes of the period—the Night Wind and Black Star of the magazines, and Nick Carter and other dime novel wonderfuls. She may not be physically in their class. But she is completely equal to them in intelligence. She was (Spears tells us) "sternly and rigorously intelligent and intellectual."

He does admire Janie a sight too much. That's why she exceeds the bounds of probability in stories that, otherwise, pluck wistfully at the fringe of realism. Janie initially appears realistic up to the moment you see her in action. Then you realize that she is a 1930s heroine, arrived a little early. She transcends reality. She is tireless, ingenious, confident. Particularly confident, for she knows that if she gets too deeply into trouble, as in "Intrudes" and "Waning Glories," a golden coincidence will shimmer from the sky and resolve all. It's stimulating to be the subject of an adoring author.

For her next adventure, "The Green Sachem" (four-part serial, May 20 through June 10, 1916), the subject is pearls. Fresh-water pearls. The Sachem is that gigantic green one.

First the pearl is found. Then an unscrupulous dealer arranges for its theft. Now Janie takes up the trail, having been engaged by a dealer to locate the pearl and buy or otherwise acquire it.

Through unidentified sources of information (a fictional convention to speed up the story), she learns the name of the wicked dealer, bluffs him into admitting knowledge of the pearl. Later, not able to approach the dealer directly, she becomes secretary to a pearl collector who would just as soon buy a stolen pearl as to take a drink. By this time, the pearl has been sold to an outright crook who is negotiating with the collector, using Janie as go-between. Seeing no legitimate way of getting The Green Sachem, she decides to steal it from the thieves.

That decision precipitates a violent attack of conscience.

She had been mixed up in a number of different affairs, but had not viewed the morals of the situations with any such keenness as she did the bright moments of the work....

(But now) Instead of going deeper and deeper into the mire of wickedness, Janie withdrew more and more from the shores of perditional efforts.

In early life she had not been above sharing in illegitimate profits and in rejoicing over them. Now she shrank from the thought of taking even a commission of stolen goods—on a pearl which must ever have a cloud upon its title...."[5]

You will be relieved to learn that she tears herself free from the shores of perditional efforts to complete her assignment successfully. It's hard to be an adventuress and still observe conventional morality. But Janie manages. Janie always manages.

Give Spears credit: he has worked up a mild variation on the Bent Hero theme. As you no doubt remember clearly from the first volume of this exciting series, the Bent Hero has a tarnished past and, for various reasons, usually love, uses criminal methods to right wrongs and do justice. That is, he robs the untouchable businessman; he confounds the untouchable criminal. Thus, the Lone Wolf, the Gray Seal, the later Gray Phantom, the Saint, Lester Leith, fine fellows all.

What is acceptable behavior for them isn't quite right for a sweet young girl who was in jail only a year. So Janie walks that gray line, forever teetering above ambiguity. She is tempted to steal from crooks, but she never does. She is tempted to throw in with criminals, and sometimes appears to do so; but that is art and illusion—she never does.

You meet the illusion in full force in "Janie Frete Intrudes" (four-part serial, June 15 through July 6, 1918). An over-confident smuggler pressures her to use Two Canoe Island as a major link in a smuggling chain. She eyes him coldly. He pressed hard. Does she waver? Does she agree? He thinks so, although the reader is not convinced. The reader, that astute fellow, is correct, and the smuggler receives a severe surprise later in the story.

That is one of the two plot threads in "Intrudes." All the serials contain two or three plot threads that wander in and out of the chapters. Sometimes the threads flow naturally together. Sometimes they have to be grabbed and tied together by a sweating author whose characters seem to be ignoring him.

The primary plot thread in "Intrudes" has to do with a slippery businessman in the silk game. He has cheated one of Janie's friends. Little does he realize that Janie has slipped into his organization and gnaws from within.

As usual, the reader is loaded with facts, this time about the silk business, how silk is imported, how silk is treated, how silk is dyed. It's a real education. If anyone asks why you are sitting around reading trashy serials, you can respond with a staggering torrent of facts, shutting them up properly.

The action in "A Shortage of Perfumes" (four-part serial, February 1 through 22, 1919) leaps effortlessly from Canada to the wild West Indies. Once again Janie seeks an inheritance, this one being an iron cask of ambergris. The cask gets lost, gets found, is buried, dug up, and hauled frantically around on boats. An evil captain weaves his web; a beautiful native woman glows with jealousy at the sight of Janie's bright red cheeks. Exciting.

During the course of the action, Janie burglarizes the Captain's house, casually buys a motor launch the way you would buy a box of tissues, shoots a knife from a killer's hand, gets clutched by a multi-armed devilfish but blasts her way free (using a large pistol that had been concealed in her blouse), and mushes up the plots of the wicked. At the end, all the bad people reform for love, love, love, except one or two who get taken dead along the way.

"Perfumes" has a more tightly integrated plot than the three earlier serials. As is usual in a Spears' production, the point of view is fragmented. For a while, the story lingers with Janie. Then it ricochets off into the story of the young man who married the native girl. After some chapters focused on his difficult life, the narrative bounds back to Janie, except for one or two minor excursions into the adventures of other characters.

Although "Perfumes" contains a few gliches, it is more coherent than, for example, "Otter Pelts." In that story, it is nearly impossible to identify the lead character. You know the lead is supposed to be Janie Frete because that's what it says in the magazine. Still you wonder about all those long stretches of prose where you follow the story of the corrupt warden, or go lost-girl hunting with the splendid young investigator. Janie keeps appearing and reappearing, nearly becoming a secondary character in her own serial.

Although the point of view is as unstable as a mirage, you can be certain of one thing—Janie Frete is a true free spirit.

That means little these days, when all the girls feel free to wear pants and plan mergers and spit through their teeth. But back in the 'Teens, things were somewhat different.

It was taken for granted back where (Janie) came from that a girl could just cook, be a wife, and have children—no more. That was what the community had tried to make of her, and she had rebelled.

That town has a different idea about girls now. They know what a girl can do—they know better than to try and tie a girl up in the log-chains of convention. Janie was still traveling secretary of the Ladies Independence Society, which she organized, and to the members of which she taught the value of cooperation.

But even so the habits of centuries enthralled the home-town minds. So she had to go forth and see, live, make life. She reverted now to her adventures. They were all amusing, of course, but some, she realized with a pang, had been diverting because they were lawless, wicked, and worse yet, unbecoming.[6]

Lawless and wicked but not unprofitable. Like other bent heroes, Janie has been able to make some provision for her old age: That neat little house on Two Canoe Island. A turquoise mine that pays her daily operating expenses. A cask of ambergris. A formula or two for industrial processes that trickle royalties into her bank account. A ranch in Nevada. Only a few simple possessions, but her own.

Whoever knew Janie Frete knew that she was a business woman and that her economic independence was her most precious possession. She had kept herself free, retained her own liberty—except for that brief and difficult interval over there in Kingston.[7]

That "brief and difficult interval" lies at the core of the following serial, "Janie Pays a Debt of Honor" (four-part serial, August 23 through September 13, 1919). Faces from Janie's past return to tangle her present. The story of her crime and imprisonment is detailed more elaborately, embellishments flying.

As dedicated series readers know, background stories can hang around for years, being alluded to in every story. By repetition, the background grows so familiar that you hardly realize how skimpy it is. Then, for some reason, the writer bursts into flame and redoes the whole thing. The expanded version contains new details, sharpened characters, and adds patches to cover all those discrepancies the author discovered later.

In "Debt of Honor," Spears doesn't write up the actual diamond smuggling and Janie's arrest. But he does create more background history and tidies what he has already written, like a housewife straightening ornaments on a mantelpiece.

Back from Janie's past comes St. Lawrence Jack. We have not met him before, except in casual references. For this serial, he has been rechristened "River Jack," but it's the same fellow. Spears tells us so, and if Spears doesn't know, who does?

For the first time, we also meet Mrs. Parkway, who took Janie into her home after our heroine got out of jail. Now Janie can do something to repay that act of generosity. In specific, she can locate Mrs. Parkway's daughter. That young lady, itching for adventure, has run off to boat alone down the Mississippi River, a minnow in a world of pike.

The first part of the serial is dominated by Janie's chase after the daughter. Potential rape looms behind the paragraphs, in the familiar tradition of the high-action story. For in the wake of young Miss Parkway sniff dirty, rotten, vile men, strange light in their eyes.

But you mustn't get worked up. Out on the river, that tiny, distant boat approaching with serene speed—that's Janie, cautiously tracking out the young Miss's route.

In spite of Janie's protestations, the grapevine along the river tingles:

—Sweet young quail coming downstream. All alone in a nice boat.

—Hear Janie Frete's on the river, too. She's a jailbird, one of us, very sharp.

Then Miss Parkway's boat is discovered empty. She has disappeared.

Investigating, Janie plunges into a web of trickery and crime. It's been spun by River Jack. He is determined to become the kingpin of Mississippi bootleggers. It is his idea to recruit Janie as his queen, exploiting her intelligence and contacts, and keeping her barefoot in the winter. With Janie's help, River Jack and his tough thugs expect to rule the stream from Natchez to Mobile.

It does not quite work out that way.

Eventually the blithe Miss Parkway gets saved. Before that happens, Janie teeters at the lip of real trouble with the authorities. If you were unsophisticated, you'd swear that she has fallen in with River Jack's plans. But her adroit manipulations, plus a few miracles, twist matters to a happy ending.

Spears, himself, had boated alone down the Mississippi, paddling with one hand and taking notes with the other. Informed description fills the serial. How to load a boat; the changing look of the shoreline; how light looks as it falls on the water and how the sky changes during the day; how you read the water; how shadows shape along the shore. What Spears did and saw, Janie does and sees. The descriptions are by someone who has been out there and collected specific information. And a lot of adjectives.

The characters of the story are not quite as successful as the nature descriptions. Tough guys crunch through the chapters, chewing iron bars and gulling the innocent. For purposes of the plot, these hardcases tend to crumble easily. Like cast iron figures with cream centers, they collapse under stress, spewing sentimentality across the prose.

Almost all of Spears' tough guys have that trait. You notice it particularly in "Janie and the Waning Glories" (six-part serial, May 15 through June 19, 1920). In this story, we meet a grim female villainness resplendent in the name Uintah Forelane. Other cast characters include a cunning male liar, a cowboy wanted for murder, assorted tough ranch hands, possemen, and a sheriff cut of old leather.

When gently bumped by plot, their hardboiled facades disintegrate. A mighty reek of sentimentality rises, as if you had tipped over a quart of dime-store perfume.

But to the story.

To Janie's amazement, she learns that she owns a ranch in Nevada. How that happened, she doesn't know. But with Janie, to be amazed is to act. Away she drives cross country (even as Spears, himself), in a splendid little automobile that never gets a flat or runs out of gasoline.

On her way through the desert, Janie picks up a sore-footed cowboy who is on the jump. Close behind him rages a posse. He has killed a mean ranger in self defense, not that anyone believes him. Out West, as you know, they hang first and consider later.

Even in 1920—or especially in 1920—you'd think that a young woman driving alone through the Big Lonesome would hesitate to pick up a tough-looking puncher. But not Janie. Adventuresses sense when they are protected by the author. She gives the cowboy a ride, feeds him pork chops, and earns his admiration. But naturally:

> She was fearless, for one thing, and she was on the level, for another thing; she asked no questions; her quick sympathy and understanding. . . were sincere and guileless.[8]

After dropping off the cowboy, she drives on to her ranch in the Waning Glory Mountains. There she finds water, grass, scenery, almost no cattle, and not that first ranchhand. The place is densely enveloped in schemes and counter-schemes. To be blunt, the ranch is a cleverly cocked legal trap, a pure swindle erect on forged documents.

Immediately the male villain comes smiling up, asking Janie to pay a trifle on the mortgage. (If she does this, she's legally liable for a bale of debt.) Always cautious, Janie begins a detailed study of the fine print. Meanwhile, the female villain, Uintah the Sinister, lurks inconspicuously. (It would appear that she had been intended to play a larger role which accidentally failed to develop.) Uintah is master-minding the swindle. Already she has smudged Janie's name by citing her as correspondent in Uintah's divorce suit. Janie has never heard of Mr. and Mrs. Forelane, although Mr. F. has heard of Janie and expressed his admiration and his wife, twisted by neurosis, thought up this intricate plan etc. etc. etc.

Back at the ranch, Janie is counting fence posts for lack of anything else to do, there being no help on the spread. Then arrives the lone cowboy she befriended in the desert. Startling, isn't it, how these things work out? Before you can say "Jesse James," the cowboy has collected a choice bunch of rustlers, gun-slingers, and short iron specialists to work the ranch.

This crew immediately sets to work collecting a herd for Janie. They ride out to grab choice cattle from three other ranches. That causes hard feelings. Complaints get back to the sheriff, who, with posse, swoops down on Janie's men, just as they are moving out a huge herd of cattle.

Running gun fight. Janie's crew is shot to ribbons. Into the Waning Glories thunders the posse. Janie becomes their prisoner.

These good-hearted men of the West don't hardly know what to do with her. She may be a Rustler Queen, but they can't hang a woman; and it sure is sorry to send a nice-looking little woman like that to the pen. But, Lord, rustlin' is rustlin', even if you can tell by lookin' that they's no harm in her.

At this critical point, like the final chapter of a serial story, a friendly lawyer reins up in a cloud of alkali.

Now the story shudders all over and does a back flip. Black becomes white, sour sweet, and the improbable even more improbable.

Those rustling cowpokes were only retrieving cattle rustled from Janie's ranch.

That smiling fellow urging on the sheriff is really a crook.

The ranch deed was hocused. (But Janie saw through that and called the lawyer in, you see.)

In an instant the real criminals are exposed. Stripped of wealth and position, they fume in jail. The Forelane divorce is cancelled and Janie's reputation refurbished. The curtain closes on virtue rewarded—except for a few shot-up punchers.

All brought about by a good lawyer.

Well, this is fiction, of course.

When the serial ended, so did the Janie saga. Only hours away, the Roaring Twenties shouted. Before long, lipstick, bobbed hair, and gin-drenched petting parties would give new meaning to the word Adventure. Aggressive young girls would find ways to tarnish their reputations other than by wearing pants and tricking criminals. How dull, then, stories about feisty business women adventuring alone in the wilds.

After 1920, the adventuring woman survived mainly in detective stories and Pearl White movie serials. The impulse which had thrown up Janie Frete as a series lead in *All-Story Weekly* smoothed silently away, a modest wave in the ocean of fiction. For about fifteen years, the series adventures was mainly represented by Mother Hansen (*Detective Story Magazine*), an unlikely enough heroine. Not until the Lady from Hell and the *Scarlet* magazines did the adventuress return, her eyes brilliant, her reputation shady.

The detecting woman, however, did handsomely. It is worth noting that the popular Madame Storey series, which began in the 1920s *Argosy All-Story*, may have contributed to the abrupt end of Janie's adventures. It seems improbable that the magazine would run two major series featuring woman, in addition to a scattering of minor short-story series. But that is speculation.

Whatever the cause, Raymond Spears moved on to other things. And we suspect that apple-cheeked Janie continued her own life in her own way, accumulating capital, walking with exquisite precision the line between crime and virtue, accepting the adulation of men, and having a splendid time adventuring through this naughty world.

Chapter 6
Cowpunchers of Desolation

The final Janie Frete serial is a western, replete with ranches, rustlers, posses, gunmen, and thundering herds, just as in the stories of Raine, Seltzer, and Grey.

That such a city-oriented heroine as Janie Frete plunged into western adventure seems faintly improbable. She seems vaguely uncomfortable out there by the Waning Glories, as if her jeans were too tight. Although the story line seems contrived, the descriptions, for all their fustian, are specific, concrete, and convincing. Spears tended to build his fiction around his personal experience; his characters performed where he put them, on the Mississippi or out west.

In any case, the western was a sure-fire form. It was, of all fictional subjects in the popular magazines, the most often requested and the most often printed. The western story was a staple, familiar as potatoes on an Irish table.

Sensitive as always to readers' wishes, such all-fiction pulps as *Short Stories* and *Action Stories* packed their pages with westerns; *The Popular Magazine*, *Top Notch*, *Blue Book*, and *Argosy All-Story Weekly* relentlessly published tales of western adventure. It was usual that those accounts contained a higher percentage of drinking, shooting, card playing, and rushing about on horses than real cowboys enjoyed. But such exaggerations did not bother even those actually out there sweating among the cattle; they, the cowboys, themselves, devoured enormous stacks of western fiction. They read the magazines to tatters, untroubled, as it seems, by the discrepancies between the fictional lives and their own.

The western fiction that they devoured was a product of more complex evolution than the simple prose might suggest. The dime novels had created the larger-than-life western hero sweeping triumphantly through an environment of constant action and danger; the novels of Owen Wister and Zane Grey established basic scenes and character types; B.M. Bower's Flying U stories provided a taste of actual working conditions on a ranch; and the Hopalong Cassidy series celebrated the quick-draw artist and made the roving cowboy familiar to the most casual reader.[1]

As western fiction poured through the slick and pulp magazines, a similar tidal wave passed through the silent movies of the period. As yet the western moving picture proceeded at the level of a comic strip. Stereotyped characters chased and pummeled each other. Heroines cringed and posed; the evil swaggered toward their ultimate punishment at the hero's hand. Not much time was spent in the company of cattle. Behind the silver screen glimmered the covers of a thousand dime novels, their chases and innocent certainties vividly recreated.

The visual appeal was intense. However limited was the realistic content of a silent film, the images seared themselves upon the minds of the viewers. Riding and fighting occupied much of the story; character complexity, ambiguity of choice, emotional interaction, realistic constraints of time and strength—all were trimmed from the story line as by the surgeon's blade.

In decades to come these elements would be returned to the filmed western with considerable fanfare. But in the 1920s, they were conspicuously absent. Not that it made any difference. Few appeared to notice the moving picture's hollowness. And this in a period when popular magazine writers were experimenting with varieties of western narrative: Max Brand with moral complexity and myth; Johnson McCulley with the costumed avenger; Clarence Mulford with a realistic portrayal of the fast-draw justice figure; and W. C. Tuttle with the farce and the western detective story.

The western detective story, that curious combination, first appeared in the dime novels, as did so much else. Deadwood Dick, Buffalo Bill, Young Wild West, Young Sleuth, Old Sleuth, Nick Carter, himself, and a rich mixture of other series characters, met mystery out west and discovered who and why, each and every time. It was wonderful.

However efficiently plainsmen and cowboys may have solved range mysteries, they were not primarily detectives. Adventure was their business: ranching and Indian killing and such pleasurable activities. When a real detective investigated a case out west, he came from some other place; or he was in the West for a visit, for the sport shooting, or to aid a friend or pursue a criminal. While doing these things, he stumbled over at least one crime a page.

Eventually all detectives returned East, leaving local range mysteries to solve themselves. So matters remained until 1920, when a long series of western adventure-mysteries opened in the pages of the *Adventure* magazine. These, by W.C. Tuttle, featured Hashknife Hartley, a wandering cowboy of endless curiosity.

Hartley refused to call himself a detective. Considering himself only as a drifting cowboy, he was an amateur puzzle-solver who spent three decades probing range mysteries for the pleasure of it.

Cowboy: 'That Hashknife feller is queer, don'tcha know it...? Last night he just sat there and never paid no attention to anybody. We was all a-talkin', but I betcha he never heard a word we said. And all to once he kinda jerks himself almost out of the chair and says,' like he was talkin' to himself, 'Why, of course! Any damn fool ought to have seen that.'[2]

The mystery fiction reader instantly recognizes this moment. It is the familiar instant of insight, when suddenly the mind lights and all things become clear. Every fictional investigator has experienced this joy as the links connect— although his pleasure is frequently expressed in more elegant language.

The moment of insight after thought connects Hashknife Hartley solidly to that celebrated international type, the amateur investigator. Like most amateurs of the 1920s, Hartley found mysteries wherever he looked. Nor was he able to rest until he had probed a problem to its final whisper. Like many other fictional investigators, he achieved his wonders by a combination of deduction and intuition, often substituting brilliance for solid evidence. It was use of common sense, he said. Others, observing this prodigy at work, announced that he was a mind reader.

Other characteristics link him with the great amateurs of the period. He shared their usual disdain for the Law's official representatives—the judges, sheriffs, deputies, and lawyers. And in common with all amateurs, he traveled in the company of a faithful Watson, here named Sleepy Stevens.

In other ways, Hashknife is the familiar cowboy hero of the western action adventure. Homeless as a cloud shadow, he wandered from the Canadian border south to Mexico, spending much time in Arizona. Along the way he concerned himself with the kind lady about to lose her ranch, the fortunes of the foolish young city fellow, the half-breed girl's love life, the arrest of that innocent old man, the activities of the wastrel son. Wherever Hashknife rode, he discovered drama, conflict, and action in the Old West which survived so long in fiction, if not in history.

Tightly woven into these traditional subjects was the mystery. This gradually developed from the events of the western story: Men are shot dead, some mysteriously. Cattle are stolen by hands invisible in the night. Hapless girls vanish, leaving behind no clue and much anxiety.

Hashknife's curiosity flares. He wonders about the bottle that survived a hundred-foot fall into a rock shaft. He is troubled by the unfired pistol which the sheriff saw used to shoot down a man. He considers the appearance of gold in the wrong kind of rock and the strange angle of bullet wounds in a dead man.

Unanswered problems swarm. Even out west. Even as cowboys ride hard and guns hammer and bodies thud into that prickly stuff, it is proper to ask who did it? How was it done? Why?

These are formal mystery problems to think over while the horse opera rages. Then insight. "Why, of course. Any damn fool ought to have seen that." Clear indication that terminal revelations are only pages away.

The Hashknife Hartley series, written by Wilbur C. Tuttle, began in *Adventure* and continued in that magazine until the mid-1930s. The initial short stories soon expanded to full-scale novels, complete in each issue. Later in the 1920s, the novels split into serials. Other serials found their way into *Argosy* at the end of the 1920s and were followed by short stories. By mid-1939, the series switched to *Short Stories* magazine, where it appeared irregularly through 1951. Appearances in other magazines is possible.

More than a dozen of these magazine novels were published as books in the United States; about two dozen were published in England, making available many of the early *Adventure* novels. Publication dates of the books and the date of the original magazine appearances have little in common.

The writer, W(ilbur) C(oleman) Tuttle, was born November 11, 1883, during a blizzard in Glendive, Montana Territory. His birthplace was the family's living quarters over the county jail, his father being sheriff of Dawson County.

Tuttle saw the west, the real west, the unglamorized west, from close range. His memories, if not romantic, were vividly realistic:

On the Cowboy: ...the cowboy was a hired man on horseback. He wasn't always in town humped over a saloon bar or enjoying a honky tonk show. In fact, if he got to town once a week, he was lucky. Saturday wasn't a loafing day, and if the Old Man had fences to fix or water holes to dig out on Sunday—there was the cowboy....

And in winter on the northern ranges—what a job! Forty-a-month plus frostbite. Out of the sack about five o'clock in the morning, the temperature about zero in the bunkhouse; outside ten or twelve below, and a wind blowing. You shiver into frozen overalls, fight your way down to the stable, where you harness a team of frosted horses, take 'em out and hitch them to a hayrick wagon....

...Then you ride, always into the wind, and scatter hay for the half-starved cows.

Man, was it romantic! Even with burlap sacks wound around your boots and a strip of blankets around your head, you usually came in to breakfast with a frozen nose and numb feet.

Then there was wood to be cut, stables to be cleaned, fences to be repaired, along with chopping holes in the ice so the cows could get water. And you usually received forty dollars a month, your grub, and a hard bunk to spread your bedroll.[3]

On General Armament: Six-shooters were common as eyebrows, and some men would catch cold if they forgot to buckle on their belts in the morning. Gun fights were rare but fist fights were common.[4]

On Two-Gun Men: My Uncle Bill was the only man I ever knew who wore two guns. You can watch pictures or television today and call me a liar, that all cowboys wore two guns—but they didn't. I asked him why he wore two guns and he quietly replied:

"I own two Colt .45s—and if I don't wear both of 'em, some dad-blamed rannahan will steal the other one."[5]

On the Posse: ...a lot of my life was spent around a sheriff's office, and I have yet to see a sheriff's posse—except in pictures. Why should a cowboy be anxious to wear the hoofs off his horse, shoot away his precious ammunition, and take a chance on his life just because the sheriff yelled:

"Come on, men, we'll get him!"

...At a salary of forty a month (cowboys) couldn't afford to buy cartridges. And with whiskey at twelve-and-a-half cents a drink, they didn't hang long at the bar. And if a cowboy had any silver on his saddle or chaps—he was a damned dude.[6]

On Education: My education was all garnered in a Montana cow-town school, where you stayed till the seats got so short that you grew callouses on your knees. No graduation—you quit.

After quitting, Tuttle sampled the writer's usual potpourri of jobs. He was a cowboy and a herder of sheep, worked for the railroad, was a forest ranger, a baseball player and manager, a newspaper cartoonist, and a writer of silent film story lines. In 1915 he began contributing humorous short western fiction to *Adventure*, farcical accounts of the lunatic proceedings in Yellow Rock County, Montana.[7] Over the next fifty years, he would publish more than eighty western novels and better than a thousand stories in such magazines as *Adventure, Argosy, Big-Book Western, Western Story, Max Brand Western, Short Stories, Thrilling Western*. His work also appeared in *Liberty* and he conducted a department in *Field and Stream*—for Tuttle was a fisherman and duck hunter of formidable dedication.

During his extended career, he spilled out series characters—gunman and cowboy knights, amusing sheriffs and eccentrics. Most were brushed with humor. All were sharply outlined, their speech habits and attitudes drawn from living models, although exaggerated, by the writer's usual license, in the name of art. His people are a fraction more complex than required by the simplicities of 1920s action fiction. Like most long-enduring series characters, they changed over the years.

Hashknife, in particular, changed. Between 1920 and 1924, his personality altered drastically—as did that of his partner, Sleepy. Thereafter, modification was less dramatic, although some degree of change can be noticed as late as the mid-1940s.

As to the creation of Hashknife and Sleepy, Tuttle remarked:

We went on an excursion to California in February (1919), leaving Spokane in below zero weather and reached Los Angeles in 90 degrees in the shade. When chilblains overlap hot feet, something has to give, and I was crippled. So I laid off the sightseeing, got me a typewriter and wrote the first serious piece of fiction I had ever tried. It wasn't funny. You can't suffer in the feet in a hot hotel room and be funny. I selected two characters I knew well, and wrote the first of the 'Hashknife' series, destined to run for about a hundred novelettes and book-length tales.[8].

The earliest stories were told first-person by Dave "Sleepy" Stevens, so called, by perverse western custom, because he was alert. As an author, Sleepy is rather more articulate and thoughtful than he later appears. He is of medium build, chunky, with heavy shoulders, and "bow legged enough to fit a horse perfectly." His face is rather square and wrinkled, his wide blue eyes innocent of guile. But you can't trust eyes. Behind that childlike cheerfulness lies a mind quick to sense impending violence and the most strategic position. He is a masterful back-up man.

Born near Pocatello, Idaho, on the Snake River, Sleepy started drifting early, ended with the Hashknife outfit in Arizona. There he became a top hand and there he met Hartley.

Sleepy: I dunno just how or why he picked up with me, but we've been together ever since.

Hashknife: I felt sorry for yuh.

Sleepy: Yeah, and I've felt sorry for myself ever since.[9]

George "Hashknife" Hartley, subject of this chapter, is a bony, angular man, nearly six and a half feet tall. Long nosed, large mouthed, he has gray-blue eyes and hair first described as roan, later as neutral. Born on the Milk River in Montana, he is the oldest of ten children. His father, a preacher, carried the Gospel throughout the region.

Hartley grew up in the cattle business, being one of the best riders in the region at sixteen. Curiosity also grew in him, large as the Montana sky, an urge to see other places, other people. Drifting south more than a thousand miles on horseback, he wandered onto the Hashknife range which would give him his nickname.

Hashknife had been born with an analytical brain. Any mystery was a challenge. In any other environment he might have been famous as a detective. But he was not a man-hunter. The punishment of a criminal was of no interest to him. Psychology, his ability to connect small details, and what he was pleased to term 'lucky hunches' had solved many range mysteries.[10]

In the first stories, Hashknife is as volatile as ether. Touchy of his honor, given to violent pranks, he sparkles with gleeful violence—a trait drawn, in part, from the original Hopalong Cassidy, Clarence Mulford's brightly drawn character who first appeared in 1906. The early Cassidy and the early Hashknife prance with boisterous youth, although in both men a part of their minds remains calm and dispassionate and watching, calculating as an alligator's eye among the swamp bubbles.

Cassidy was also a roamer, although he retained the Bar 20 as home base. Hashknife and Sleepy enjoy no such stability. They drift, curious to see over the next hill. This is rarely the way to affluence, in cow country or elsewhere. They seldom have much money and their dress reflects their modest resources:

Their raiment was nondescript. The wind and dust of the dim trails had scoured and faded all the color from their shirts, their bat-winged chaps were worn and wrinkled, and their sombreros were flopping and shapeless.[11]

Hashknife wears an old weathered, hand-made cartridge belt, long used. It supports a worn holster and a single Colt revolver. His boots, extra high of heel, are ancient, and the spurs are worn to circles of steel.

As Sleepy remarks early in the series:

Soldiers of fortune? Naw, sir, we're cowpunchers of disaster. Fortune's never smiled on us. At time's she's busted out laughing when we've doubled our trail and left some anxious sheriff barking up a tree, but otherwise she's had her back turned to us....

Right now our combined wealth won't total over seventeen dollars. We've got two Winchesters, a .41 and a .44 Colt, and Hashknife packs a .44 derringer in his pocket.

Under us we've got two jug-headed broncs and two good saddles...."[12]

The suggestion is that we are in the presence of ambiguous heroes, mingling good qualities and bad. The character type was widely recognized in 1920, having been popularized in the novels of Zane Grey. It is roughly the same "good-bad" character played by William Hart in his silent films. During the 1920s-1930s, Max Brand would elaborately develop the character in all manner of fictional settings.

While neither Hashknife nor Sleepy is bad in the sense of ferocious law breaking, each is casually disrespectful of authority, reputation, and the majesty of the law. Hashknife has the popular hero's contempt for the legal system:

Law ain't always justice. I don't believe in hanging a man. To me, there's no greater premeditated murder than hangin' by law. Two wrongs never make a right. The law can't make right; so what right do they have to take it? Imprison a man so he can't do any more wrong—that's enough punishment.[13]

The emphasis on justice rather than legal forms, the selective attitude toward obedience to law, the rootless status of Mr. Hartley and Mr. Stevens outside established communities, the vigor with which they defend the luckless—all these points identify the two cowboys as justice figures, a sprightly type of fictional hero. The justice figure steps in to cure disorder whenever the law and its official representatives have failed. Possibly he may bend a few laws while committing justice. No matter. If Hashknife occasionally steals the evidence, forges a will, cons a crooked rancher, tells an artful story, only a narrow bigot could consider these actions crimes. Even Sherlock Holmes, even Dr. Fell, diddled the law for justice.

As the series begins, Hashknife is very much an exuberant justice figure. "Hashknife—Philanthropist" (*Adventure*, Mid-July 1920) contains much more action, quantities of humorous dialogue and sassy talk, but little mystery. The mystery elements included are common to innumerable other westerns: who rustled the stock? Who shot at those nice cowboys? Why?

By the second page, unknown men are blasting away at our heroes and they are blasting back. From this promising beginning, they ride into Badger City, there encountering crooked officials, a plotting ranchman, a festering injustice (a cowboy framed to prison), a victimized rancher and his pretty daughter. All these elements will become nearly permanent features of the series.

There follows conflict with the authorities. The plot advances from violence to violence. Hashknife deduces sharply. The angle of a bullet wound, the sheriff's willingness to pay a bribe, the shape of a brand pour out their message to him, if to no one else.

At the ranch where so many cattle have vanished, Hashknife closely studies local cattle brands. Later, through a series of only faintly credible bluffs, he wrings written confessions from each of the criminals—the crooked rancher, the crooked sheriff, the scowling minion. These confessions will free the framed cowboy. And the girl rejoices as the angels sing.

Such a summary omits all the rich juices flavoring the story. Humor sweetens the pages. Violence is playfully presented, and corruption, easily exposed, is easily discomfited. Numbers of single-trait characters rush past, each brightly drawn, perhaps from life. Dialogue, descriptions, opinions, attitudes gleam with authenticity, never quite overwhelmed by plot requirements.

So much action packs the story that it is difficult to follow Hashknife as he performs his miracles. He is as tight-lipped as Holmes. His habit of never explaining anything enrages Sleepy:

> You sure can talk above a whisper but you has too many secrets. You won't tell me a danged thing, will you? No, of course not.
>
> I follers you just like a sheep. When you say 'Shoot,' I shoot. I'm weaned and rope-broke, Hashknife, and able to take nourishment without getting the colic, and still you won't tell me anything.[14]

It is Watson's eternal complaint.

The reader knows as little as Sleepy. Tuttle makes no effort to spread clues for the reader to snatch up. Let the reader marvel, not think. When Hashknife recognizes a notorious brand-altering expert, when he works out how the Cross L brands were changed, he uses special information never offered the reader.

Granted that it was only 1920, and the Detection Club had yet sworn to avoid such crimes of composition.

The series is still green, however, and Tuttle is feeling his way into the story form. Two years later, in "The Ranch of the Tombstones," (*Adventure*, December 30, 1922), he has devised a more complex story and pointed up the mystery elements. Slightly.

One Halloween, someone scooped up all the tombstones in a small cemetery and planted them in Bliz Skelton's front yard. It was still another effort to force him off his ranch, Skelton thinks. Hashknife agrees.

He and Sleepy have just ridden into the region and find Skelton's hired man, fatally wounded, on the road. They carry him into town. There they meet an arrogant gambler and a second plot line—this one dealing with the fortunes of Lonesome Lee, a drunken rancher in mortal fear of the gambler.

In short order, Hashknife has knocked the gambler flat, insulted the sheriff, spoiled a plot to frame Skelton for the murder, and prevented the gambler from taking advantage of Lee's daughter.

Such selfless behavior unsettles the sheriff, who has certain secrets to hide. He makes a weak attempt to arrest Hashknife and Sleepy:

Sheriff: I got to do m' duty.... You're resisting an officer, if you only knew it.

Hashknife: Ain't nobody resisted you—yet, but if you don't crawl to your horse and rattle your hocks out of here, I'll nail your pants to the floor and leave you there to starve.[15]

Between bouts with the sheriff and sassy talk to other principals, Hashknife takes time to investigate the cemetery. There lies the concealed motive for all this foolery—a rich reef of gold. With that evidence, Hashknife faces a 50-man posse and explains who did what and why. A little shooting flares up at the end, but no one of any consequence is killed.

As these early stories often do, "The Ranch of the Tombstones" ends with rewards raining down on Hashknife and Sleepy. It would seem difficult to remain poor when grateful friends load you with checks and titles to ranches. Eventually, Tuttle faced this unexpected anomaly by allowing his heroes to glide quietly away at story's end, unembarrassed by worldly possessions.

To speak plainly, "Tombstones" is repetitious and dotted all over with bits of undeveloped plot, like buds frozen on a branch. The action ambles engagingly along, shedding humorous scenes during which Hashknife baffles the plotters each and every time. It all seems easy. The emphasis is still on western adventure, not mystery. As a result, the minor mysteries and their solutions are treated as decorations to the main narrative, interesting but not of primary importance.

By this date, 1922, Tuttle has dropped first-person narration. This is the first of many changes, continuing into 1924, which will modify the characters, complicate the stories, and finally establish a permanent prose tone. Another major change occurs when Tuttle tangles the straight-line adventure with a secondary plot. In time, this second strand will grow as richly complex as the primary story, expanding the cast of characters and their interrelationships, developing emotional intensities of considerable strength, when the action does not interfere.

Most changes are in place by the end of 1924. Now begins an intricate string of novels and long novelettes containing strong mystery and action lines and secondary plots concerned with inappropriate love and distressed families.

"Hashknife and Fantom Riders" (February 29, 1924, *Adventure*) brings Hashknife and Sleepy to a town bent by invisible terror. Unseen, untraced raiders rustle and kill. No ranch is safe. There are no clues. Soon Sleepy has been severely wounded and Hashknife must work alone to make sense of this complicated mess. The situation is even more confused by the problems of the half-Indian girl who is loved, or perhaps not, by the rich young wastrel.

In "The Medicine Man" (March 30, 1924), so much stock has been stolen from the Triangle D that the ranch is flat broke. The owner, Bud Daley, feels he is a failure who has condemned his wife to misery because of his lack of ability. After which the bank is robbed. On the vault floor is discovered a decorative rosette from one of Bud's chaps. He is promptly arrested by the sheriff for robbery and murder, since no sheriff, in this series, ever does other then the obvious.

Again Hashknife has doubts. Riding to a nearby town, he attempts to trace the route along which the stolen cattle were shipped. He finds only a dose of knock-out drops in a hostile saloon.

Such set-backs are nothing to a dedicated amateur investigator. In a few more chapters, he understands all. And   explains all to an enthralled bar room crowd, as he plays two-handed poker with the villain, the table littered with $500 chips.

In the November 30, 1924, "The Trey of Spades," the Trey is a bandit who leaves that playing card at the scene of his outrages. A drunken young man of bad reputation is suspected, arrested, almost lynched. Hashknife gets most of the story sorted out, after much trouble. And no wonder, since the problem includes a dance hall girl who isn't, a preacher who doesn't, and a killer who won't.

Of all the changes introduced during 1924, the most remarkable is the extensive reworking of the two lead characters. Many of Hashknife's personal traits are transferred to Sleepy—including the roan-colored hair (which Hashknife borrows back during a few later stories). Hashknife also relinquishes most of his frivolous pleasures, such as girl watching, most of his fractious behavior, and much of his playful backtalk.

Now it is Sleepy who baits the sheriff in those dialogues where ridicule seethes beneath genial nonsense. As in this meandering conversation with a sheriff who has just lost a prisoner:

Sleepy (to Hashknife): Don't antagonize him, I tell yuh. He's the sheriff, and he's got an awful mad upon himself.

Sheriff: You think you're smart, don't yuh?

Sleepy: Well, maybe I ain't so smart, but I'm sure cautious. As far back as we've ever traced our family tree, there has been a cautious streak. Yessir, the old sap just fairly oozes caution. Now—

Sheriff: Aw, to _____ with your family tree.

Sleepy: That's what I always told Pa. I don't hold with no—

Sheriff: My _____![16]

The dashes conform to *Adventure*'s policy, during that remote period, of never permitting profanity on the page. As a result, some of the chapters look like letters passed by censor—more dashes than content. The omitted words are so innocuous, by present standards, that you suspect Tuttle of fudging his profanity, after all.

Not only does Sleepy take over Hashknife's habit of prodding a stiff forefinger into the bulging waistcoat of the Law, but he also appropriates Hashknife's eye for the girls. For a few stories, Sleepy grows uncommonly susceptible to skirts and smiles, eliciting the usual ponderous witticisms:

Sleepy: Dang you, can't I admire beauty if I want to? I've got eyes and a heart.
Hashknife: When they passed around eyes and hearts, yuh robbed the platter, but when brains came you was all filled up.[17]

Which is distinctly unfair. For a second banana, Sleepy is foresighted in danger and quick-witted in action. Granted that he is no hand with puzzles. Few of us are. Hashknife's ability to tease out a hidden situation from thin air frets Sleepy. He cannot quite see how the trick is done, and his chronic inability to see through granite sharpens his tongue:

Sleepy: The stage just left and that big Chinaman was on the seat with the driver.
Hashknife: Didja want him for anything?
Sleepy: Not that anybody knows about. I jist said that he went away on the stage. If you'd 'a' told me that, I'd be supposed to marvel to beat hell and lose sleep over it, wouldn't I?[18]

The fact that the big Chinaman rode off on the stage happens to be one link in Hashknife's thought concerning drug smuggling (of all things) through the region. Not one hint of this escapes him. Neither Sleepy nor the sheriff nor the reader find much illumination from Hashknife till the story is ending.

Perhaps this wall of silence accounts for the rather tedious carping that wells out whenever Sleepy detects a new mystery in the offing:

Sleepy: It makes me tired. Every time we go anywhere, somethin' happens. There's no peace anywhere. When them fellers was tellin' about that hold-up, your nose was twitching like the nose of a pointer dog. Dang it, me and you didn't come here to hunt bandits.[19]

Not that there is any way of deflecting Sleepy from adventure, once it has been scented. He registers his complaint in the tradition of the grumbling sidekick (another innovation of the dime novels) and his eyes brighten and go round with innocence. He has stated his pleasure in the inverted language of the West. "Lordy," he says, "I was scared everythin' was going to be all right."

It is the last thing that need concern a character in this series.

Hashknife's personality alters even more drastically than Sleepy's. His initial high spirits, as frothy as those of a twenty-year old with a sports car and $10,000, gradually settle. He grows less demonstrative, more self-controlled, more inclined to deception than defiance. In four years, his behavior ages fifteen. Chronologically he hardly ages, beginning the series when he is something over thirty and ending, some decades later, in his early forties. A successful series preserves a man wonderfully.

That longevity is not because of his skill with the pistol. Neither Hashknife nor Sleepy handle a gun with the greased facility of the usual western hero. "Neither of them could split a second on the draw. There was nothing uncanny about their ability to draw a six-gun, nor were they of the dead-shot variety. The West knew many gunmen who were swifter, more accurate than these two. Yet these two lived unscathed."[20]

Usually unscathed. Old wounds scar them both. They are forever being shot at by ambushers. It is a tedious story when a bullet doesn't whiz past a cheek, past a neck, draw a blood line along the ribs. But the more common face-to-face, stand-up-and-draw gun fight does not often happen. Hashknife and Sleepy are thinking men, not duelist. They anticipate trouble and take action before people start snatching out weapons.

That sharply reduced the number of stand and shoot scenes. If you enjoy those, read Hopalong Cassidy. Hashknife is interesting in less obvious ways.

Although they avoid bar room gun brawls, their lives are more than normally violent. Both men are confirmed fatalists. At one time, Hashknife read the *Rubaiyat of Omar Khayyam*, which left a lasting impression on him:

Hashknife: Ever read that poem which was written by a feller whose name sounds like an answer in Chinese? Something about the moving finger writes and having written moves on. I don't know the rest, Sleepy, but she means that it's all cut and dried and it don't make no difference if your gun does stick.[21]

For a man who believes in predestination, Hashknife takes a most aggressive role in the problems he faces. No Eastern passivity here. Although he might be the puppet of a larger fate, that does not diminish the zeal with which he attacks problems. If he fails, it will be the fault of Fate, not his own inactivity.

He is an enthusiastic and unskillful pool player. He drinks modestly and with care. His major vice is roll-your-own cigarettes, Bull Durham and papers. Both ingredients he constantly bums from Sleepy. He is a competent poker player, not flashy but reading his opponents with accuracy.

His growing reputation as a range detective is an embarrassment. "Must be some other fellow, not me. I'm just a cowboy." When identified as the Hashknife Hartley all the stories are told about, he can assume the role of a gullible fool or a conceited fool or a slow wit hopelessly confused. It depends on the audiences. He works best sitting quietly, asking questions, watchful at the edge of action, studying men and wondering. When not investigating, he is sociable enough and so quick to sympathy for those in trouble that Sleepy never lacks for a complaint:

Sleepy: (Hashknife), you always go kind of out of your way to bother into other folks' troubles. Every dang place we go you gets into some dang kind of mixup, and she's always because you feel sorry for somebody. If it was only you I'd say for you to go to it and grab a tombstone but, blast it all, you always drags me into it.[22]

But what else is a justice figure for if not to get into a mixup because you feel sorry for somebody?

The Hashknife stories written between 1924 and 1933 are the heartwood of the series. The characters have stabilized. The tone of the stories has grown firm, the characteristic themes and conflicts developed. The improvised narrative bounces along, filled with surprises for the reader—and for Tuttle, who refrained from detailed plotting ahead of time and tangled up the story as he went along. Or so he claimed.

Tuttle: I have never mapped out a story in my life.

I do not bother about plots nor situations. A typewriter and some paper seem to be all I require, and I let the story tell itself. When my lead character gets bothersome enough to worry me I know he is ready to tell me the story.[23]

I have never dictated any copy. I am not fast on a typewriter—using only two fingers and profanity—but I am never more than two chapters behind my imagination. Seriously, I never know what the next paragraph is going to contain.[24]

Such stories as the 1925 *Hidden Blood* are so complex, you wonder how he ever found the ending. The novel abounds in criminal problems. Unfortunately most of them are answered within a chapter. No sooner is a mystery stated than the narrative, panting audibly, shows us those responsible talking it over. The reader knows most of it; Hashknife is not so favored, although he keeps up with the reader very well, thank you.

The story concerns theft, murder, miscegenation, rustling, and smuggling as two gangs collide down by the border. Gang One is making a nice thing of drug-running; Gang Two attempts to hijack its way into the profits. Caught in the eye of the action are Hashknife, Sleepy, and the squawman Hawkworth.

Hawkworth has two children—a beautiful half-breed daughter, and an unconfessed son who is being raised out on the West Coast by Hawkworth's best friend, Meline. The best friend is a two-faced criminal, deeply involved in drug smuggling. He has embezzled all the funds Hawkworth sent to him for banking and has turned the son into a dope addict. Then Hawkworth writes asking for $20,000 to buy into a mine. That request precipitates a fake holdup, a real shooting. After that, the blood-letting begins.

By the final chapters, things are black for the forces of good. Hashknife is tied up in a cellar; Sleepy has fallen down a disused mine shaft; the two gangs have temporarily united and captured Hawkworth; and the beautiful half-Indian Miss Hawkworth, is being forced, at gunpoint, into a disagreeable marriage.

Virtually the entire cast is crammed into one large room, strangely like a moving picture set. There, Hawkworth's son finds the forced marriage not to his taste. He is in love with the girl, not knowing that she is his sister. He gets to shooting by way of protest, is shot several times in response. Then Hashknife and Sleepy take the evil from behind:

The room was choked with smoke, through which darted flicks of flame, and the old adobe walls fairly shook from the concussion of the guns.

Then the reports ceased. It was like the touching off of a pack of firecrackers, a blending of many explosions for several seconds, which died away to individual reports, unevenly spaced—then silence.[25]

Everyone is killed who would, in any way, obstruct a satisfactory ending. All open questions of mixed-race marriage are swept away out of sight, and the story ends in tight-lipped sentimentality, not a detective story, not much of a mystery story, but action all the way.

"The Buckaroo of Blue Wells" (*Adventure*, November 23, 1926) is James Legg, a young bookkeeper who is offered ownership of the X Bar 6 if he can prove, within a year, that he can run a ranch.

With his dog, Geronimo, James leaves for Blue Wells, Arizona. At once he blunders into a robbery of the train's express car, is chased by men with guns, stumbles into the protection of some drunken cowboys who begin his initiation into the life of a cow puncher.

Soon he is courting the beautiful girl at the next ranch. Her father, and all the ranch hands, have been arrested for the train robbery. That being the case, James does the only thing possible for a gentlemen—he moves to the ranch to help the girl out, with the aid of that taciturn drifter, Hashknife Hartley, and his cheerful friend.

In short order, mysterious bullets sing around James' ears. The bunkhouse is blown apart and the admirable girl kidnapped.

All this action is complicated by the story of Tex Alden, an unsuccessful rancher who seems to have lost $8,000 at poker on the night of the robbery. Worse, Tex knew that the money was on the train. Immediately, everyone glares suspiciously at Tex, except the sheriff (whose capacity for error is awe-inspiring) and Hashknife, who never shows who he suspects until just before the final guns go off.

In "Shotgun Gold" (November 1, 1927), a crafty plot is afoot to get two ranchers fighting, so that a third ranch can step in and scoop up a concealed gold mine. Unsigned threatening notes flutter about the cowtown. The sheriff is scared out of office; the county judge is white with fear, although still holding court. Soon a gambler has been murdered by hands unknown. Then a killer with a .22 begins slaughtering cattle.

Clues swamp Hashknife: dead steers with the brands cut out, a .22 cartridge, a reef of gold-bearing rock. All clues are fakes and the truth comes out in the courtroom, where guns crash and marvelous revelations are made.

In the five-part serial, "Bluffer's Luck" (*Argosy*, July 13, 20, 27, and August 3 and 10, 1929), an ex-convict returns from prison. Shooting begins promptly. But matters are not simple. Tangled together are such characters as a young lady impersonating a deceased young lady, a tricky ex-prosecutor, a crooked gambler, and a drunken cashier, all twisting and turning wildly.

At this point in the series, Tuttle does not piddle away the secondary mysteries as rapidly as in *Hidden Blood*. Now he allows them to accrue, incident by incident, as pieces of the larger mystery. The narrative is no longer a succession of loosely associated scenes, but tightens to a more artful structure—"more," in this case, being a relative term meaning better than chaos.

Tuttle's gradual technical maturation brings on other problems, as maturation always seems to do. While individual stories are more thoroughly developed, they also show a tendency to reflect situations and character types from past stories, which is understandable, and future stories, which is regrettable.

Even improvised fiction requires form—if for no other reason than to placate the editor, who plans to publish the story as a four-part serial. That immediately requires a suspense break at the end of each serial part. Since all parts are about the same length, these secondary climaxes tend to appear at rather mechanical intervals, giving the effect of ticking clockwork.

The mechanical requirements of serial parts resonated through the entire story: Introduction of initial characters, action, complication the first, action or humor, complication the second.... Since Tuttle was improvising within a fixed form, like a chef specializing in 9-inch fruit pies, he tended to favor certain character types. These could be depended upon to introduce the problems and complications needed, exactly on schedule.

One such character was The Flawed Father—a drunk or suspected criminal, or, more usually, a rigid old hardnose, pig-headed and intolerant. It was the Flawed Father's destiny to be forever manipulated by the forces of darkness. He frequently ended up shot.

Equally familiar was The Neer-Do-Well Son, hot tempered, rejoicing in liquor, cards, and bad company. These dubious pleasures lead him directly to peril, jail, flight from the law, and/or personal disgrace. In most cases, The Son redeems himself by sacrifice. He does not always survive the gesture.

The Inappropriate Hero is callow, energetic, clever, and totally uninformed as to how life is lived in the Great West. He fumbles along, toppling off horses, blundering in and out of gun fights. Frequently battered, he is never extinguished.

The Older Woman, a frequent character, is of forcible personality and strong opinion. Always sympathetic, she provides stability in a seethe of confusion and violence.

The Beautiful Half-Breed Girl, part Indian or part Mexican, is altogether lovely, a glorious object to be contended for. She frequently faces a forced marriage to a worthless man.

Equally beautiful is The Splendid Girl. She is also afflicted with love problems and displays a sublime ability to get engaged to a plausible villain. Moreover, she has a tendency to get carried off by wicked men for wicked reasons.

The Coldly Competent Rancher may be either villain or victim. Exercising real political power in the region, he conducts himself with the high arrogance of a Feudal Baron. Slippery foremen assist him. Also a few scary gunmen, who ride around in the chapters like detached bits of Hell.

The Blackguard Sheriff of earlier stories has been transformed to The Befuddled Sheriff. Usually befuddled. He is an amiable dub, teased by his deputy, pitied by the community. He lurches boldly about, arresting at random, welcoming Hashknife's cryptic suggestions.

These primary characters are supplemented by a swarm of bit players—humorous drunks, cowboys, cooks, bartenders, narrow-faced lawyers, and Mexicans significantly fingering their knives. Each is distinctly, if not complexly, drawn. Each gives a single, vivid glimpse of a human face.

Humor is used freely. Tuttle began his work for *Adventure* by writing short stories that closely resembled silent movie comedies. The Hashknife series is considerably more restrained, although humor persistently bursts from the paragraphs.

Much of that humor is tossed out in passing, sudden sparks flicked from the blazing narrative:

Charlie yawned widely and rubbed his nose. Charley had not been slighted when they passed around noses.

Just that: a casual observation *en passant*. Similar sparks flash from the dialogue:

Any man that wears a mustache like (the sheriff's) couldn't find his own socks inside his boots. That man has gone all to hair.

Humor adds an agreeable richness to the dialogue. The effect is of people talking naturally, rather than characters conversing to advance the plot. Even when a joke has clearly been starched and ironed ahead of time, it slides as neatly into place as if it had been improvised on the spot:

Cowboy, cowpoke, and cowpuncher mean the same thing—a bunch of ignorance, with hair on one end and toenails on the other.

Less off-hand, and usually less successful, are the brief comic scenes introduced to break up the action and vary the mood. Two or three of these scenes appear during a novel. Most are obvious, uncomplicated stuff, self-conscious humor at the level of an Abbott and Costello routine:

—The ranch owner's ritzy wife orders filet mignon and cavier to the bafflement of the ranch cook.

—A pair of cowboys, shimmering with whiskey, have a succession of mishaps.

—A tough sheriff is accidentally knocked down, dazed out of his wits, and otherwise treated as if he were surrounded by Keystone Cops.

All this is loose-jointed, unsophisticated stuff, part physical comedy, part vaudeville sketch. But even when Tuttle is constructing set pieces, his touch is engagingly light.

At the end of the 'Twenties, he heard a pair of Mexican workmen speaking their own variety of English. Delighted with the sound, he brought them into his fiction, under various names. The comedy lay in the garbling of the language, not in the character of the Mexicans. As characters, they are uniformly tough and ruthless, and there is little amusing about their actions. The contrast between their speech and their behavior is intense.

Miguel found Ricardo outside the door, and they went back to their room, where they finished up the bottle of *vino*. . . .

'I've been theenk quite some lots,' stated Miguel, missing his head entirely with his big hat.

'Good!' exclaimed Ricardo. 'I'm glad for hearing. W'at you theenk?'

'I'm theenk,' he replied solemnly, 'eef those *Americanos* fin' out we gots those weemen—we bot' gets hong.'

'Mm-m-m-m-mha!' agreed Ricardo solemnly. 'Hung by the neck until you are died. That ees wort' theenk about. W'at you suppose Porfiro steel those weemen for? Young one wort' looks at, but the ol' one ees not wort' damn. . . . Bimby t'ree, four damn cowboys come down here—*wham, bam, boom!* Where we be then?'

'Porfiro feex everytheeng.'

'Feex the bosted necks? Bah! Onkle Porfino be beeg helps to us, w'en crazy cowboys got rope on necks. . . .'

'Maybe Porfiro save us.'

'*Idiota!* Porfiro save rope—that ees all.'

'W'y he save the rope?'

'So they hang him, too.'[26]

All this is pleasant and delightful, no doubt, lace over iron, light foolery frosting grimmer reality. It is typical of Tuttle's humor. Like the physical comedy of the silent movies, the laughter barely conceals an undermass of violence and pain.

We have glanced at some of Tuttle's continuing character types and at his habit of easing high-action narrative with humor. At this point, we turn again to Hashknife Hartley, for a few words about his methods of investigation.

Every detective develops a particular style in the practice of his art. So it is with Hashknife—although his style is often so vague as to be invisible.

By the time Hashknife and Sleepy enter the story, it is usual that complications are long underway. People from two or three ranches have been introduced and ground one against the other. One ranch seems inhabited entirely by hard men wearing black hats. Another ranch reels from the effects of mass rustling. A tempest of murder and robbery leaves suspicion pointing squarely at the innocent. Two separate story lines have formed. One of these concerns the fortunes of a trusting young woman; the other, of an ill-advised young man. And danger walks.

As sub-plots twist like demented snakes, Hashknife ambles on stage. Soon he has declared for the side of the beleagured ranch. He may even accept a job there, although he does precious little work. No time to work. He is investigating in his own oblique way.

Slowly he rides into town. He dawdles over the pool table. He yarns casually with bartenders, stable hands, town bums. He lounges in the sheriff's office, listlessly fingering the murder weapon, examining firing pin marks on the shells found at the death scene.

Or he inspects cattle brands. No detective in literature ever drew such vast amounts of information from a brand. Perhaps once a story, he gathers up Sleepy and they ride to a nearby town, there to wander bonelessly around, loafing and talking in dusty indolence until a few invisible threads have been collected. Invisible to Sleepy. They are visible enough to Hashknife.

During the final quarter of the story, Hashknife begins to sing. He is not musical. As Sleepy remarks, he is unable to tell "Home Sweet Home" from "Little Brown Jug." But when his voice rises in a droaning wail, Sleepy brightens. That dismal sound indicates the end is near. The problem has been worked through and Hashknife is ready to pounce.

He pounces as he investigates—obliquely.

Since Tuttle has seldom bothered to plant much in the way of tangible evidence, Hashknife rarely weaves a traditional deductive web, clue by clue, around the guilty. More usually he reveals the guilty by shocking them from cover. To do this, his favorite device is forgery.

Few investigators practice the art of forgery as industriously as Hashknife. Wills, letters, notes, receipts flow smoothly from his fingers, the content based on his intuitive understanding of the concealed situation. He is never far wrong, and his conscience never pangs.

The forgeries lever open secret criminal conspiracies. The conspirators, sniffing betrayal, explode to confusion, panic, gun violence. The stage is now set for the just and unjust to face each other at the hidden ranch house, the forgotten shack, or down at the center of town in the courthouse.

Bring Hashknife to a courthouse and be prepared for revelations and gun fire. In "The Tin God of Twisted River," he graphically demonstrates how the brands were faked and who did the deed. In "Shotgun Gold" the court hazes with powder smoke as men struggle and shoot and marvelous explanations spurt forth. In "The Cross In a Box Mystery," Hashknife and Sleepy miss the gun battle at the inquest but arrive soon enough to explain all obscurities. Although Perry Mason might not approve of these loose judicial proceedings, justice is served, one way or the other.

At the end of the 1920s, Hashknife began bobbing up in *Argosy*. For about six years, his series wavered between that magazine and *Adventure*. It was the same series, the same characters, the same scene, the same author. Yet there were differences. After a serial or two, the *Argosy* stories shrank to novelettes— or so-called novelettes; they were really short stories. Appearing irregularly through 1938, these were strongly action oriented. Mystery flared at once with much physical activity.

Hashknife and Sleepy arrive early on the scene. Wandering has taken its toll. Shabby, ill equipped, nearly penniless, they drift into town, eager to glimpse the other side of the hill. Their reputations echo through the west, larger and grander than the men, themselves, as seems often to have been the case back then. Things are different now.

"Hashknife Plays a Hunch" (*Argosy*, November 4, 1933) tells how an ex-convict returns to his home town. An explosion of murder results—including a man shot by a pistol that lacks a firing pin. There follows dirty work at the Pueblo village; a kidnapped girl lies unconscious among ancient ruins while a dirty-necked bad man and a hardboiled ranch owner struggle to cover their tracks. Then they begin biting each other. In the final pages, a pair of drunken cowboys in a buggy collide with a house, just as an innocent man is about to be shot.

For part of the story, Hashknife pretends to be dead. He has figured out most of the plot from such unlikely clues as an ink-soaked letter, a case of cartridges with gold slugs, and the murder of a little rabbit of a storekeeper. At the root of all the scheming is a mine stuffed with gold.

In "Deception Trail" (*Argosy*, December 15, 1934), a decent man is framed to prison for the murder of his brother—by his brother. The story begins in Beverly Hills, California, where Hashknife is offered the job as foreman of an

Arizona ranch. When he accepts, he finds the ranchlands overrun by the other men's cattle and evidences of crooked dealing everywhere. Complications immediately develop in the interesting form of two wives and two daughters, and only one husband to go around.

Hashknife performs brilliantly in this story. As foreman he is so straight talking and blunt that you would like to nominate him for President. The final confrontation takes place in the lobby of the cowtown hotel and Sleepy has a chance to do some shooting for a change.

"Hashknife Pays A Debt" (*Argosy*, February 2, 1935): When Hashknife had a chest full of broken ribs, Old Mrs. West visited him. Now she is in trouble, her husband dead, her ranch stolen from her, her son on the run.

So it's off to Diamondville, Arizona. While camping in a barn, Hashknife and Sleepy are fascinated observers as unseen men plot and murder. All the wrong people get blamed. It is the work of that crooked ranchman, Diamond, who owns every horned toad in sight.

But Diamond's luck runs out. He meets an honest coroner and he meets Mr. Hashknife Hartley, who has suddenly acquired the ranch that Diamond thought he owned.

After that, Hashknife forges a little note to Diamond, causing general panic. Diamond slaps the wrong man and gets shot dead by a reformed crook. Neither Hashknife nor Sleepy have to pull a trigger at the end, although they burn up plenty of ammunition during the story.

The *Argosy* short stories are condensed, simplified, and hyperthyroid. Stripped of secondary characters and multiple sub-plots, with descriptive material omitted, familiar scenes compressed to lines, time frantically accelerated, the stories whiz hotly along, miniatures of their former selves.

This was typical of most of *Argosy*'s non-serial fiction during the 1930s. It was pared to a minimum of everything but conflict and action. Even major series characters who had survived from the 1920s—among them, Madame Storey and Peter the Brazen—adapted to the frantic pace. But the strain showed; one by one they fell away.

By the mid-1930s, Hashknife and Sleepy had also vanished, popular as they had once been. Perhaps Tuttle had finally tired of them. Or perhaps *Argosy* was more enthusiastic to Tuttle's new character, Henry, a comic, fat, quick-talking slickster of a sheriff. Whatever the reason, Hashknife and Sleepy stayed absent until the end of the 1930s. By then they had shifted operations to the *Short Stories* magazine, and there they remained until the early 1950s.

Short Stories was already home for Sad Sontag, another of Tuttle's wandering cowboy adventurers. The magazine was a bit less frenetic than *Argosy*, contained somewhat longer stories, with a trifle more character drawing and motivation, and a trifle less action and peril. Each story expended enough plot to fuel an entire novel.

As usual, the shift to a different magazine brought changes. Not many but some. In *Short Stories*, our heroes are not quite the purposeless wanderers of the past. Much of their time is spent looking into things as a favor to the Cattlemen's Protective Association. Strictly to oblige Association Secretary Bob (or Buck) Marsh, understand.

Sleepy is much irritated by Marsh's requests, which are always vague, always dangerous, and never involve pay. Hashknife scorns pay. He is a free-lance, tied to no man. And besides, roving knights are out for the scenery and adventure, not cash.

So Sleepy seethes and Hashknife grins and Bob Marsh, far off and invisible, manipulates their travels through the pages of *Short Stories*.

These late adventures are smoothly written, with prominent mysteries, elaborate plotting, and ideas occasionally borrowed from previous 1920s stories. "Passengers for Painted Rock" (April 25, 1939) pits Hashknife and Sleepy against the three White Masks—killers who rob and shoot and write fierce notes and kidnap pretty girls and tie Sleepy up in a mine with only some fizzing dynamite for company. Hashknife saves him. Nothing saves the Masks.

In the July 25, 1947 "The Menace of Spirit River," a drunken young tenderfoot seems to have gunned down both the sheriff and his deputy. Improbable? Hashknife picks at the matter and uncovers a plot to sneak sheep onto the cattle range. The idea is a first cousin to that told in richer detail in "The Dead-Line" (*Adventure*, October 20, 1924).

The novel, *Mission River Justice* (1956), tells how a young ex-convict returns to town the very day that his father is shot and killed while holding up the stage. The young man declares himself an outlaw and takes to the hills. All turn against him—except the sheriff's daughter, who believes him innocent. She is right. Hashknife proves it so, and also that black is white, and upside down is rightside up, all amid frequent bullet showers. The story has not been traced in the magazines but was probably written during the 1940s. The prose is quick, clean, and pared until only the structure of the story remains, like a leaf reduced by the art of the botanist to a fragile transparency of itself.

For nearly thirty years, Hashknife and Sleepy roamed the fictional west. They performed in three or more pulp magazines, two or three dozen books, and an eighteen-month radio series that aired during the 1940s. Today they may still be found in your library. Look under westerns, not mysteries. The books are primarily reprint editions from England.

Hashknife and Sleep have endured well. They traveled a timeless west, only lightly touched by Twentieth Century change. The infrequent mention of airplanes, automobiles, parachutes, and typewriters place the period between 1905 and 1920. We need not press Tuttle too closely on the dating.

The West he offers is a dream and a fiction, decorated by glinting bits of reality. But he is not writing history. He is providing mystery-adventure for our pleasure. In that world, death and violence arrive on schedule. Perils loom hourly. All problems may be dissected by thought. And a hero, indestructible as a god, can survive the years on no funds at all.

In the course of the series, Tuttle got hold of the essence of two men. They are not deeply realized. Certainly they are not fleshed out in the psycho-sexual habit of today. They are simple men, poor and uneducated, only partly explored by their author. They are also skeptical of mind, ironic of speech, independent of nature. However casually they were cast onto the page, they pulse with life. There is blood in them and quirky personality. They draw you back—the essential test of a successful character.

For that reason, the books are still to be found. The two horsemen still ride slowly through the enormous country toward distant hills. They converse sparingly. They have ridden together for years and need little speech.

Tomorrow, another town, another problem, another chapter. Beyond that rises another range of hills. And so the books multiplied through the long years.

Like Peter the Brazen, Hurricane Williams, and the Major, Hashknife Hartley is one of that minute group—the Grand Adventurers. He is less celebrated than Alan Quatermain, but his adventures are no less energetic and dangerous.

It is characteristic of the Grand Adventure that it is far away, distant and remote—among the blood-splattered islands of the South Pacific or fanged mountains in Tibet. Our minds create the scene from a few words of description. But whether we visualize the locale or not, the narrative action roars on. For wherever the Grand Adventure is found, the opponents are murderous, your death a strong possibility, and your judgment of others a main factor in surviving the afternoon.

Grand adventures necessitate grand risks. Habitually its heroes stride magnificently through the action. They are of high excellence and drawn to an outsized scale. However the adventure story does not always demand the grand treatment or characters to meet that demand. The fabric of fiction contains innumerable characters. Only a few of these are, in any sense, outsized, and only a few reach celebrity status. The rest twinkle through a handful of issues, only to be replaced by other hopefuls.

All characters have an affinity for the odd situation. They have the gift for adventure—if not for Great Adventure. For adventure is not always a quest beyond the scowling mountains; a gifted person can stay close by home and experience marvels.

In the following chapter, we will meet a few people who did that. Firemen, stenographers, gold-diggers, ball players, and bums. Some labor in romantic occupations. Still others slave at routine.

All of them tingle with a special sense for adventure.

They find it easily. It lies all around, apparently, glowing like opals scattered on the lawn.

For example....

Chapter 7
Right in Your Own Backyard

1—

Over the years, the pulp magazines published a series on every conceivable profession. Or perhaps it only appears that way, so astounding was the variety. If a subject seemed in the least liable to tickle the public chin, it promptly materialized in the pages of *The Popular Magazine, Top-Notch Magazine,* or some other worthy title.

As you might suspect, the subjects selected often echoed the public's current fads and entrancements. A popular stage sensation, a successful moving picture, a national news story would provide the seed. From such enticing stimulation, a series leaped.

We have long forgotten the precise grain of sand that formed these pearls. Perhaps an assiduous examination of newspaper headlines might suggest why *Blue Book* offered stories about a diver or secret service operative in 1910-1911. Or *Short Stories* a 1923 series about a reporter. Or the 1924 *Snappy Stories* series about a gold-digger.

Series were often laid in small towns, as are the stories of Eddsfield politics. The reader could identify immediately with the people, depicted by a carefree use of stereotypes. Other series confined themselves to big city neighborhoods, themselves small towns in concrete. In those places characters, like Mother Hansen or Spud McGee, enjoyed their rather peculiar adventures amid surroundings reasonably familiar to all readers.

Sport stories swarmed. In the formative days of the general-fiction magazines—roughly a twenty-year period beginning about 1904—nearly every issue offered a sports story, particularly about baseball, the King of Games. Nurtured by Merriwell and other game-oriented dime novels, and by a growing American preoccupation with the hitting and catching of balls, a wave of sports fiction spilled sweatily through the pulps. Capable heroes slammed the ball at the last moment, or duelled teammates, or did valiant things to win for the home town team. The tone of these stories was between Ring Lardner and Frank Merriwell, without the satire of the first or the innocence of the second.

Still other series concentrated on small adventures in western towns. Or life behind the circus flaps. Or how they made movies or worked the 5-a-day vaudville stage. (All the actors, it seemed, were just home folks, after all; just what you had suspected.)

Were you curious to learn the details of a stenographer's life? Or a musician's experiences in a dance band? Perhaps you yearned for the active life of a reporter or salesman.

Wait patiently. Soon your favorite magazine would print a series about that job. And when you read that series, you learned that, as you had always expected, stenos and salesmen and political bosses led remarkable lives, darting from excitement to triumph, a giddy whirl. Adventure was as close as your heartbeat. Especially if you were fortunate enough to work in an intrinsically thrilling occupation.

As a fireman, for instance. Imagine living the life of a fireman....

2—

Ned Holly, that dashing young giant, enjoyed a six story run in *Blue Book* from November 1910 through April 1911. "Holly of the 'Big Nine' " was the series title; by Frank Finnegan.

"The Big Nine" referred to the fire section to which Holly belonged. This was back in the days of the horse-drawn engine, with boilers that must be fired. As the rig raced along, it streamed smoke as densely as the structure it was attempting to save.

Fire Marshall Doyle, that irascible veteran, is in charge of operations. He glares at Holly with an uncharitable eye. It is the old familiar story—the young man must battle his way to acceptance. And so he does, his deeds dazzling. This is called "The Boys' Book Syndrome."

Doyle's daughter, Marguerite, loves Holly and he loves her. But the Marshall doesn't want her marrying a fireman. No, sir. He resists and resents, generating tense pages of copy.

Till Holly saves the old codger from drowning during a lumber yard fire. That turns the old man's head around. So Holly and Marguerite get his blessing and the ethereal joys of marriage loom.

By that time, Holly has earned a medal of honor from the city and become a lieutenant in the department. The men regard him as sports fans regarded the Merriwells.

Comes the night of the wedding dinner....

Ah, you sly fox, there's no surprising you.

You're right. It is one of those things predestined. The fire bell rings out. After a certain amount of agonizing, so that you might appreciate his mettle, Holly leaves for the fire dressed in a tuxedo and silk topper. Once there, he saves a young boy from Fearful Doom. He, himself, is plunged into flaming wreckage. But the faithful fire dog, Roxy, sniffs him out and he crawls to safety, singed but triumphant.

Other firemen series cropped up through the years. Among them was "Yellow Pup—Fire Eater" by Carlton Mattis, in *People's Favorite Magazine*, the series beginning February 10, 1918. The Yellow Pup is a rich man's son who is determined to become a fireman. They all think him a coward at first. He isn't.

About ten years later, *Top Notch* published another fire-fighting series, this one by Vic Whitman, who snapped out series about firemen, policeman, musicians, this and that, in a delightfully casual way. During 1927-1928, he ground out a competent group of stories about fighting fires in 1908. From the stories, it is clear that fictional heroes are all the same, whatever the date.

The subject proved popular enough for Harold Hersey, distinguished publisher of short-run titles, to bring out the *Fire Fighters* Magazine in 1929. The magazine did not long linger in this demanding world, even though glorious with front covers painted by Walter Baumhofer.

If your tastes ran to water rather than fire, Frederic Reddale wrote a series about professional diving for the 1910 and 1911 *Blue Book*. The 1911 series (January to May or later) was titled "The Further Adventures of Matt Bardeen." Old Matt has retired and, with his wife, works as the assistant keeper of the Ponquogue Light House. He tells these stories to the narrator.

Although Matt is just that bit long-winded, his tales have the ring of truth. If they weren't his adventures, they were surely experienced by another diver. As stories, they are as thin as a politician's excuse for stealing, yet each has an authentic ring. Such as Matt's experience in the Thames River.

He's working a sunken ship full of copper ingots (April 1911). The divers are wiring the ship to blow it apart. Just as they complete the wiring, Matt slips and ends chest deep in mud. For a moment, he feels endangered—but only for a moment. As a story, it is trifling; as personal reminiscence, it is fascinating. So are Matt's experiences with sharks while working on a Samoan breakwater (May 1911).

Few technical details seep into these stories. But that can be forgiven. These slender delicate fragile pieces would snap under a mayfly's weight; what really counts is the feeling of authenticity, which leaves so clear an impression of how it was to work under water in 1911.

A major figure of American folklore is the traveling salesman. Of that legendary crew, Professor Harold Hill (the Music Man), and Alexander Botts (of the Earthworm Tractor Company), are transcendent examples.

In the long-ago past, readers of the *Top-Notch Magazine* followed "The Adventures of Steve Blake, Traveling Man." The series, by J. A. Fitzgerald, ran from October 15, 1913, to the end of that year, or perhaps a few issues more. Blake was no Harold Hill, but he had his moments.

Each story jogs brightly along, full of obvious humor, easy solutions, and slangy fresh dialogue. Each is peopled by characters wearing large signs:

> *Bad Man*   *Pathetic Woman*   *Good Darky*   *Weak Man*

The day of the traveling man rises around us. Through the paragraphs ring the voices of the commercial travelers. They are jaunty, if worn, riding the trains from city to city across the mid-west.

Blake travels for Hinkle and Company: notions and house furnishings. He's a star salesman, filling the order book where others sweat hopelessly.

It is not easy out there on the road. Competitors' dirty tricks slow Blake up. Natural disasters threaten his schedule. But he has a clever mind. And he's glib as Eden's snake.

In his lapel shines the button of the Commercial Travelers Association. He is as proud of that button as of a halo. "You're a disgrace to that button you're wearing," he snarls at a salesman who is treating a poor old woman ugly. That rascal deserves to be pitched from the great CTA fraternity.

Success does not always come to Blake. He fails at love. The sweet girl will not wed him until the world realizes the splendor of her voice. Unhappy day, her voice is a caricature. To pry her from the clutches of a fake voice teacher, he invests $1500. But it is money wasted. She is determined to wait for the world's admiration. Her decision means good-bye money, good-bye girl.

Heart ravaged, he swings out across the territory, selling until sorrow is forgotten, a matter of one story.

December 1, 1913: he meets a salesman who is conning a poor alcoholic fellow trying to make a comeback. Blake shows up this bad apple before a Board of Directors—although why the salesmen are pitching to a Board of Directors isn't clear. Exposed, the scoundrel slinks away into the night. In appreciation, Blake's company sends him to England. The series continues from that point. . . .

The stories are shameless hackwork; the characters simple cut-outs: white struggles with black and, in an obviously staged scene, overcomes. But you can forgive this. The stories remain worth reading for the glimpses they give of a salesman's life in 1910. It is fascinating. The banter, the incessant movement, the abrupt bright little pictures of other times. Those descriptions of that long-vanished world justify the effort to read the story.

Top-Notch had been around since 1910. It was intended as a successor to the *Tip-Top Weekly*, the dime novel title which had published so many of the thousands of adventures of the Merriwell boys.[1] *Tip-Notch*'s editor was identified as Burt L. Standish (the pseudonym signed to the Merriwell series and usually employed by Gilbert Patten). In this case, however, the name Standish concealed the name Henry Wilton Thomas.

Editor Thomas pressed his writers to turn out adult adventure fiction. Regrettably, what he bought classifies as "juveniles of a rather superior class."[2]

That is certainly true of the Frank Hawley (The Camera Chap) series. Frank is a newspaper photographer, thus combining interest in that new-fangled photographic stuff with interest in the newspaper game.

Hawley serials have been noted in *Top-Notch*, 1913 and 1923, and, obviously enough, scattered in between, since the letters column of the magazine often mentions his name in admiring and reverent tones.

In the stories examined, the plot struggles gamely along, energized by a few incidents and a great deal of description. Scenes are so heavily padded as to obliterate the action. As in "The Big Bet Snapshot," a three-part serial, November 1 through December 1, 1913. The serial is credited to Bertram Lebhar, or, at least, that is the name signed to it.

Frank is seeking the photograph of camera-shy Rufus P. Winger, The Copper King, who has made a $200,000 bet that it can't be done. Frank does—after difficulties; and manages to survive Winger's pressures on the *New York Sentinel* to quash the photograph and, incidentally, Frank's job. It's all predictable stuff, too heavy for the young reader and too vapid for adult fiction. Hawley, however, is resourceful/dashing/clever and uses his social contacts most adroitly. He has everything a hero requires, except characterization.

A later serial, "The Haunted Diamond" (five parts, September 15 through November 15, 1921), is signed Burt L. Standish. In this adventure, Hawley uses his camera to investigate the dismal collapse of a baseball team. They fall down. They throw weirdly. They reel insanely about. Frank's pictures reveal why: a plotting gambler has buried remote-controlled electromagnets all about the ball field, the rascal.

A less romantic occupation than newspaper photographer was pursued by Mr. Langhorne "Steer" Lyte. Mr Lyte was a barber in Anson, a small town vaguely on the fringes of civilization. The date is 1917-1918.

Lyte is an unusual barber with an unusual background. Over six feet tall, he is built like a battleship. Formerly he was a heavyweight prizefighter with seven KOs. He owns an outsized medal to prove that.

Lyte appeared in a handful of stories written by Holman Day. These began in the December 20, 1918, issue of *The Popular Magazine* and ended early in 1919. Through the stories shine glimpses of small-town America—a scene of horses, genial inefficiency, and patriotic fervor. And also, if the stories are remotely accurate, a non-stop flow of connivers and con men.

Lyte, himself, was With It on the carnival circuit. Hulking, fierce faced, he was the enforcer, who lumbered forward working his huge hands, whenever the sucker squawked about that extra squeeze inside the Professor's phrenology tent.

That work slowly galled his conscience. He left the carnival business, absently pushing in the Professor's face. ("Steer Lyte's Bit," December 20, 1918.) He buys into a barber shop in Anson. His first act as a new resident is to warn town officials that the carnival is ringing in crooked gambling games.

In order to increase the suspense and complicate the story, it is customary, at this point, for the city officials to ignore such a warning. And so they do.

Lyte makes alliance with the local Fire Department, he being the kind of big, bellowing, cheerful realist that they like.

Now, into his shop steps a bearded lady—The bearded lady. She has had it with show biz. To help her along, Steer gives her a clean shave. He further obliges her by hurling her protesting husband into the street—the husband being, at the moment, dressed as a chicken.

The ex-bearded lady, moist with gratitude, tells Steer that a carnival gang will hit the town that night, sniffing for trouble. She's right. The gang does come to town that very night. And when they come, they find trouble. Backed by the Fire Department, Steer confronts the 7-foot carnival champion, pulls his whiskers, breaks up the march, and runs the crooks out of town.

Next story, two weeks later: "Handling Pidgin the Hot End" (January 7, 1919). Into Anson slides a golden-tongued promoter, promising to turn the town into Eden. Steer immediately disgraces himself by upending a bowl of oatmeal on the promoter's head.

After that gaff, it takes fully six pages for him to redeem himself by chasing away the con man—just before the citizens are picked clean.

At heart, Steer Lyte is less a barber than a knight in dusty pants. He has adopted Anson and will protect it from harm. Doesn't matter whether the city fathers approve. They are gullible as pan fish, anyhow. Not so Steer Lyte. His heart may be golden mush, but the carnival has burnt all the sentimental fog out of his head.

If a certain amount of that fog clings to Steer's stories, you need only smile and read on. Any series describing a man in a chicken suit sailing into the street is a series to be cherished.

3—

In a three year period, the Street & Smith magazines ran three separate series with political settings. Two of these demonstrate rather sketchy ideas of how things happen in a free society and feature feminine leads who are gifted manipulators. The third series tells you so much about how things actually happen that, as you read, you can feel your morals mildew.

The earliest stories concern Blackstone Paget, Governor of New State. The series was written by David Douglas for *People's*; it began August or September 1916 and apparently ended with the December issue.

Governor Paget looks like Abe Lincoln, being tall, homely, and a disorderly dresser:

His long, black, poorly fitting mail-order frock coat, and much wrinkled, baggily kneed trousers made his huge frame seem grotesque.

What's more, he is a native Kentuckian, full of idealism and simplicity, which fits the mythical, if not the historical, Lincoln.

(Paget's) inauguration suit had been paid for out of his first month's salary.

Right from the start, he's in conflict with the vested interests. New State has just joined the Union, created from a chunk of the Indian Territory. The money interests have swarmed in, eager to bribe, corrupt, exploit.

Since they can't buy Paget, they set out to discredit him.

(Yes, yes, it is perfectly clear that this is fiction—1916 fiction. A politician who pays for his own clothing, who refuses bribes and will not be corrupted. What could it be but fiction? Inept fiction, for true fiction gives the illusion of reality. No glimmer of reality hides in this story, did you strain for it with the finest mesh sieve. We have seen too many politicians, heard their rich voices, watched their faces as they twisted and grinned before the jury, observed the despicable compromises that are their lives and the silken ease with which they betray their position, their society, their constituency, their friends, their wives, and any aspect of human life, where decency, trust, honor, and similar obsolete nouns, might be expected. We have observed too many politicians. They crawl through the newspaper headlines, dragging behind a fetid stench of reputation. They lie in public and are not blasted by Heavenly wrath. They negotiate in private for private advantage. How merrily must Plato view them from Eternity's balcony, these leaders of our nation, in whose presence we rise to applaud and envy and admire. We have seen many politicians, but nowhere have we seen a Blackstone Paget.)

For the purposes of the story, Paget resists those corrupting bribers. So does his secretary and former law partner, Norman Talcott. Old Norm is an ex-drunk and a great admirer of Paget's wife, Patty.

Since this series was published ever so long ago, it causes no hardship to reveal that Patty becomes the true lead character in the series. Governor Paget gradually shrinks away to a secondary character, little in evidence during the final stories.

At the beginning ("Mate and Checkmate," November 1916), Patty surprises a pair of burglars robbing the governor's safe. During the scuffle with them, she is shot gently in the right arm. During the excitement, she picks up a piece of evidence they dropped. The reader learns nothing more about this until the final page.

What the thieves were after—and what they took—was a piece of paper which is the only evidence that Paget did not accept a $5,000 bribe.

(Five thousand dollars! In our decade, you couldn't dare bother the City Editor with a story about a mere five-thousand dollar bribe. We have learned not to be concerned with penny ante crime.)

Things look grim for the Pagets. But Patty speaks severely to the dissolute son of Senator Rutherford. By and by the son brings in the Senator for a conference with Patty. It is retribution time. Patty reveals that during the struggle with the robbers, she had torn a monogram from one of them—and it is yours, Senator Rutherford, you—one of the thieves!

With this evidence, the Senator is forced to withdraw all those charges he had brought against Paget. He also resigns.

Were this not a rather simple-minded story, the Senator would utter hooting jeers and Paget would get himself booted into the alley. Since this is fiction with a clever heroine, the Evil Senator is foiled and Talcott appointed to fill his unexpired term.

The next story leaps ahead several years ("Patty Exercises Her Wits," December 1916). Paget's term of office is almost up. The crooked interests have introduced a bill to squeeze the state dry. The question is whether Paget will veto it.

Patty decides to save him the trouble and scuttle the bill, herself. Maneuvering in a most hazardous fashion, she drops broad hints, through channels known to politicians' wives, that the Pagets might be susceptible to a bribe. And the same time, she turns Talcott loose to prove that the bill conceals a massive swindle.

Gracious, yes! He does this handily. When the bill comes to a vote, the evidence of corruption can be flaunted in the law-makers' faces.

As the voting gets underway, Paget has been invited to a meeting of all the chief crooks. There he is given the option of accepting a huge bribe or being shot dead. In a brisk Wild West ending, he overpowers the gunslinger and is busy slugging heads when in burst Patty and Talcott. They bristle with pistols—and the news that the dirty work has been voted down.

All this high drama may not accord with your view of politics. If so, you will not much appreciate the merits of "A Petticoat Boss," either. Written by Albert E. Ullman, the series began in the First August 1918 issue of the *People's Favorite Magazine* and continued twice a month into 1919, fifteen or more parts being published.

Rosie Maroney is our heroine, a tough-headed young lady, unsentimental as a fish knife. She enters local politics when only 18, working with ex-judge Phineas Reese, who advises her as her career progresses. Rather immediately, she outwits the corrupt Boss Cronin of Belleville. As a reward she receives a minor political job.

Gradually she learns to handle herself in the political environment, an education experience equivalent to learning to swim in a privy. Boss Cronin is tough, his ring entrenched, immersed in graft and abuse of power in the tradition of politics as the Great American Game.

"Two Can Play the Game" (October 25, 1918) describes how she helps the reform party almost get in. They don't. That's because they campaigned on all the things they were going to forbid people to do. Boss Cronin does little but watch and grin as reform scuttles itself with its mouth. They must have been Democrats.

From this debacle, only Rosie survives. She is elected city auditor and afterward gives the Boss fits.

"A Case of Fifty-Fifty" (January 25, 1919) allows Rosie a single good blow against the machine. She is barely able to prevent the Boss, the state politicians, and the railroads from stealing a valuable property. When certain information is needed, she slips aboard a private train and eavesdrops on a private conversation. She is most determined.

The adventures of Rosie reflect more of the real world than the Blackstone Paget series. But not until the Eddsfield stories does a series come close to reflecting the actualities of daily politics.

The series was written by J. Frank Davis for *The Popular Magazine*. It began about the First October 1920 issue and continued into the early months of 1921. The initial stories are complex almost beyond summarization. Beginning with a simple problem, they gradually expose all the interlocking and competing interests that operate within Eddsfield to make the problem almost insoluble.

The Eddsfield political scene is a combination of self interest, graft, spite, payoffs, maneuvering for position, deceit, greed, rampant privilege, trickery, and opportunism. Just like your home town. The description is all the more loathsome because the situations ring with the white sound of truth.

Leading the reader through these ripe tangles is the newly elected young Mayor of Eddsfield. Mayor Kendall, still unsophisticated, is learning to handle himself at city and state levels. He is one of four members of the informal Eddsfield Republican council. The dominant council member is "Web" Judson, bald treasurer of the Republican City Committee, seasoned and shrewd. The other members are Merril Hart, local bank president, and Lawrence Neal, the Eddsfield member of the state Senate.

"The Zamboanga Wild Man" (October 20, 1920) traces the far-reaching political consequences of a negro taking a job with the carnival. Featured as a wild man, he is required to gnaw a raw beef bone five times a day. His stomach rebels. He complains. And because he assists his ward to bring in the colored vote, an opportunistic ward heeler sees the chance to make a small power grab. From there, the story gathers momentum like a snowball rolling down a hill of dung.

"A Purely Moral Issue" (November 7, 1920) begins with Rev. McNutt's crusade to regulate dance halls. It expands to a major double-cross in the State Legislature. McNutt's Law and Order League thinks that they are going to name a police commissioner for Eddsfield. But the ex-mayor has paid off the Governor to have himself appointed—there being riches in the police commissioner business. Only narrowly is this crook headed off. Mayor Kendall manages to get a subtle unconstitutionality written into the commissioner's appointment bill. After the bill is passed, it can be voided. Tricky.

In "The Yarboro Flop" (November 20, 1920) that same ex-mayor, a "brilliant, unscrupulous demagogue," seems close to winning the Governor's office on the Democratic ticket. Only if a few votes can be switched to the Republican candidate, can ex-mayor, Curtley, be stopped.

The Republican state committee sends Kendall to the town of Yarboro with $30,000 bribe money. Seems that the political powers of Yarboro are inflamed against the Republican candidate. About them, he remarked in his artless way:

> Yarboro is so rotten and corrupt, Republican and Democrat alike, that whichever faction has the biggest bundle could always carry the town, and (if) either side (didn't) have a single dollar to spend, the election could be swung by the gang that had the biggest box of cigars.[3]

The Democrats have already bought off Yarboro, but Kendall pays a trifle more and, by that green logic, draws them into the Republican camp. After much arguing, he pays only $11,000 and proposes to return the rest to the State committee. That unworldly idea horrifies Eddsfield's leading politician. He tells Kendall to donate half to the state Republican campaign fund, the other half to the Eddsfield fund.

> ...and they wouldn't be shocked if we didn't make any report (on the money's disposition) at all.... If they even heard of your talking such nonsense as returning the money, they would make up their minds you were too much of an amateur ever to be trusted again. Giving the money back! My boy, it isn't done.[4]

The stories are fascinating. But be warned: read them and you will never again scc a politician without wanting to knock him down.

4—

Gold-digging was a less reprehensible profession than politics. In this context, gold-digging doesn't refer to the laborious job of cracking rocks and sieving creeks for gold, but to the gentle art of separating a rich old fellow from large amounts of cash.

It helps if you are slender, blond, and have great melting eyes, you little feminine delight.

Anita Loos sparked national attention with her book, *Gentleman Prefer Blonds* (1925), which had been published, bit by bit, earlier that same year, in *Harper's Bazar* under the title of "The Illuminating Dairy of a Professional Lady." The diary gave every evidence of being written by a young blond type whose prose was unsteady but whose assessment of gentlemen was accurate to the nearest thirty-five cents.

Slightly before *Gentlemen Prefer Blonds* reached the quality markets, numbers of sprightly little blonds had flooded the pages of *Snappy Stories*. At least one of these damsels published a diary two years before A. Loos' more celebrated effort. That diary, "Keeping Tabs on Maudie: The Diary of a Slip of a Girl," began in the Second December 1923 issue of *Snappy Stories*.

Other girls couldn't be bothered to write things down. They were far too busy with art as applied to life:

Then she ran into the bedroom and donned a transparent negligee, one of those negligees designed for the trapping of men.

That sentence suggests that the adventure about to be narrated is rather different from the adventures already met in these chaste pages. Certainly *Snappy Stories* differs from all the other magazines we have met. It was, in fact, one of the early specialized pulp magazines, appearing about two years before the somewhat different specialization of *Detective Story Magazine*.

The initial issue of *Snappy Stories*, dated August 1912, was slanted toward males with twenty cents and no objection to coy prose. The subject was women, sometimes from his point of view, sometimes from hers, always with the delightful possibility of bare skin and sexual experience on the next page, if not the next paragraph. It never came but it always might.

These stories were dense with tease: girls taking drinks; girls kissing; girls dropping away filmy garments; girls inviting men to their apartments; girls painting their faces; girls flirting.

...her cheek upturned to his lowering cheek, her body swaying in pliant response to his....

The sex situation was a great central glare around which the heroine fluttered, splendid in high heels, lipstick, cigarettes, gin, filmy underwear, and advanced ideas. Although the line between purity and degradation was perilously thin, a heroine never quite tumbled over. A girl might revel through glittering adventures, very madcap. But if she fell, she did it in the decent obscurity of the white space between the paragraphs.

As far as darker material was concerned, *Snappy Stories* was completely pure. Read what you would between the lines, nothing more than flaming kisses and scalding embraces happened during the stories, after which the amorous pair tottered apart. Endless variations were played on the theme of near seduction, the complexities of male-female relationships being reduced to a naughty giggle.

> *The Lady Who Would*
> *Sally Delivers the Goods*
> *Married Men Are So Safe*

However mild these stories now appear, they found an audience and *Snappy Stories* found success. Similar magazines soon followed, among them *The Parisienne Monthly* and *Breezy Stories* (1915), *Pep Stories* and *Saucy Stories* (1916), *Gay Paree* and *Zing* (1920).

Breezy Stories was closely modeled after *Snappy Stories*. The first issue was dated September 1915, the magazine continuing through 52 volumes to 1941. At first, the stories were mildly pleasant trifles about young women elated by the vote, their new social freedom, and the merry game of love. Later, during the 1920s, the merry game became vividly tinged with sex. Not that any heroine actually stepped over that boundary. But she came close. She might.

Late in 1933, the venerable *Young's Magazine* (1897-1933), which had begun using suggestive, girly fiction around 1903, merged with *Breezy Stories.* By then the 1920s flapper had given way to the 1930s sophisticate. Now the compromised wife, the casually unfaithful husband, filled the stories with suggestive teasing. Adultery, that great indoor sport, flourished in an atmosphere of cocktails, parties, and daring conversation. In spite of all temptations and opportunities, the heroine evaded carnal love, in an accidental sort of way, and found true, honest, and legal love in the final lines.

In most magazines, the art work was splendidly stylish, the line drawings beautifully done. Few of them showed nudity. The prose was far less artful. It strutted with a sophistication that must have dazzled the high school fraternity crowd:

We're all trying to find something glamorous and piquant and bizarre in life. The quest takes us into strange by-ways. Life with us is experimental, and we can only forget it when the experiment goes badly.[5]

At times, the prose reached 9.6 on the Richter Scale.

...at twenty-two Claire was a raving beauty. Tall, slim, and exquisitely modeled. Brown hair, the color of autumn leaves. Great big blue eyes, darkly fringed with long lashes. An entrancing mouth, though perhaps a trifle big. White hands with long, slim fingers. A complexion comparable with the proverbial roses and cream. A bright and vivacious manner and a musical speaking voice. All these things were Claire's.[6]

More often, the tales of girls who have gone wrong, want to go wrong, don't know whether they have gone wrong, were rendered in the language of a Dick-Jane primer:

The head waiter bowed me to a table and I ordered the table d'hote dinner. The food—Russian—was delicious, and I saw several people drinking quite openly out of glasses. I needed cheering up and I ordered some red wine. Instead of receiving the usual horrible red ink, they brought me quite a good claret. This cheered me....[7]

It would appear that *Snappy Stories* constantly kept a gold-digger series simmering in its pages, like a pot of chicken soup on a stove. "Her Oyster Knife" by Veron Tankeray is reasonably typical. Beginning around October 1923, it ran in five or so parts. Part V, "The Adventures of Dr. Quex" (Second December 1923 issue) tells how frigid Hazel marries a painter sick with love for her. She appropriates his income, supplements this by contributions from other men who appreciate her glowing eyes. When husband eventually catches on, he poisons her wine, killing her dead. But she is revived by that odd Dr. Quex. The point of all this is elusive, unless it is to point the moral that wine is bad for you.

"Confessions of a Gold-Digger" by One of Them, ran from May 1924 to near the end of the year. Lovely, hardened Gloria of the shining golden hair plans to retire a wealthy woman. Money flows in and out of her life, like the tide undulating upon a beach. At length she nails a rich fish. Loses him. Collects a bankroll. Loses that. Undaunted, she begins again:

It was high time that I got an apartment.... Still I did not care to draw on my own slender resources to pay the rent in advance, and I would have to wait for someone to do it for me.[8]

Gets a job modeling dresses, an admirable place to be seen by wealthy men. The manager of the dress shop sets her up in an apartment, saying: "Be happy in your little nest... and sometime ask me to come and have a cup of tea on Sunday."

After getting the apartment, she soon finds a wealthy fellow "who seemed about sixty (with) a red face and white hair."

Gloria's on her golden way but where's she going? Will she land as big a fish again? See the next *Snappy*.

5—

While Gloria stalks her elderly prey, across town the antithesis of these beautiful young gold diggers hunches grimly behind a cash register. The register is in Mother Hansen's Kitchen, a regrettable restaurant, and the long-chinned old woman behind the register is Mother Hansen, herself. She is no gold digger, hunting apartments, Daddies, and silk underwear. She is a tough old, stone-eyed owner/cashier/peacemaker of a restaurant located where the New York slums blend invisibly into New York's crooktown.

Mother Hansen was the star performer in a series written by Paul Ellsworth Triem for *Detective Story Magazine*. Like other series in this magazine, the adventures of Mother Hansen continued for an extended period, roughly from 1923 to 1930, with one or more stories later reprinted in *Best Detective Magazine*.

Mother Hansen is a wonder. You think her asleep behind the cash register. But not so. Her opaque black eyes are shut but her mind is wide awake. Occasionally she dips a hand into a side pocket for a pinch of caraway seeds. These she chews slowly, not having many teeth.

She watches. Her restaurant is small and not very prosperous in a tough section of New York City. Many of her customers know what the inside of jail looks like. Others will shortly learn.

Mother Hansen will not. Back in her girlish days, years and years ago, she was on the wrong side of the law. They never caught her. Later she gave up that chancy life, being a woman of cold sense and inflexible will. She made her private reformation and has not slipped again.

She kept all the old contacts, however. She knows all the tough men, young and old, the safe crackers and the second-story men: they come to her for favors. In return, she exacts assistance from them in solving her own problems.

Frequently she has problems. You might say that she is problem prone— or even adventure prone.

In the late afternoon, she leaves the restaurant smell of fried meat and coffee. She stalks firmly through crowded streets, a tall old lean crone wearing a black bonnet. She invariably carries an ancient umbrella with a large crooked handle.

At a push-cart she buys a packet of crystallized ginger. Very fond of strong flavors is Mother Hansen: Caraway, ginger, peppermint—they cut the taste of a day's grease fumes.

Home is a small two-story house, very old, standing by a vacant lot. She shares her premises with Dick the cat, Sylvia the canary, Tiger the bulldog. Inside, she sniffs the odors of old wallpaper and wood with relish. She brews tea.

A narrow life? Not at all. It is stuffed with adventure. For an old lady with bonnet and umbrella, she saw an amazing amount of action.

As when Crooked Colonel Russel decided to steal his own jewels for the $50,000 insurance. He framed dim-witted Tom Piehl for the job. Now Tom was a check artist, not a box man. Fleeing the hue and cry in dismay, he told his story to Mother Hansen. If Tom didn't understand what he was up against, she did. At once.

And made arrangements with a friendly robber to steal the jewels from the Colonel. Immediately the Colonel assumed that Tom did the job and went hunting for him with a large-calibre pistol.

Mother Hansen anticipated that, too. She cracked the Colonel's head with a vinegar bottle, just as police swarmed out of the woodwork.

The police hadn't been fooled by the Colonel, either.

Unfortunately, the jewels causing all this trouble aren't recovered. It would have been awkward to return them, Mother Hansen realized. So she kept them.

The story, "Mother Hansen Swings a Mean Bottle," may be found in the November 3, 1923, *Detective Story Magazine*.

In the story, "With Her Boots On," January 17, 1925, she makes herself such a pain to the fake medium, Professor Davalle, that he poisons her with preserved ginger. Would you believe that she is too tough to die? After a horrible day spent writhing around on the floor, she recovers and goes after the Professor. Thinking her a ghost, he leaps from a third-floor window. The fall doesn't do him a bit of good.

"Dark of the Moon" (October 31, 1925) sees our heroine arrested. Accidentally she interrupts a robbery by a negro. In the delightful way of 1925 blacks, he leaves the scene with the speed of light, leaving behind a sack full of silver. Before Mother Hansen can return the loot, she is arrested by an ambitious patrolman.

She is immediately freed, of course. Everyone knows that she's honest. But the newspapers rib her unmercifully. Boiling for vengeance, she searches a month for the thief. Locates him, too, on top of a building. Only to discover that he is a she.

He or she escapes again, once more leaving a sack of loot behind. Mother Hansen leaves this sack just where it has fallen and goes home. She has had enough of the whole affair.

"Mother Hansen's Yuletide" (December 25, 1926) is one of those crime-flavored Christmas stories that *Detective Story Magazine* felt impelled to publish annually. The level of sentiment in these stories often resulted in cramping and nausea.

In this tale, Mother Hansen punishes a vindictive drug fiend. She also gets an ex-con a parole and refurbishes the reputation of a young man who has been framed. By a magic which can only be ascribed to the season, she collects members of the Parole Board to observe all these heated goings-on.

All Board members come willingly. Perhaps they were afraid that she would put the umbrella handle around their necks and jerk. It is her characteristic attack mode, effective as a karate chop.

For bootleggers, however, she needs more than an umbrella. A blind pig (a speakeasy to you) opens on her street and begins flooding out poisoned booze. Enlisting a batch of young blonds, Mother Hansen wrecks the place *a la* Carrie Nation.

Inflamed by this significant social gesture, Big-Neck Sam attempts to shoot her, run her down with an automobile, and, when these efforts fail, has his boys take her for a ride.

Mother Hansen comes back none the worse for wear.

Seems she is carrying a vial of nitroglycerine. The bootleggers decide that they want nothing to do with an old broad as salty as all that. ("Mother Hansen's Bite," June 15, 1929.)

Unlike Mother Hansen, Miss Maisie St. Claire is a professional woman of extraordinary charm. Maisie is a stenographer, precariously employed in the law office of former judge George Dorsey. For two years, she has worked there, being in charge of the office, of scrambling the files, and of giving customers her opinion of what the law is—or ought to be. She is blithe and opinionated. She is out to do the world a favor, and the world ought to be glad. As a matter of fact, she is a charm and a delight, being a bright, slangy, up-to-date flapper of the Jazz Age kind:

Maisie: 'Ain't dancin'—much. Why it ain't once a month I shake a Charleston now. When I ain't tendin' to business it takes all my time takin' a private course on how to tend it better. And when I get where I'm aimin' at, I won't care if the shimmy's gone outta style or any other dance....

'...I'm gettin' my brains manicured so they'll have sharp points on 'em, and some day I'll sit back and let 'em support me. I'm workin' in the law business....'[9]

The Maisie stories, written by Nell Martin, appeared in *Top-Notch Magazine* in late 1927 and the first months of 1928. Maisie is a circus girl, her mother a performer on the calliope, her father an acrobat. Given such parentage, the baby could hardly be more With It. Yet she is headed for higher things and, deftly skipping over some years, she ties onto the law firm of Judge George Dorsey.

On her way, at last.

On her way out, if Dorsey has a say in the matter.

He fires her once a week, and once a week she becomes so valuable that he must take her back. In that office there is an inordinate amount of crow eating, and the Judge is well acquainted with the taste of feathers.

If all this sounds like situation comedy, you are entirely correct. All that it lacks is the small screen and commercials. Such a story as "The Hand Is Quicker Than the Eye" (January 1, 1928), for example, could slip without change into a 6:30 family-time television program.

Thus: Dorsey falls into the hands of a designing woman and is as putty. She plans to use him as a catspaw in a stock swindle. Beguiled by her rich voice, he is willing to babble that the useless stocks she has allowed him to hold for her are entirely sound. He hasn't checked, being occupied with staring into the deep pools of her eyes.

Maisie, more practical, discovers that the lady has a fortune-telling racket on the side. She sees stock quotations in the glass ball. Maisie lifts a list of these stocks from under the good woman's nose, just in time to save Dorsey from making a fool of himself. Instead, he becomes a hero—thanks to Maisie. It all happens in the final column.

"All Is Not Wasted That Leaks" (February 15, 1928) tells about this poor fellow who has a leaking artesian well. A mean neighbor has hauled this unfortunate fellow into court. Until something is done, the poor chump must pay a big fine every single day. Dorsey, however, does nothing. Fortunately for the firm, Maisie reads law books, finds a technicality and dramatizes it with a basket of live fish, and saves the day. Again Dorsey shines with reflected glory.

In "Move the Whole House" (June 1, 1928), Maisie is back reading law books again. She gets fired because she gave the right advice to the wrong client over the telephone—a grievous error. This fellow is escaping Dorsey's clutches by dodging among tricky legal points.

Escaping Dorsey is easy. Escaping Maisie in her own series is impossible. Just as the evil fellow is having his house moved, Maisie attaches it, complete with writ and sheriff. In a scene of gorgeous low comedy, straight out of the silent movies, she drives the truck, trailer, and house across town during the rush hour. It's an adventure that should have appeared on *I Love Lucy*.

6—

Street & Smith Sports Stories (1923) and *Sports Story Magazine* (1924) are part of that movement toward single-subject magazines which began, in earnest, immediately after the First World War.

Several specialized pulps had already appeared: *Railroad Man's Magazine* (1906), *Snappy Stories* (1912), and *Street & Smith's Detective Story Magazine* (1915). With the lifting of wartime paper restrictions, and a horde of returning readers, came a rush of new magazines: *Western Story Magazine* and *Thrill Book* (1919), *Black Mask* (1920), *S&S Love Story* (1921), *Sea Stories* and *War Birds* (1922), *Weird Tales* and *Detective Tales* (1923).

Each magazine concentrated on a segment of the market, each small, yet sufficiently large enough to yield profit after production and distribution costs.

Long before 1923 publishers had included sports stories in their general-fiction magazines. As noted elsewhere, these magazines went to great lengths to please everyone. All manner of fiction for all manner of different tastes, packed tightly together in the same magazine. If the cat could read, they would have included stories for her, too.

Contents of the 1910-1912 *Popular* and *People's* featured one or two sports stories an issue. When *Top-Notch* was introduced in 1910—with its bias toward juvenile fiction—much more sports material was pumped into the magazine. By 1913, it was not uncommon for more than half the magazine contents to be devoted to football, basketball, cross-country running, and baseball.

At first, the sports were for amateurs, college-based *a la* the Merriwells. Professional sports crowded in quickly, particularly stories about baseball, baseball teams, baseball players. At that time, a swarm of minor professional teams filled the country and similar teams thrust into the popular fiction of the day.

Two series from the 1919 *Top Notch* may serve as example.

In mid-1919, *Top Notch* featured a series signed Bert L. Standish and featuring that deadly slugger and second-baseman, Jack "Slash" Triebault. Jack was supported by his friend, Eddie "Wizard" Wing, a center fieldsman and also a deadly hitter. These gentlemen played for the Sharks, a professional team, in the April, May, and June issues of 1919 *Top Notch*.

At this time, the Sharks were competing with Eastern clubs in a league circuit. As they battle their way to success, Slash and his friend share a number of strangely similar experiences.

The series is titled "The Baseball Adventures of Slash Triebault." The May 1, 1919, story, "Boots and Bones," opens with Slash in a deep slump. Eddie Wing is much concerned and eavesdrops on a heated argument between Slash and his wife, Kate.

Slash: "I will have that girl!"

It could mean only one thing. Obviously Slash has lost his heart to a bit of fluff and is casting away a perfectly good wife, only a year married.

Wing is filled with dismay. The old friends pass sharp words. Wing does not speak directly to the subject, however, since to clarify the situation would be to end the story before its time. Instead, the misunderstanding is inflated still more.

Wing trails Slash to a lurid dive. There the beer flows and the jazz band blares and Slash hunches over a table with a bold young thing.

At length—for even bad stories end at last—we learn that the young thing is a former maid who stole Kate's diamond ring. ("I couldn't help myself. It was so beautiful. I never had nothing like that.") To get the ring back, Slash has secured the services of a friendly detective. And isn't Wing covered with well-deserved embarrassment.

That is a typical story. Through a determined misunderstanding, one principal suspects the other of folly, then is astounded by an innocent explanation.

"Make 'Em Be Good" (May 15, 1919) makes Eddie Wing the subject. Now *his* game is off. Slash discovers that he is slipping away to a seedy place where he consults with a bold woman. Worse still, Eddie's dear darling love, Peggy, is emotionally wrapped up in a rich old fellow, almost forty-five. But a clever widow helps Peggy see where her heart really is. And Slash regrets that he suspected the worst.

You would think that the plot couldn't be squeezed for another drop. But you would be wrong. It's Katie's turn in "Use Your Bean" (June 1, 1919).

As we open, Slash is gnawed by jealousy. For Katie has been slipping stealthily away to town. For no admitted reason.

Slash fears the worst. In torment, he enters the final game, playing with ferocity, raging and snarling.

He gets beaned by the opposing pitcher. Staggers to his feet and makes a thrilling speech to the crowd: It was an accident. My opponent is a noble fellow, too fine a pitcher to hit me deliberately.

Cheers.

He finishes the game with a concussion and the Sharks win the series.

From the ball park, Slash staggers home, seeking his erring wife.

Perhaps he can forgive her, too, as he forgave the pitcher.

But God, Dear God, there she is, in the house. With a man. Another man!

Actually a French chef.

She is taking cooking lessons, all for Slash's sake.

Well, now if that ain't a laugh on Old Slash, I'll swallow that old horsehide.

The formula is as predictable as an American breakfast.

For the purposes of the story, each character behaves so immaturely that you suspect they wear diapers. Slipping in among these infantile spasms are crisp descriptions of game high points. Those, at least, are vivid stuff. The baseball part of the story shines with sunlight, noisy crowds, men straining in sweaty competition. The baseball part of the story is fine.

During 1919 and 1920, the *Popular Magazine* published a long series by Raymond J. Brown, about the Red Legs, a professional ball club.

The stories were as varied as the Triebault stories were not. Brown seems familiar with the Ring Lardner baseball stories (which first appeared in the *Saturday Evening Post* and later collected in the book, *You Know Me, Al*). However, Brown's stories lack the searing edge of Lardner's prose, and he handles the Red Leg players far more gently. Brown understood that readers respected ball players and wanted to grow up to be like them and would not enjoy seeing them depicted as monuments of ignorance and conceit.

So they were not so depicted. But the stories do not show ball players as monuments of good sense, either.

At story center jitters the Red Leg's manager, tubby little Matt McCoy, the primary continuing character. He is not, however, the lead character. That varies with each story. The lead is played by assorted ball players—faces in the passing crowd. They step forward, tell their story, vanish into the series.

That device permits an agreeable flexibility. Many different personalities in a variety of stories and moods, all stabilized by the faces of a few familiars.

One issue offers you a comic story—such as "A Nine with The Upper Ten" (October 7, 1919). This tells how a player gets tired of Sunday exhibition games and frames a fake invitation for the team to play at Chicago's exclusive Forest Hills. He's set for a day of rest. Only, when they arrive, they find a team there waiting for them.

Next issue, the tone is different. "A Straight Game" (October 20) concerns a pitcher who accepts a bribe and how his father straightens him out. It's a sober story with occasional flashes of realism working up to a sentimental ending.

"Mister Hoyle" (August 7, 1920) is about courage, always a popular subject for a sports story. The new recruit is considered yellow—he sticks to rules, will not fight. During a ball park riot, he proves otherwise, just as you knew he would. The other players are shamed and the reader glows with self-appreciation.

The September 7, 1920, "The Bread of Jeremiah" is a quietly humorous story. Tells how a big-bearded Bible-spouting giant comes to play ball for the Red Legs. In the September 20 story, "Dummy Dickinson's Home Run," a pitcher, hard pressed for money, hires out as the Sunday pitcher for a deaf and dumb team. McCoy discovers this contract violation and cooks up a fiendish punishment.

These are simple little stories concentrating on personalities, rather than descriptions of games. They are not heavily fettered by formula. What a far cry they are from the ancient formula of the good ball player versus the bad ball player, and how the big game was almost lost before it was won. You can read the Red Legs stories over again. It is a tribute to Mr. Brown.

Or perhaps to Mr. Lardner.

7—

It is axiomatic that any profession of interest to the public may become the basis for a story series. Whether the series will be interesting is another matter that, together with astrology and the secrets of the pyramids, will not be considered here.

It is no surprise, then, to discover various series featuring vaudevillians, musicians, motion picture companies, and circus folk. They were staples of entertainment back then. The following decade would add radio folk. Were the pulps active today, series would be written about television groups—which, of course, television has already done, in its unique role as America's contemporary illustrated pulp magazine.

Long ago, the mid-1919 *Blue Book* ran a short series by I. K. Friedman, titled "Adventures in Vaudevillainy." It featured the slippery Art Furber, sometimes a performer, sometimes a promoter, always a dedicated scoundrel. His conscience, like a pet rock, was small, hard, and easily mislaid.

The August 1919 "Giants and Midgets" tells how he borrows a side-show's midgets and giants to perform in a vaudeville sketch. For three months, he deftly evades paying salaries, commissions, or related costs. He ends strewing midgets and giants from Florida to California. All profits stuck permanently to Mr. Furber.

The adventure is written as a series of letters from Furber to his side-show source. Through the correspondence he begs, wheedles, evades, castigates, and double crosses—an amazing record. While the story told through letters is old as the hills, Mr. Friedman uses it with great effect.

During 1920, Hamish McLaurin signed a series of stories for *Popular* that concerned people in the entertainment business: musicians, singers, actors, and other such romantic folk. Continuing characters did not appear. The subject was the entertainment business and the method was a surprise twist at story's end.

For the most part, these stories are conventional boy-girl things, brightly spangled by behind-the-scenes views. Each story contains a greedy bad person you can dislike and a hero whose position becomes downright miserable before success kisses him.

"Old Lily-of-the-Valley" (March 7, 1920) is a broken-down camel rented for a vaudeville turn. The camel is needed in an act the hero has created out of his own head, leaving the strong impression that his head has experienced a profound malfunction. The act includes the camel, desert scenes, a beautiful girl, and a canvas airplane to fly away with her. It is necessary that this mess become a hit, so that the hero can marry *Her*. Well, it is a success. But then the villain jabs him full of morphine. But then the camel kicks the villain smack in the face, sort of evening things out.

"Twisting Out of It" (March 20-April 7, 1920, a dual date issue) features a contortionist. He wants to marry the girl but has a contract with a bad act. Quietly he revises his act, giving the girl a fat part. Then he pretends to be drunk. Gets fired. Turns out that his new act is a comic drunk routine.

"Making It Hot for Mowery" (August 7, 1920) tells how a young man, trained in the handling of dice, punishes a gambling, no-good, fire-extinguisher salesman. The scene is Rangoon; the story is told back stage. The September 7, 1920, "Boomerang Ballad," is in the first person, being Tony Costello, a brilliant piano accompanist. After he satirizes a species of love song, he ends up with a hit, prosperity, and a perfectly splendid wife. Which you anticipated right from the beginning. "One on the Booking Office" (September 20) tells how a wandering chimpanzee spices up a miserable act that has accidentally been booked into a major theatrical circuit.

In all stories, accident rules. Problems magically shimmer into golden coins. They get married at the end.

Similar stories are reworked in various series about moving picture groups. As those of you remember, who paid attention to your Nick Carter lessons, several of Nick's adventures intersected moving picture groups shooting films in the streets of New York City. They took an outline of suggested action, and improvised a story against real backdrops.

The Adventures of the Picture Players (by Albert Dorrington) appeared during late 1919 in *Top Notch*. The film makers skate here and yon, exposing tremendous quantities of film. Their preparations are as sketchy as a fish-net blouse. You run up. You fall down. Then everybody fights.

As in the Red Legs series, the Picture Players activities frame the stories of various individuals. For example:

Mr. Denham, scenario writer, finds himself in North Australia and tied to a chair. He is the victim of a fiendish Jap. From the swamp nearby comes the massive splashing of crocodiles. But in the nick of time, the lovely Japanese daughter frees him. It's as exciting as a silent movie.

And that's what's been going on—the filming of a silent. Although Denham didn't know it.

The Perfect Picture series stays closer to home than the Picture Players but is not a whit closer to real life. The Perfect Picture adventures were written by Thomas Thursday for the late 1920s *Top Notch*. All stories examined were narrated by the red-headed cameraman, Oscar.

These are feather-headed fictions. The characters are too lightly sketched to be one dimensional. Events dance along. Figures described as actors and directors and writers appear. They wring their hands. They whoop. Off they dart. It is all bright surface writing, lightly amusing, leaving not a trace behind once the story is read.

"When Tangle Meets Jangle" (October 1, 1920) shows how a fast-talking con man becomes a featured comedian. "Mail and Female" (November 15, 1920) concerns the singular courtship of a rich boy, who woos a star to win her stand-in.

Thomas Thursday published largely in *People's*, *Popular*, *Top Notch*, and, later, *Argosy*, *All-Story Weekly*. He specialized in mildly haywire characters.

Only a few of these worked for the movies. Others were carnival or circus folk, their days eventful and exciting.

The Move-A-Long Greater Circus and Side Show paraded through *Top Notch* during the latter half of the 1920s. Doc Ramble, side show manager, narrates the stories. As in the Red Legs series, each story focuses upon a different person. Life under canvas is only the incidental backdrop.

Thus—in "Gipsy Stuff" (July 15, 1920), Princess Mahulogoo, Gipsy Psychic, predicts a glowing future for a tongue-tied farmboy. Fortunately he does not know that her real name is Theda Blimpgay. (These are humorous stories; hence the witty names.) Immediately the farm boy becomes confident and glib. But not quite glib enough to propose successfully to her—nor is she psychic enough to understand what he is fumbling to ask her.

"Shorter Hours, Longer Pay" (September 1, 1920) is about labor agitation at the side show. The trouble is stirred up by a competitor, marvelous in a false beard. Under his evil eloquence, the freaks and roustabouts want—well—shorter hours and longer pay. They are disappointed. The competitor eventually loses his beard and gets hit over the head with a tent stake. Always something.

In later years, Thursday moved to *Argosy*, which published a few 1926-1927 stories featuring circus characters. "Sis Boom - Florida" (April 17, 1926) is another flimsy entertainment describing how some circus folk get involved in a Florida land deal and swindle the swindlers.

It is surprising that more series about musicians did not appear. Jazz was a force in the land, although little distinction was made between the classical forms, now celebrated as New Orleans, Chicago, Kansas City, *et al*, and equally popular orchestras which put on funny hats at 2:00 AM. They were all jazz bands—which is to say they played the "Tiger Rag" four times a night.

Stories featuring musicians suffer from the common paradox that rarely is the story about a musician being a musician. More usually, he is a musician being a hero or a detective. By definition, a musician must perform music, an activity which tends to produce blocks of descriptive narrative. No action narrative, however.

Customarily, then, the musician is involved in non-musicianly things. The idea may be self-defeating.

Vic Whitman wrote a scattering of stories that featured dance hall musicians. "At Dawning" (February 15, 1928, *Top Notch*) concerns a drummer who is forced to leave the business. Dance hall dust is bad for his lungs and his love life. But can he stay away? You wonder why he is affected only by dance hall dust. Why not farm dust or house dust or even West Fifth Ave. between 45th and 47th on the west side of the street dust? The obvious answer is that we are confronted by another of those stories which sets up a conflict and resolves it, to the general delight of the population. Whether it is a real or imitation conflict makes no earthly difference. Conflict is required: conflict is provided. That the resulting story is a shallow imitation of fiction seems irrelevant. Admittedly this story is a shallow imitation of fiction and is regrettable.

Whitman also wrote a brief series about Larry, the Syncopatin' Kid. This appeared early in 1929, again in *Top Notch*. The writing is primitive enough to be collected as folk art.

The Kid (we are told) "swept through life on a current of hot music. The life of the dance hall had always been his."

He was a piano player. Nice-looking fellow with a clear tenor voice; he was slim, debonair, immaculate, sober. And white. Remarkable.

The fiction is hacked from standard boilerplate, being uninformed, riddled with awful gaps in logic, and dressed in ghastly scraps of jazz slang.

The Kid plays at the Gondola Dance Hall. This is owned by Warren Plaining, the Dance-Hall Magnate. His lovely, unspoiled daughter, Stella, loves the Kid. And Stella "meant all things to him." All night, she moons around the dance hall, listening to the band laying it down:

It was the cake-eater-type number, replete with saxophone breaks, hot trumpet, and weird wailing clarinet, a number that was primitive in appeal, one that started shoulders waving and knees buckling fantastically.[10]

Since the band includes two violins and plays from stock arrangements, we may assume that they offered no real competition to Johnny Dodd's Blue Washboard Five.

All this background is synthetic and carelessly sketched in. The Kid lounges at the piano in an attitude that would effectively immobilize his left hand, if the description is correct. But no matter. He does not function as a musician but as the stock juvenile hero. In that capacity he may be anything from an adventurer to a psychologist to a detective. Anything but a musician.

In "Red Hot Blues" (February 15, 1929), he interrupts a set to leap from the dance hall into the river, saving a drowning boy. Later he proceeds remorselessly on the trail of the murderous ukulele player, the fiend responsible for setting fires everywhere.

At the risk of being exposed as dogmatic and uninformed, this commentator knows of no series characters featuring jazz musicians. There was Saxophone Smithers in *Argosy*, a bum who lugged a sax along through hobo jungle and freight yard, puffing melodiously upon the instrument. It isn't recorded, however, that he played jazz, and considering the environments to which his horn was exposed, you wonder that he could force any sort of tone from the pitiful thing.

The first respectable series about jazz musicians seems to have been Jack Webb's 1950s radio series about Pete Kelly, a hard-bitten Kansas City cornetist who solved mysteries between sets. Kelly faced Prohibition gunman, who were tough, in stories hardboiled enough for *Dime Detective*. The moving picture, "Pete Kelly's Blues," spun off from the radio series and demonstrated what could be done with the material.

They played jazz on that program. Good, biting, small band jazz, with never a funny hat or a violin on the stand.

8—

The profession of bumming is full of amusing adventure. So legend tells us.

Legend is silent about malodorous clothing, wee bugs, road encounters with crazies of unique sexual interests, and madmen grinning for blood. Nor does legend address that character erosion peculiarly caused by lack of direction.

The bum, the tramp, the hobo—three variants of the wandering man—picked up a sort of glamour from Chaplin's silent movie tramp character. The Little Tramp was a sort of mute minstrel. The social material from which the character was fashioned was less innocent.

In both England and the United States, unemployment accompanied every depression, recession, and panic. Each economic event released hordes of men to tramp scavenging across country.

They searched for Big Rock Candy Mountain and that great gold mine in the sky.

They rode the freights. Clustered in the farmer's barn. Filled the farmer's wife with unease.

They strayed into the dime novels, as in "Hobo Harry, the Beggar King" (*Nick Carter Weekly* #451, May 11, 1907).

And they filled boys' books with stereotyped figures and easy menaces:

...a bloated face covered with very dirty whiskers leered suddenly from behind the bushes. Mildred cried out and gripped Richard's arm.... (from *Richard Minter and the Mystery of the Pawned Collection*)

A few names entered popular mythology—Weary Willy, Happy Holligan, Number One, Pete the Tramp, The King of the Road.

And the idea, much watered down, got into the pulps through John H. Thompson's extended series about Bill and Jim.

"Drifters" they are called in the series. The first-person narrator, Jim, is a big idle fellow with no last name. His partner, William Harrison Higgins, is not described. But he is an opportunist, quick-witted and lucky.

Various artists illustrated the series, each with a different version of our heroes' faces. The 1927 *Flynn's* shows them looking vaguely like Laurel and Hardy. The mid-1930s *Argosy* shows Bill as a fat man in a checked suit and Jim as a big, long-faced hard guy.

The pair appeared in *Flynn's* and *Argosy* from (within generous limits) 1924 to about 1934. The stories are the most fragile of any sustained pulp series. Between 1,000 and 1,500 words long, they are fictional wisps, hardly more substantial then mist.

The story situation is simple. The boys are broke and hungry in the city. Bill then stumbles on a way to get them dinner.

Jim: Our perspective, financially speaking, seldom extends beyond the next meal.

They are urban types, please understand. They are not ragged outcasts shuffling along dirt roads. They are shabby, not dirty. Friendless but not criminals. Just two men who have drifted around the country together for about twenty-five years.

The first Bill and Jim story noted is "Dinners For Two" (November 8, 1924, *Flynn's*). They have been stranded while traveling with a small-time mid-West vaudeville circuit, their act unstated.

They are broke, broke, broke. And having nothing to lose, they decide to shoot the works and panhandle at a mansion. Selecting a calling card from his collection, Jim sends it in, hoping to bluff his way in to the millionaire owner and beg half a dollar. Instead, the millionaire personally returns the card, plus a hundred-dollar bill.

Figuring that this opportunity is too good to leave, the two return that night. They are just in time to see the police carrying the millionaire away. He is screaming that he had paid for protection. . . .

Jim checks the returned calling card and discovers that the name on it is the town's Chief of Police.

Flynn's saw little of the pair. *Argosy All-Story Weekly* was their real home. "A Draft on the Past" (April 10, 1926, *Argosy*) reworks well-worn material. Bill wins fifty-odd dollars in one-dollar bets predicting the next play of a ball game. He's listening to the telegrapher's transmissions and bets before the transmission is posted. Unfortunately, the fellow he's betting with is totally broke.

Occasionally they raise money by selling in the street. In "Diamonds Are Trumps" (August 7, 1926, *Argosy*), they are peddling metal polish and blunder into the robbery of a fancy jewelry store. "Guesswork" (March 12, 1927, *Flynn's*) is primarily style, having the least content of any story in the English language. Bill is convinced that he has thought out the solution to a prominent murder case and phones his idea to the police. Then the pair of them begin worrying that the police will haul them in as suspicious characters. They decide to flee the city. But they don't. And the police don't. All that worry for nothing.

During the 1930s, a steady parade of these fragile scraps ran in *Argosy*. Usually Bill and Jim occupied the final two or three pages of the magazine. As the series continued, original ideas slowly dwindled to borrowings from two-reel movie comedies and dramatizations of familiar anecdotes.

In "The Literary Racket" (May 31, 1930, *Argosy*), Bill finds a way to sell books so remarkably bad that they can't be given away. The gimmick, old as the hills, is to pretend that the books contain blue material. "The Clutch of Circumstance" (July 12, 1930, *Argosy*) tells how they do a good deed and move a car parked in a No Parking zone. The machine belongs to bank robbers and our boys become accidental heroes, although memory whispers that Laurel and Hardy did it first.

Well, on and on and on. Dozens of these trifles, all in *Argosy* now.

July 30, 1932, "Hush Money": They see a thief steal something from a house. Turns out that he stole a bagpipe. The neighbor pays them not to identify the thief.

August 19, 1933, "No Funds": They think they've discovered the kidnappers and their victim. They report their findings to the police and are allowed to use the police meal ticket while the cops pull a raid. The police find a man fretting over a sick dog. Before they return grumbling to the police station, our heroes have eaten the meal ticket completely out.

June 2, 1934, "Winner Take All": Jim tries to save his suitcase full of Higgins Peerless Indian Oil from their blazing boarding house. He is attacked by the landlady's vicious dog. To get to the suitcase, he must bundle the dog in a coat and carry the howling beast. When he stumbles outside, smoldering dramatically, Bill promotes a collection for the brave fellow who risked his life to save that dog.

December 15, 1934, "Stifling Competition": Bill spoils the machinations of a crooked carnival manager by giving him exploding cigars. These the manager gives to the town mayor and the Chief of Police.

Familiar jokes. Worn out anecdotes. As short-short stories, they have a mild silver glitter, like your memory of school days. Incredible that so many appeared. And in *Flynn's* and *Argosy*, of all the strange places. Apparently they filled a need.

9—

The fabric of fiction contains innumerable characters. Only a few of these reach celebrity status. The rest twinkle through a handful of issues and are replaced by other hopefuls.

All of them, successful or not, have an affinity for the odd situation. They have the gift for adventure—and, as we have seen, adventure is not always a quest beyond the tall mountains. A gifted person can stay close to home and experience excitement every day. Spud McGee did. Spud was a cab driver. Worse, he was a cab driver in New York City. Still worse, Spud had no instinct for danger. That may be what makes for adventure, for an incautious cab driver is destined to experience a lot of it.

Spud is an incautious cab driver. His wife, Sue, says that he is tender hearted. His pal, "Chunky" Schmidt, thinks that Spud is a mark. Spud, himself, thinks that the tenderness is in the region of his head.

McGee is a stocky little freckled redhead. In practice, he is a good deed doer. He has, in consequence, become an accomplished adventurer on the streets of New York City.

He drives for the Meteor Cab Company. Their stand is over at the edge of Central Park—the blue-painted machines. While waiting for fares, Spud fusses around his machine, polishing the glass, sweeping out the interior. The company is picky. Spud wears a neat blue uniform with black puttees, no less, clearly placing the era in the 1920s. He is as nice about that uniform as he is about his machine. He is quite unlike his friend Chunky, who looks like a rag-bag and whose machine resembles "the tag end of a prairie storm." Chunky is too busy reading pulp detective magazines to pay much attention to maintenance. He stays out of trouble that way.

Spud does not. Spud is constantly in hot water. The world sizzles with people anxious to get him into trouble. If you read *Detective Story Magazine* from about 1928 to 1932, you must have read some of Spud's first-person problems.

Although Spud got the credit for narrating these stories, the name signed to them was Charlotte Dockstader, who had been contributing to the magazine since the middle 1920s. Charlotte gave Spud no peace. But he would have got himself burned even without her help. As mentioned, he just had no instinct for self-preservation.

"R.S.V.P." (August 25, 1928) tells how a steady passenger drops his keys in Spud's cab. The keys are fastened to an address tag and are picked up by a crook. This fellow directs Spud to the apartment and cleans it out. When the truth dawns on Spud, he is looking down the barrel of the crook's gun.

Off they go to the center of Central Park. There our hero is to be shot down. Fortunately, he has been able to signal to Chunky, who bends a case of tools over the criminal's head.

The story is in the best McGee tradition—straight into trouble, from which, by a near miracle, his friends or his wife manage to extract him at the last possible moment.

"The Acid Umbrella" (June 15, 1929) features Spud, Sue, and Chunky tracking down a ring of thieves—radio stealers, they are, very ferocious. The main thief carries a sulfuric acid squirter up his sleeve. Mess with him and you end up looking like the Phantom of the Opera. This sweetheart has killed a policeman, a close friend of the McGee's. Nothing will do but Spud and company must try to run the fellow down.

They set a trap that works so well the thief comes after Chunky's expensive radio, gets the radio, takes away the radio. Spud gets his head rapped. After that, they take the police into their confidence. In a rousing ending, half the precinct closes in on the criminals, after Spud and Chunky identify them at a ball game.

The theme of "The People vs Spud McGee" (September 7, 1929) recurs throughout the series. Through no fault of his own, Spud gets arrested and jailed. Without a smart wife, he'd be serving time yet. In this story, the cab company gets held up. All in innocence, Spud carries the thief as a fare. The fellow spins such a hard-luck story that Spud takes him home. When the police burst in, there's Spud with the murder weapon and a feeble story. The loot has vanished. After Spud gets bailed out, Sue reasons that the money has been hidden in the cab all this time. The thief will return. And sure enough, he does. Gets caught. Confesses. Thank Heaven!

So matters go. Spud is just standing there, a simple smile on his not unhandsome face. Then trouble rears up and falls all over him. In a desert, he'd be troubled by tidal waves.

1930: He is back in jail.

"Spud McGee's Danger Signal" (August 2, 1930) tells how he helps this poor little old out-of-luck fellow move some furniture. It isn't his furniture. Spud is arrested for the theft. He would be a jailbird today if Sue hadn't gone out and caught the real thief. She arrived just as the judge was passing sentence. It's highly dramatic and if the formula hadn't been frayed by considerable use, you might even have been excited and leaped up from your chair to buy another issue of the magazine.

As a hero, Spud lacks aggressiveness. He doesn't mold his fate so much as stand there fecklessly while fate slops all over him. Fortunately Mrs. McGee is a bright, active woman and C. Dockstader can always be relied upon to help, even though it's always at the last minute.

But really, a hero should have more to say about his fate than does Spud.

10—

Minor figures, the people of this chapter. Their adventures began no trends. The future was not shaped by their past. Within the stream of popular literature, they bobbed briefly, bits of painted wood riding the flow.

Minor stories. Most of them work within the grip of formula's steel clutch—as the Slash Triebault or the Bill and Jim stories. Only occasionally, as in Eddsfield, does the fiction turn from market requirements to less predictable paths.

These are adventure stories of modest dimensions. They do not aspire to the incandescent drama of Hurricane Williams or the deadly decisions forced upon Peter the Brazen. Around home, the adventures are less intense, calmed, perhaps, by familiar cityscapes and routines of life that are novel but not so far from those of the readers. Frequently, folk elements are included, either familiar elements from the past (Bill and Jim) or new elements developing from the present (the gold-digger stories). In most of the other stories, the adventure and its dangers are implicit in the protagonist's job, with a certain amount of romanticizing on the writer's part to keep matters interesting.

Where danger is unlikely to exist, artificial complications are used to create conflict. That common device, the Good Us versus the Bad Them, appears as frequently as the theme of Ravel's "Bolero." The Good Us-Bad Them device allows an easy source of conflict and an excuse for continuous action. It permits motivations to be reduced to a thread. For if They oppose Us, Their intentions are dark and Their character lamentable.

That being the case, elaborate characterizations may be ignored. The characters become simple as rubber stamps, identified by tags selected from stock. Such figures may be manipulated through chapters of strong narrative movement. They chase about enthusiastically: the Good Us minding our own business, constantly harassed by Those Other People. All is subordinated to action, human experience being expressed as activity of the body's primary muscle groups. Or so matters are conducted at simple fictional levels, as in boys' books, television series, and such basic series fiction as we have met in this chapter.

For all practical purposes, these stories are best described as juveniles for adults. Each story is a frenzy of movement, confrontation, struggle. Through this turmoil move purported adults pursuing their mysterious desires and pleasures. If you examine them closely, you will note that these characters are simply older juveniles who crave wealth, love, and community approval. Their reactions are immediate and athletic. They show no foresight, only a complex slyness. They inhabit no known society but only that strangely limited world of a magazine short story.

These characters and their adventures filled the pages of the less exacting popular magazines—and a fairly substantial percentage of the more exacting magazines, as well. For human experience, they substituted action. They did it well. But it remained enhanced boys' fiction.

Afterword

When the pulp magazines first appeared, the adventure story was waiting for them, polished by accumulated centuries of story telling. Adventure fiction is very old. It is perhaps the oldest of all story types, with the possible exception of that fiction which begins, "Dearest, I love only you...."

But there is no need to probe the deep past for origins. That adventure fiction published in *The Argosy, The Popular Magazine, The Monthly Story Magazine,* and the later rest, was rooted in the immediate past. It was influenced by Stevenson and Kipling, Doyle, Old Sleuth, Haggard, Buffalo Bill, Wister and Henty, and the myriads of boys' fiction specialists who scribbled their fantasies on both sides of the Atlantic.

No sooner did the adventure story enter the pulps than it began changing. The boy-oriented story, full of slap-dash derring-do, abruptly adopted a more resolute adult tone, rather like a chick imitating a rooster. The tone of the fiction became darker, the action more violent. The stories were populated by brave Irishmen, faithful natives, hyperactive Americans, and a rare host of eccentric sea captains.

Still, characteristics of boys' fiction remained embedded in these stories. Without much trouble you can make out such familiar things as the excellent younger hero and the doting senior male, the search for wealth in dangerous distant places, the villain, the chase, the flare of last-second ingenuity, and those obligatory final scenes when the hero, modest as a saint in silver, stands glittering in the admiration of his friends. And enemies.

These matters were quietly combined with the romantic melodrama, long beloved of stage and newspaper serial. In most cases, the fictional heroes took on at least a superficial resemblance to adults. Love, suspense, and violence bloomed together, like morning-glories tangled along a fence. Frequently characters did things under the influence of strong emotions, rather than a need to advance the plot. If a man loved a maid, he occasionally clasped her cautiously in his arms, both of them fully clothing, in the sunlight, and guarded by chaperons and a careful author from the brambles of passion.

These changes appeared side-by-side with serialized reprints of H. Rider Haggard's novels. These dark visions told of explorations in lands as foreign and unforgiving as the moon and as dangerous. These remote lands, fabulous as the centaur, came alive in sharp descriptions. Concealed within them lurked civilizations lost for a thousand years, strange peoples, treasure beyond desire, magic, death, love, and violence.

Invariably, violence. The appearance of the European outsiders into these closed communities triggers all their latent violence. The society bursts like some horrible egg and death bounds howling out. From these accounts of butchery and horror, Haggard distilled a certain moral grandeur. When Umslopagaas stands alone on the queen's stairway in Milosis, slaying dozens as they rush against him, you are present at one of the peaks of adventure fiction. He fights and he dies, as he lived, in nobility, for principle.

Other authors in other stories followed the way Haggard had opened. Burroughs, Worts, Greene, Wirt, Stilson, Gisey, Cummings, Farley—each in his own way adopted the Haggard model to his own needs. If they did not quite clamber to Haggard's heights, perhaps that failure can be blamed on the First World War.

That war reduced Haggard's bloodiest slaughters to a squabble between sparrows. The war changed the technology of killing, changed attitudes toward killing, changed attitudes, even, about society and man's place in society. A new kind of hero appeared. He was disillusioned, hard-boiled, self-contained, often savage, as Hurricane Williams, or as emotionally insulated as Peter the Brazen or the Major; or, like the Friel adventurers, alienated from society.

Even in such a generally amiable series as Sanders of the River, the murderous face of the war shows in the use of modern weapons and tactics. And in that fiction sited in South America—as in the Geoff or Billy June series—the hero must maneuver among violently politicized social fragments which howl and snarl and kill brainlessly.

This is not to insist that post-war adventure fiction sagged into universal gloom. That fiction contained more than automatic weapons cutting down endless waves of natives. Or tormented heroes baring their teeth against their irrational lives.

True, the story of hard-boiled, realistic violence continued through the work of Gordon Young (Hurricane Williams, Don Everhard) and W. Wirt (Jimmie Cordie). But stories featuring less ferocious heroes were equally popular. Peter the Brazen, that fine young man, found frequent occasions for violence. He was, however, primarily a figure of whirlwind adventure melodrama, disrupting Oriental snares, sniffing out new experiences, evading doom by a split hair, protecting the honor of all those fool women. By some curious process of de-evolution, his stories grew ever more shallow and fantastic as the 1930s sped past.

Both the Major and Janie Frete continued the tradition of the crooked hero, that character type beloved of the 1906 silent movies. Janie reformed, pretty much, more or less. The Major never pretended to reform. Time and a sympathetic author gradually allowed him to sink into the quicksands of honesty to become a Savior of the Empire. In both cases, the hero's self interest was superseded by those more luminous abstractions of justice, decency, and honor.

A similar progression, even more accelerated, is found in the history of Hashknife Hartley. He began scoffing caustically at the law, was transformed to a knight errant and justice figure, and ended as an unofficial detective for an official organization.

Most of these series figures operated at the fringes of civilization. Other characters, however, were solidly based in urban life. Their adventures rose from the streets and buildings of the city. Their professions provided the sand grain about which condensed the pearl of fiction. Secretary, politician, gold digger, ball player, musician, bum, cab driver—the way they earned their living generated long sequences of adventures.

The urban adventures seem somewhat trivial when compared to the sweep of other series. Explorations in unknown Africa or secret struggles in China rise like basalt cliffs above milder tales of how two bums got dinner or how the dim-witted taxi driver got blamed for something he didn't do. But there is room in fiction for the minute, as well as the epic.

The few examples of adventurers selected for this volume by no means exhausts the genre. At about the same time that Quatermain, O'Rourke, and Sanders confronted their respective Africas, the diplomatic agent was born. E.P. Oppenheim had popularized the story form but the pulps pursued it, with usual vigor, through extraordinary variations: Norry, fashion plate and secret agent; Trevor, an American impersonating an English Lord; John Solomon, the Cockney genius who repeatedly saved civilization; Jimgrin who preserved the political stability of Arabia and India through extended excursions into craft and violence.

In the next volume, we will meet these splendid people. We will also re-encounter the bent hero, as that character type emerged in ever new variations— which include the inhumanly strong Night Wind; the mysterious Zorro, laughing in black; Bulldog Drummond, that hard-boiled beer-swiller; and Lester Leith, the wit of crime.

We will also meet formidable warriors: Khlit and Kirdy, Cossacks in seventeenth century Russia; Tros in the time of Caesar; Luigi Cardossa, tricking his way through ancient Italy. We will view the beginnings of the air combat short story and meet that renowned aviator and infantryman, T.X. O'Leary, whose adventures reeled madly into science fiction. And we will travel with Jimmie Cordie and his deadly friends, as they apply World War I machine-gun tactics through the Far East.

All these and others, Secret Service, Bent Heroes, Warriors, in *Violent Lives*, the next volume of *Yesterday's Faces*.

Notes

Chapter I

[1]The description of O'Rourke is drawn from two stories by Louis Joseph Vance: "The Further Adventures of O'Rourke: In Which O'Rourke Sheathes His Sword," *The Popular Magazine*, Vol. III, No. 2. (December 1904), p. 123; and "O'Rourke, the Wanderer: I— The Pool of Flame," *The Popular Magazine*, Vol. VII, No. 1 (November 1906), p. 2.

[2]Vance, *Terence O'Rourke, Gentleman Adventurer*, NY, A. Wessels (1905), p. 28.

[3]*Ibid*, p. 327.

[4]*Ibid*, pp. 158-159.

[5]*Ibid*, pp. 170-171.

[6]Vance, "The Pool of Flame," p. 33.

[7]Frank Luther Mott, "The Argosy," *A History of American Magazines, 1885-1905*, Vol. IV, Cambridge: Harvard University (1957), pp. 417-423.

[8]Sam Moskowitz, "A History of the 'Scientific Romance' in the Munsey Magazines, 1912-1920," *Under the Moons of Mars*, NY: Holt, Rinehart and Winston (1970), p. 310. This long essay is essential to any serious study of the early magazines. Part 3 discusses early years of *The Popular Magazine*, when it "afforded *Argosy* with the first direct competition it had ever had."

[9]In 1905, Charles Agnew MacLean became editor and the golden age of *The Popular Magazine* began. By the end of 1906, the magazine had expanded to 224 pages and 15¢. Twice-a-month issuance began with the October 1909 issue, and increased to weekly with the September 24, 1927, issue. From this high point, the frequency of issuance slowly declined, becoming twice-a-month once more with the July 7, 1928, issue. Then it became a 25¢ monthly with the February 1931 issue. The final issue was dated October 1931. These variations in issuance were paralleled by several title changes. With the September 24, 1927, issue, the magazine became *Popular Stories*. It was changed to *The Popular*, January 7, 1928, and to *The Popular Magazine*, October 20, 1928.

[10]Cutcliffe Hyne, "The Trials of Commander McTurk, VI—The Sultana," *The Popular Magazine*, Vol. V, No. 4 (February 1906), p. 165.

[11]Gordon Young, "Savages," *Adventure*, Vol. 22, No. 3 (First August 1919), p. 130.

[12]Young, "Wild Blood," *Adventure*, Vol. XXV, No. 2 (Mid-April 1920), p. 113.

[13]Young, "Savages," p. 131.

[14]The fourth volume of this series, *The Solvers*, briefly discusses the influence of Gordon Young's Don Everhard on the character of Race Williams.

[15]Until the latter part of 1921, *Adventure* was published twice a month, the issues being identified as First-... Issue and Mid-... Issue. These dates corresponded to the 3rd and 18th, which dates were cited on the table of contents for some years. In 1921, the magazine frequency of issuance was increased to three times a month, the issues being dated 10, 20, and 30 (except for the February 29th issue).

[16]Young, "Savages," p. 122.

[17]*Ibid*, p. 132.

[18]Young, *The Vengence of Hurricane Williams*, NY: Doran (1925), p. 158.

[19]"Wild Blood" was published in the Mid-March, First and Mid-April, and First June, 1920, issues of *Adventure*. No magazines were published dated in May 1920. A printer's strike in 1919 had created a discrepancy between the published date and the date of issuance; the May dates were omitted to adjust that discrepancy. (The magazines were dated a month ahead of issuance.) Volume numbering was not affected.

[20]Young, *The Vengence of Hurricane Williams*, pp. 19-20.

[21]Fiction requirements as stated in "The Camp-Fire," Vol. XXIX, No. 4 (Mid-May 1912), p. 184.

[22]T(homas) S(igismund) Stribling, *Laughing Stock*, edited by Randy K. Cross and John T. McMillan, Memphis: St. Luke's Press (1982), pp. 150-151. Stribling's facetious remarks purposefully ignore the extensive contributions of feminine writers to the detective, fantasy, and love pulps.

[23]Arthur Sullivant Hoffman, "The Camp-Fire," *Adventure*, Vol. 94, No. 1 (November 1935), pp. 164-165. Further Hoffman commentary on this subject may be found in *Adventure*, Vol. XLVI, No. 3 (April 30, 1924), pp. 182-183.

[24]P(elham) G(renville) Wodehouse, *Author! Author!*, NY: Simon and Schuster (1962), p. 32. The quotation is from a letter, dated July 23, 1924, to William Townend, who published a number of stories in the 1920s *Adventure*.

[25]Stribling, *op. cit.*, p. 153.

[26]*Ibid*, pp. 151-152.

[27]Hoffman, November 1935, p. 163.

[28]Stribling, *op. cit.*, p. 156.

[29]The purpose of The Legion was given in *Adventure*, Vol. 11, No. 1 (November 1915), pp. 217-218, as follows: "The Legion believes in making instantly available to our country, in case of war, all men who already have military or technical training valuable in modern warfare by land or sea. Members of the Legion enroll themselves in advance for the purpose to be used as the Government (not they themselves) may see fit, according to their qualification." To omit no one, Legion membership was also extended to men experienced in "trades, businesses and professions."

[30]Stribling, *op. cit.*, pp. 155-156.

[31]Ibid, p. 202.

[32]In 1928, publisher Hearst sold *McClure's* to the Magus Magazine Corporation, which promptly vulgarized the publication.

[33]Editors after Hoffman were Joseph Cox (July 1 to October 1, 1927), Anthony Rud (October 15, 1927, to March 1, 1930), A. A. Proctor (March 15, 1930 to 1934). The dates are approximate. After *Adventure* sold to Popular Publications, William Corcoran served briefly as editor. He was succeeded by Howard V. L. Bloomfield (August 1934 through 1940), Kenneth White (1941 through 1948), and Kendall Goodwyn (1949 to September 1951). Later editors included Ejler Jakobsson (November 1951 to March 1953), Alden Norton (August 1954 to August 1964), Peter Gannett (October 1965 to October 1970), and Carson Bingham (December 1970 to April 1971).

Chapter II

[1]George Bronson-Howard, "Plantagent Hock: Hero, Madame Mandarin," *The Popular Magazine*, Vol. IX, No. I (July 1907), p. 112.

[2]George F. Worts, "The Men Who Make the Argosy," *Argosy*, Vol. 209, No. 5 (January 25, 1930), p. 718.

[3]The six "Peter the Brazen" novelettes were ruthlessly pruned into a book of three parts. Various names were changed with reckless hand and several enticing bits of Peter's early history were omitted. A discussion of these deletions is given in a two-part article

by Rick Lai titled "Peter Moore, The Other Man of Bronze," and contained in *The Pulp Collector*, Vol. 3, #3 (Spring 1988) and Vol. 3, #4 (Summer 1988).

[4]Loring Brent (pseudonym for George F. Worts), "Peter the Brazen: The Princess of Static," *The Argosy*, Vol. C, No. 1 (October 5, 1918), p. 20

[5]*Ibid.*

[6]Brent, "Peter the Brazen: V. The Golden Paw," *The Argosy*, Vol. CII, No. 1 (November 30, 1918), p. 31.

[7]*Ibid*, p. 29.

[8]Robert Sampson, *Yesterday's Faces, Vol. 3: From the Dark Side*, Popular Press/Bowling Green, Ohio (1987), pp. 8-14.

[9]The ship, the Latonia, was rechristened the Vandalia in *Peter the Brazen*, Lippincott (1919) by George F. Worts.

[10]Brent, "Princess of Static," p. 34.

[11]Chungking has since been renamed Chongquing.

[12]Brent, "Peter the Brazen: II. The City of Stolen Lives," *The Argosy*, Vol. C, No. 3 (October 19, 1918), p. 419.

[13]Brent, "The Golden Paw," p. 27.

[14]*Ibid*, p. 36.

[15]*Ibid*, p. 43.

[16]*Ibid*, p. 45.

[17]Brent, "The Man in the Jade Mask," *Argosy*, April 26, 1930, Vol. 211, #6, p. 762.

[18]Brent, "The Sapphire Smile," *Argosy*, February 8, 1930, Vol. 210, #1, pp. 48-49.

[19]Brent, "Sting of the Blue Scorpion," *Argosy*, November 26, 1932, Vol. 234, #3, pp. 68-69.

[20]Brent, "The Master Magician," *Argosy*, February 25, 1933, Vol. 236, #4, p. 38.

[21]Brent, "Kingdom of the Lost," *Argosy*, September 1, 1934, Vol. 249, #4, pp. 47-48.

[22]"Kingdom of the Lost," August 25, 1934, Vol. 249, #3, p. 22.

[23]"Kingdom of the Lost," September 22, 1934, Vol. 250, #1, p. 121.

[24]*Ibid*, p. 123.

Chapter III

[1]Higgins, D.S., *Rider Haggard*, Stein and Day, New York (1983), pp. 22-4. Higgins remarks: "It became obvious in the following weeks that the real purpose of Shepstone's mission was to achieve the annexation of the Transvaal by the British." That annexation, so it was said, would have brought in the British military presence to stabilize the region. The gold and diamonds of the Transvaal might also have encouraged this worthy desire for tranquility. Annexation became a fact in April 1877.

[2]Edel, Leon, *Henry James, A Life*, Harper and Row, New York (1985), p. 324.

[3]Wallace, Edgar, "The Seer," *Sanders of the River*, Doubleday Doran, & Co., New York (1930), p. 227.

[4]Lane, Margaret, *Edgar Wallace*, William Heinemann, London (undated), p. 225.

[5]Hogan, John A., "From One Thing to Another," *Edgar Wallace Society Newsletter 39* (August 1978), p. 2.

[6]Wallace, Edgar, "The Affair of the Lady Missionary," *People of the River*, Ward, Lock & Co., London (undated), p. 40.

[7]"The Dancing Stones," *Sanders of the River*, pp. 118-9.

[8]*Ibid*, pp. 239-40.

[9]*Ibid*, "The Loves of M'Liuno," p. 219.

[10]Refer to Volume 1 of this series (*Glory Figures*) for a discussion of the Just Men and their prodigious effect on mystery-action fiction in the popular magazines.

[11]With the December 1915 issue, the *New Story Magazine* changed its title to the *All-Around Magazine*. Whatever its title, the magazine published fourteen Sanders stories, most of them having previously appeared in the 1911 *Sanders of the River*.

[12]Hogan, John, "The Saga of Sanders, Part II," *Edgar Wallace Society Newsletter No. 22* (May 1974), p. 3.

[13]Lofts, W. O. G., "Francis Gerard, Lover of Sanders and Africa," *Edgar Wallace Society Newsletter No. 12* (October 1971), pp. 1-2. Born in London of an Irish mother and a French father, Gerard was raised in France and read all of Wallace's books during his teens. His own first mystery novel was written in 1934, and he published extensively in *The Thriller*. During the war, he served at Malta as a major and later in the War Office, London. In 1946, he emigrated to South Africa, settled in the Natal region, becoming a citizen in 1948.

[14]Hogan, John, "The Saga of Sanders, Part I," *Edgar Wallace Society Newsletter No. 21* (February 1974), p. 5. In this article, Hogan gives the recommended reading sequence of the River series:

Sanders of the River (1911)

The People of the River (1912)

Bosambo of the River (1914)

Bones (1915)

Bones of the River (1923)

Sanders (1926)

The Return of Sanders of the River (1938—Gerard)

The Law of the River (1939—Gerard)

The Justice of Sanders (1951—Gerard)

The Keepers of the King's Peace (1917)

Lieutenant Bones (1918)

Bones in London (1921)

Sandi the King-Maker (1922)

[15]Wallace, "Hamilton of the Houssas," *Bones*, Ward, Lock, and Co. (undated), p. 31.

[16]*Ibid*, "The Man Who Did Not Sleep," p. 124.

[17]Hogan, *EWS Newsletter 39*, p. 2.

[18]Wallace, "The Tamer of Beasts," *The Keepers of the King's Peace*, Ward, Lock and Co., London (1919), p. 156.

[19]*Ibid*, "The Hooded King," pp. 245-6.

[20]Wallace, "The Queen of the N'Gombi," *The People of the River*, Ward, Lock & Co., London (undated), p. 122.

[21]*Ibid*, "The Sickness Mongo," p. 214.

[22]Wallace, "Bones Changes His Religion," *The Keepers of the King's Peace*, p. 29.

[23]*Ibid*, p. 51.

[24]"The Crime of Sanders," *The People of the River*, p. 234.

[25]L. Patrick Greene, "Lines of Cleavage," *Adventure* (First February 1921), Vol. XXVII, No. III, p. 109.

[26]Greene, "Tools," *Adventure* (First August 1921), Vol. XXX, No. 3, p. 102.

[27]Greene, "Squeeze," *Short Stories* (August 10, 1934), Vol. CXLVIII, No. 4, p. 145.

[28]Greene, "Lines of Cleavage," p. 102.

[29]Greene, "Major Methods," *Short Stories*, Vol. CXVII, No. 1, (October 10, 1926), p. 30.

[30]Greene, "Crooked Barrels," *Short Stories*, Vol. CLV, No. 2 (April 25, 1936), p. 37.

[31]*Ibid*, pp. 20-1.

[32]Greene, "Pestle and Mortar," *Short Stories*, Vol. CCXIV, No. 3 (September 1952), p. 64.

[33]Greene, "Crooked Barrels," p. 37.

[34]Greene, "Kaffir Orange," *Short Stories*, Vol. CLV, No. 4 (May 25, 1936), pp. 161-2.

[35]Greene, "The Lake of the Dead," *Short Stories*, Vol. CCXV, No. 4, Whole Number 1984 (April 1953), p. 21.

Chapter IV

[1]Wilbur Hall, "Around the Campfire," *Adventure*, Vol. 11, No. 4 (February 1916), p. 215.

[2]Hall, "Billy June and the Private Document," *Adventure*, Vol. 11, No. 4 (February 1916), p. 41.

[3]*Ibid*, p. 43.

[4]*Ibid*, p. 41.

[5]Hall, "Billy June and the Amazon River Scandal," *Adventure*, Vol. 13, No. 1 (November 1916), p. 148.

[6]Two minor characters of "The Pathless Trail," Pedro and Lourenco, had previously appeared in nineteen short stories published in *Adventure* between mid-September 1919 and Mid-July 1921. Later, in 1929, Friel called back the pair for an additional four-story series.

[7]Arthur O. Friel, *Tiger River*, Centaur Press, New York (1971), p. 18.

[8]The grandson of McKay returns to the lost kingdom of Hoseran some seventy years later in the three-part *Adventure* serial, "In the Year 2000" (May 15 through June 15, 1928).

[9]Arthur O. Friel, *Fiction Writers on Fiction Writing*, edited by Arthur Sullivant Hoffman, Bobbs-Merrill/Indianapolis (1923), pp. 56-7.

Chapter V

[1]One issue was published of *Sheena, Queen of the Jungle* (Spring 1951). The magazine contained three novelettes. A fourth novelette later appeared in the Spring 1954 *Jungle Stories*.

[2]Anonymous, "The Men Who Make the Argosy: Raymond S. Spears," *Argosy*, Vol. 221, No. 1 (May 16, 1931), p. 140.

[3]Raymond S. Spears, "Janie and the Waning Glories," *All-Story Weekly*, Vol. CX, No. 3 (May 22, 1920), p. 339.

[4]Spears, "Trail of the Otter Pelts," *All-Story Weekly*, Vol. LIV, No. 4 (February 12, 1916), p. 664.

[5]Spears, "The Green Sachem," *All-Story Weekly*, Vol. LVIII, No. 4 (June 3, 1916), p. 686.

[6]*Ibid*, p. 687.

[7]Spears, "A Shortage in Perfumes," *All-Story Weekly*, Vol. XCIII, No. 3 (February 1, 1919), p. 366.

[8]Spears, "Waning Glories," *All-Story Weekly*, Vol. CX, No. 2 (May 15, 1920), p. 161.

Chapter VI

[1]Early themes and characters of western fiction are discussed in *Glory Figures*, Volume 1 of this series.

[2]Tuttle, W.C., "The Cross in a Box Mystery," *Adventure*, Vol. LXXXII, No. 1 (March 15, 1932), p. 24.

[3]Tuttle, *Montana Man*, Avalon Books, NY (1966), pp. 27-8.

[4]*Ibid*, p. 26.

[5]*Ibid*, p. 9.

[6]*Ibid*, p. 29.

[7]For a discussion of Tuttle's Yellow Rock series, refer to "Pandemonium in Yellow Rock," *Deadly Excitements* by Robert Sampson (Popular Press, Bowling Green, 1989).

[8]*Montana Man*, p. 161.

[9]Tuttle, "The Buckaroo of Blue Wells," *Adventure*, Vol. LX, No. 4 (November 23, 1926), p. 50.

[10]Tuttle, "The Ghost Riders," *Adventure*, LXXXIV, No. 3 (October 15, 1932), p. 48.

[11]Tuttle, "The Tin God of Twisted River," *Adventure*, Vol. LV, No. III (October 30, 1925), p. 120.

[12]Tuttle, "Hashknife—Philanthropist," *Adventure*, Vol. 26, No. 2 (Mid-July 1920), p. 10.

[13]Tuttle, "The Finger of Fate," *Argosy*, Vol. 248, Number 1 (June 30, 1934), pp. 79-80.

[14]"Hashknife—Philanthropist," p. 20.

[15]Tuttle, "The Ranch of the Tombstones," *Adventure*, Vol. 38, No. 3 (December 30, 1922), p. 29.

[16]Tuttle, "The Medicine Man," *Adventure*, Vol. LXV, No. 6 (March 30, 1924), pp. 18-9.

[17]Tuttle, *Hidden Blood*, Houghton Mifflin, Boston (1943), pp. 34-5.

[18]*Ibid*, p. 80.

[19]"The Buckaroo of Blue Wells," p. 39.

[20]"The Tin God of Twisted River," p. 122.

[21]"Hashknife—Philanthropist," p. 17.

[22]"The Ranch of the Tombstone," p. 22.

[23]Sullivan, *op. cit.*, p. 80.

[24]*Ibid*, p. 427.

[25]*Hidden Blood*, pp. 237-8.

[26]Tuttle, *The Trail of Deceit*, Houghton Mifflin, Boston (1951), pp. 200-1.

Chapter VII

[1]The first issue of *Top Notch Magazine* was dated March 1, 1910. It was a 36-page publication in the familiar dime novel format, lean, flat, saddle stitched, and was issued twice a month, 5 cents a copy. At first directed to "older boys," it converted to the formal pulp magazine format with the November 1, 1910, issue, expanding to 192 pages. The price inflated to 10 cents. Thereafter it continued as an adventure-oriented pulp until the middle 1930s.

[2]Quentin Reynolds, *The Fiction Factory*, Random House, NY (1955), p. 165.

[3]J. Frank Davis, "The Yarboro Flop," *The Popular Magazine*, Vol. LVIII, No. 3 (November 20, 1920), p. 83.

[4]*Ibid*, p. 84.

[5]"The Mermaid's Misstep," *Snappy Stories*, Vol. LXXXV, Number 2 (Second September 1924), p. 106.

[6]"The Love Swindler," *Snappy Stories* (Second September 1924), p. 10.

[7]Anonymous, "Confessions of a Gold-Digger," *Snappy Stories* (Second September 1924), pp. 93-4.

[8]*Ibid*, p. 98.

[9]Nell Martin, "The Hand's Quicker Than The Eye," *Top Notch Magazine*, Vol. LXII, Number 5 (January 1, 1928), p. 31.

[10]Vic Whitman, "Red Hot Blues," *Top-Notch Magazine*, Vol. LXXVI, No. 6 (Second February 1929), p. 45.

Bibliography

Anonymous, "The Men Who Make the Argosy: Raymond S. Spears," *Argosy*, May 16, 1931, Vol. 221, No. 1.

Bleiler, Richard, *The Index to Adventure Magazine, Vols. One and Two*, Starmont House, WA (1990).

Cohen, Morton (Editor), *Rudyard Kipling to Rider Haggard*, Fairleigh Dickinson University Press (1965).

Edel, Leon, *Henry James, A Life*, Harper and Row, NY (1985).

Friel, Arthur O., *The King of No Man's Land*, Grosset & Dunlap, NY (1924).

———*The River of Seven Stars*, Harper, NY (1924).

———*Tiger River*, Centaur Press, NY (1971).

Goulart, Ron, *Cheap Thrills*, Arlington House, New Rochelle (1972).

Greene, Graham, "The Lost Childhood," *Collected Essays*, Viking, NY (1969).

Haggard, H. Rider, *Allan's Wife*, Newcastle Pub., No. Hollywood, Calif. (1980).

Hall, Wilbur, "Around the Campfire," *Adventure*, Vol. 11, No. 4 (February 1916).

Hersey, Harold Brainerd, *Pulpwood Editor*, Greenwood Press, Westport, Conn. (1974).

Higgins, D.S. *Rider Haggard*, Stein and Day, NY (1983)

———(Editor) *The Private Diaries of Sir H. Rider Haggard, 1914-1925*, Stein and Day, NY (1980).

Hoffman, Arthur Sullivant, (Editor) *Fiction Writers on Fiction Writing*, Bobbs-Merrill, Indianapolis (1923).

———"The Camp Fire," *Adventure*, Vol. 94, No. 1 (November 1935).

Hogan, John A., "From One Thing To Another," *Edgar Wallace Society Newsletter No. 39* (August 1979).

———"The Saga of Sanders, Part 1," *Edgar Wallace Society Newsletter No. 21* (February 1974).

———"The Saga of Sanders, Part Two," *Newsletter No. 22* (May 1974).

Hyne, Cutcliffe, *Captain Kettle, K.C.B.*, Federal Book Co., NY (1903).

Jones, Robert Kenneth, "The Lure of Adventure, Part 1," *Echoes*, Vol. 4, No. 5 (October 1985).

———"The Lure of Adventure, Part 2," *Echoes*, Vol. 4, No. 6 (December 1985).

Kirk-Greene, A.H.M., "Sanders of the River," *Edgar Wallace Society Newsletter 39* (August 1979).

———"The Story of Mr. Sanders, African Administrator Extraordinary," *Edgar Wallace Newsletter 30* (May 1976)

Lai, Rick, "The Hand of Kong," *The Pulp Collector*, Vol. 2, No. 3 (Winter 1987).

———"Peter the Brazen: No. 3 of A Death-Defying Act, Part 2," *Echoes*, Vol. 6, No. 5 (October 1987).

———"Peter the Brazen, The Early Adventures," *The Pulp Collector*, Vol. 4, #4 (Summer 1989).

Lane, Margaret, *Edgar Wallace*, William Heinemann, London, undated.

Lofts, W.O.G., "Francis Gerard," *Edgar Wallace Society Newsletter No. 12* (October 1971).

_____and D. J. Adley, *The Men Behind Boys' Fiction*, Howard Baker, London (1970).

Moskowitz, Sam, *Under the Moons of Mars*, Holt, Rinehart and Winston, NY (1970).

Mott, Frank Luther, *A History of American Magazines, 1885-1905, Vol. 10*, Harvard University, Cambridge (1957).

Murray, Will, "The Evil Lotus," *Doc Savage Club Reader*, #11.

Reynolds, Quentin, *The Fiction Factory*, Random House, NY (1955).

Sabatini, Rafael, *The Fortunes of Captain Blood*, Grosset & Dunlap, NY (1936).

_____*Captain Blood Returns*, Houghton, NY (1931).

Stribling, T.S., *Laughing Stock* (edited by Randy K. Cross and John T. McMillan), St. Luke's Press, Memphis (1982).

Tuttle, W(ilbur) C., *Hidden Blood*, Houghton Mifflin, Boston (1943).

_____*Mission River Justice*, Avalon Books, NY (1955).

_____*Montana Man*, Avalon Books, NY (1966).

_____*Piperock Tales*, Avalon Books, NY (1963).

_____*The Trail of Deceit*, Houghton Mifflin, Boston (1951).

_____*Tumbling River Range*, World Publishing, Cleveland (1944).

Vance, Louis Joseph, *Terence O'Rourke, Gentleman Adventurer*, Wessels, NY (1905).

Wallace, Edgar, *Bones*, Ward, Lock & Co., Ltd, London (undated paperback edition, #220).

_____*Bosambo of the River*, Ward, Lock, & Co., London (undated).

_____*The Keepers of the King's Peace*,. Ward, Lock, & Co. (1919).

_____*People of the River*, Ward, Lock, & Co., London (undated).

_____*Sanders of the River*, Doubleday, Doran, NY (1930).

_____*Sandi the King-Maker*, Ward, Lock & Co. London (undated).

Wodehouse, P.G., *Author! Author!*, Simon & Schuster, NY (1962).

Worts, George Frank, *Peter the Brazen*, Lippincott: NY (1919).

Young, Gordon Ray, *Hurricane Williams*, Bobbs-Merrill: NY (1922).

_____"Storm Rovers," *Adventure*, Vol. XXVII, No. VI (Mid-December 1920).

_____*The Vengence of Hurricane Williams*, Doran: NY (1925).

Magazine Appearances of Series Characters

Captain Bantam by Walter Wood
in *The Popular Magazine*, Series Title: "Captain Bantam, Kingdom Jumper"

1904

Nov   The Annexation (first)
Dec   Saving the Cargo

1905

Jan   The Cruise of the "Promised Land"
Feb   The Rival Claimants
Mar   In the Reign of King Bantam (final)

Captain Blood by Rafael Sabatini
in *Adventure*

1921

June 3	Rebels Convict
June 18	Don Diego Valdez
July 3	The Prize
July 18	Maracaybo
Aug 3	Blood Money
Sept 3	Santa Maria
Sept 18	Lord Julian's Mission
Oct 10	The Hostage
Oct 20	Captain Blood's Dilemma

Janie Frete by Raymond S.
Spears
in *All-Story Weekly*

1916

Jan 29; Feb 8, 12, 19	The Trail of the Otter Pelts (4-part serial)
May 20, 27; Jun 3, 10	The Green Sachem (4-part serial)

1918

Jun 15, 22, 29; Jul 6	Janie Frete Intrudes (4-part serial)

1919

Feb 1, 8, 15, 22	A Shortage in Perfumes (4-part serial)
Aug 23, 30; Sept 6, 13	Janie's Debt of Honor (4-part serial)

1920

May 15, 22, 29	Janie and the Waning Glories
June 5, 12, 19	(6-part serial)

Mother Hansen by Paul Ellsworth Triem
(Listings incomplete. In following, Mother Hansen abbreviated MH.)

in *Detective Story Magazine*:

1923

Sept 8	Mother Hansen Uses Her Umbrella
Sept 29	MH Meets a Fiddler
Nov 3	MH Swings a Mean Bottle

1924

Aug 23	Pie Face
Sept 13	MH Takes Up a Collection
Dec 20	MH's Holiday Party
Dec 27	MH Talks in Her Sleep

1925

Jan 17	With Her Boots On
Jan 24	MH Is Kinda Liberal
Feb 7	MH's Third Degree
Feb 28	MH Tries Truth Serum
Mar 7	MH Turns a Worm
Mar 14	MH's Honest Penny
Jul 4	MH and the Gangsters
Jul 11	MH, Art Patron
Jul 18	MH Buys a Bulldog
Aug 8	MH Meets the Angel Child
Oct 31	Dark of the Moon

1926

Jan 16	MH Swallows the Sinker
Feb 6	MH and the Snow Bird
Oct 9	MH Tries Real Estate
Dec 25	MH's Yuletide

1927

Jan 29	Weeping Losers

1929

June 15	MH's Bite

1930
Aug 23   MH's Love Birds
Oct 11   MH's China Girl

in *Best Detective*:
1936
Oct   MH and the Gangsters

Hashknife Hartley by W.C. Tuttle
in *Adventure*

1920
Mid-July   "Hashknife"-Philanthropist
First August   A Whizzer on Willer Crick

1921
First May   The Devil's Dooryard
First September   Law Rustlers

1922
Dec 30   The Ranch of the Tombstone

1923
Feb 28   Tramp of the Range

1924
Feb 29   Hashknife and Fantom Riders
March 30   The Medicine Man
Oct 20   The Dead-Line
Nov 30   The Trey of Spades

1925
Jan 20   The Lovable Liar
March 30   Hidden Blood
August 30   Hashknife of the Diamond H
Oct 30   The Tin God of Twisted River

1926
Jan 30   Vanishing Brands
July 8   The Range of Restitution
August 23   The Trouble Trailer
November 23   The Buckaroo of Blue Wells
December 31   Two Fares East

1927
March 1   The Red Triangle
July 1 & 15   Thicker Than Water
August 15   (3-part serial)
September 1   Crooked Coin

| November 1 | Shotgun Gold |
| December 1 | The Meddler |

1928
| April 15 | Buzzards |
| May 1 | (2-part serial) |

1929
November 1	The Luck of San Miguel
December 15	Mavericks
January 1 & 15	(4-part serial)
February 1, 1930	

1930
| June 1 & 15 | Bullet Crazy |
| July 1 | (3-part serial) |

1931
March 15	The Scar of Fate
April 1 & 15	(3-part serial)
Sept 15, Oct 1	The Make-Believe Man
	(2-part serial)

1932
March 15	The Cross-In-A-Box Mystery
July 15	Flimsy Evidence
October 1 & 15	The Ghost Riders
November 1 & 15	(4-part serial)

1933
| May 1 & 15 | Rifled Gold |
| June, July, August | (5-part serial) |

1934
| June | Hashknife Throws a Diamond Hitch |

1935
| March 1 | The Loot of Santana |
| July 15 | Trigger Trouble |

in *Argosy*:
1929
| July 13, 20, 27 | Bluffer's Luck |
| Aug 3, 10 | (5-part serial) |

1933
| November 4 | Hashknife Plays a Hunch |

1934

| June 30 | The Finger of Fate |
| December 15 | Deception Trail |

1935
| February 2 | Hashknife Pays a Debt |

1938
| May 14 | Short Rope for Rustlers |

in *Short Stories*:
1939
April 25	Passengers for Painted Rock
November 25	The Double Crossers of Ghost Tree
December 25	Hashknife's Partner

1940
| April 25 | Murder Map |
| October 10 | Horse of a Different Color |

1941
January 25	Plenty Rope
June 10	The Red Trail of a .41
August 25	Trail of Lies

1942
| August 25 | The Lobo Trail |

1943
| March 25 | Wolves of Lobo Butte |
| December 25 | The Double Crossers of Little Saguero |

1944
March 25	Hashknife Keeps a Faith
June 25	Border Buzzards
August 25	Fate and Some Fools

1945
January 25	Lightning Luck
April 10	The Lobo of Saquero Bend
June 10	Bullet Proof
September 25	By Executive Appeal
December 10	Death Trap at the Lazy M

1946
February 25	Crazy Moon Gold
June 25	Tenor Range
December 10	Six-Gun Law in Lazy Moon

1947
July 25   The Menace of Spirit River
September 10   The Loot of the Lazy A
December 10   Whom the Gods Would Destroy

1948
June 25   Dead Men Don't Need to Talk
October 25   Dancing Devil Range

1949
February 25   Mr. Smith of the Ten Bar B

1950
Feb   The Big Pay-Off
August   The Kingdom of Cole

1951
January   The Rattler of Fate

Note: My thanks to Walker Martin, who provided the bulk of the entries contained in the checklists.

Checklist of Books Published

Note: The following list is incomplete. Titles are cited only when known that the book is about Hashknife Hartley. It has not been possible to trace all title changes between magazine and book publications, or between the English (Collins) and US (Houghton and Avalon) editions. The information in this listing is based on that contained in Hubin's Bibliography of Mystery Fiction, with additional data provided.

Title	Date Mag Pub	England: Collins	US
Bluffer's Luck	1929	1932	Houghton, 1937
The Dead-Line	1924	1927	
Diamond Hitch	1934	1962	
Double-Crossers of Ghost Tree	1939	1965	
Hashknife of Stormy River		1931	Houghton, 1935
Hashknife of the Double Bar 8		1927	Houghton, 1936
Hidden Blood	1925	1929	Houghton, 1929 and 1943
Medicine Maker		1967	
The Medicine-Man	1924	1925	Houghton, 1939
Mission River Justice		1956	Avalon, 1955
The Morgan Trail			Houghton, 1928
(Published by Collins as Hashknife of the Canyon Trail		1928	
The Mystery of the Red Triangle	1927	1929	Houghton, 1942
Passengers for Painted Rock	1939	1962	
The Payroll of Fate		1966	
Rifled Gold	1933	1934	Houghton, 1934

The Santa Delores Stage		1935	Houghton, 1934
(also published as Twisted Trails,			
Popular Library, 1950)			
Shotgun Gold	1927	1941	Houghton, 1940
The Silver Bar Mystery	1930	1932	Houghton, 1933
(also published as The Trail of			
Deceit, Houghton, 1951)			
Thicker Than Water	1927		Houghton, 1927
The Tin God of Twisted River	1925	1942	Houghton, 1941
The Trail of Deceit			Houghton, 1951
(See Silver Bar Mystery)			
The Trouble Trailer	1926	1946	Houghton, 1946
Tumbling River Range		1929	Houghton, 1935
Twisted Trails			
(See Santa Delores Stage)			
Valley of Suspicion		1964	
The Valley of Twisted Trails		1932	Houghton, 1931
The Valley of Vanishing Herds			Houghton, 1942
The Wolf Pack of Lobo Butte	1943	1946	Houghton, 1945
(Published by Collins as			
Wolf Creek Valley)			

Geoffrey Heronhaye by K. and Hesketh Prichard
in *The Popular Magazine* (Series title: "The Fortunes of Geoff")

1906

Oct	I. How He Earned His First Wages
Nov	II. How He Played A Return Match with Dehrez
Dec	III. A Price on His Head

1907

Jan	IV. Spanish Gold
Feb	V. How He Fought for His Lady
Mar	VI. From Savage Fingers
Apr	VII. Weapons of War
May	VIII. Personally Conducted
June	IX. The Pass of the Mexican
July	X. The Insurgent General
Aug	XI. Orders to Kidnap
Sept	XII. The Last Round

Plantagent Hock by George Bronson-Howard
in *The Popular Magazine* (series title: "Plantagenet Hock: Hero")

1907

March	I. The Lady of Luzon
April	II. The Silver Princess
May	III. The Custom of the Country
June	IV. Jonah Number Two

July	V. Madame Mandarin

Spud McGee by Charlotte Dockstader (Listings incomplete)
in *Detective Story Magazine*:

1928

Aug 25	R.S.V.P.
Sept 15	The Gilded Lady
Oct 13	Wet Shot

1929

Jan 26	The Blue Cruiser
Apr 27	The Flying Jewel
May 11	Don't Tip Your Hat
Jun 15	The Acid Umbrella
Jul 20	Broadway Panic
Sept 7	People vs Spud McGee
Dec 28	Spud's Neediest Case

1930

Mar 1	White Clew
May 10	Spud's Blind Faith
May 31	Spud's White Clew
	(Not same as 3/1/30)
Jul 12	In the Lion's Mouth
Aug 2	Spud McGee's Danger Signal
Aug 9	Blinding Bandages

1931

Jun 6	Spud's Chinese Night

1932

Jan 30	Spud Gives a Lift
Mar 12	Stronger Than Bullets
Apr 9	Spud's Masquerade

Commander McTurk by Cutcliffe Hyne
in *The Popular Magazine*

1905	Series Title: "The Trials of Commander McTurk"
Sept	Annexed In Error
Oct	The Value of a Steam Blockade
Nov	The Western Ocean Pirate
Dec	The Balance of Power

1906

Jan	The Gray-Green Powder
Feb	The Sultana
Mar	Marguerita Pearls
Apr	Taking Water

| May | Manoa (Final) |

The Major by L. Patrick Greene
in *Adventure*

1919
| 1st Nov | No Evidence |

1920
| Mid Nov | Two of a Kind |

1921
1st Feb	Lines of Cleavage
1st March	Ivory
1st April	Amnesia
1st Aug	Tools

in *Short Stories*
1921
| *Nov 10* | Royal Game |

1923
| March 25 | A Matter of Range |
| July 10 | A Major Development |

1924
| May 25 | Gold from Ophir |
| Sept 25 | With One Stone |

1925
| Oct 10 | Pestle and Mortar |

1926
Feb 10	Heading North
March 10	Truth Is Mighty
June 10	Bush Shadows
Aug 10	Idols
Oct 10	Major Methods

1927
| Feb 25 | A Hottentot's God |
| June 10 | Witchcraft |

1928
| March 25 | Fool's Folly |

1929
| June 25 | The Major's Private Bank |
| Aug 10 | The Major Sets a Trap |

1930

Jan 10	Water
April 10	Shiners
June 10	Fire
June 25	Trapped

1931

June 25	Chingering Ching
Sept 10	A Major Surrender
Oct 25	Veldt Gold

1932

March 25	Forbidden Valley
June 10	Wind Falls
Nov 25	Biters Bitten

1933

Jan 10	Barehanded
June 25	A Drink for A Dog
Oct 25	Swift Justice

1934

Jan 10	Slick Fenton's Release
Feb 10	Account Paid
March 25	Flight
May 10	Laughter
Aug 10	Squeeze
Aug 25	One Thousand Pounds Reward
Sept 10	By Rule of Drum

1935

March 10	Decoy
April 10	The Miracle
June 25	The Lake of The Dead
July 10	Murder By Diplomacy
Nov 25	The Lame Boy

1936

March 10	The Oyster's Pearl
April 25	Crooked Barrels
May 25	Kaffir Orange
July 10	A Major Masquerade
Oct 10	Fog Bound

1937

Feb 10	Blank Charge
April 10	The Biggest Game
Sept 10	The Perfect Impersonation
Oct 10	The Thanks of a Bee

1938
April 10   Galloping Lions
May 25   The Last Outspan

1939
Jan 25   Major Sacrifice
May 10   Bread Upon the Waters
June 25   The Isle of Silence
Aug 25   Villainy Enforced
Oct 25   The White Ones of Bunyore

1947
Oct 10   A Major Doublecross
Nov 10   The Quickness of the Hand

1952
Sept   Pestle and Mortar

1953
April   The Lake of the Dead

1954
April   By Rule of Drum
                                            in *Star Magazine*

1930
Nov   The Seventh Plague

Note: The Preceding checklist is incomplete. My thanks to A.H. Lybeck and to Diggs LaTouche who provided most of the information cited.

Terence O'Rourke by Louis Joseph Vance
in *The Popular Magazine*:

1904
March thru June   O'Rourke, Gentleman Adventurer
                                            (4-part serial)
                                            *Under series title of "The Further Adventures
                                            of O'Rourke":*
July   In Which O'Rourke Returns To the Sword
Aug   In Which O'Rourke Serves the King
Sept   In Which O'Rourke Plays Providence
Oct   In Which O'Rourke Saves a Throne
Nov   *In Which O'Rourke Pays a Debt
Dec   In Which O'Rourke Sheathes His Sword

*Not included in book, *Terence O'Rourke,
Gentleman Adventurer*

Under series title "O'Rourke, the Wanderer":

1906

Nov | The Pool of Flame
Dec | Captain Hole of the Pelican

1907

Jan | The Gaunt Serang
Feb | The Way of the Wanderer

The Pathless Trail by Arthur O. Friel
in *Adventure*:

1921

Oct 10,20,30 | The Pathless Trail
Nov 10 | (4-part serial)

1922

Jul 20,30 | Tiger River
| (4-part serial)

Aug 10,20

1924

Mar 20,30 | The King of No Man's Land
| (4-part serial)

Apr 10,20

1925

Jan 30 | Mountains of Mystery
| (4-part serial)

Feb 10,20,28

Peter the Brazen by Loring Brent (George F. Worts)
in *The Argosy*:

1918 | (6-part series published under the title
| "Peter the Brazen")
Oct 5 | I: Princess of Static
Oct 19 | II: The City of Stolen Lives
Nov 2 | III: The Bitter Fountain
Nov 16 | IV: The Dead Spark
Nov 30 | V: The Golden Paw
Dec 14 | VI: The Gray Dragon

1919

Nov 22 thru | The Golden Cat
Dec 27 | (6-part serial)

1930

Feb 8 | The Sapphire Smile

April 26	The Man in the Jade Mask
June 21, 28	That Cargo of Opium
	(2-part serial)
Nov 22, 29	The Hand of Ung
	(2-part serial)

1931

April 25,	Vampire
May 2	(2-part serial)
May 30	Chinese for Racket
June 6	(2-part serial)
Nov 21	Cave of the Blue Scorpion

1932

| Nov 19 thru | Sting of the Blue Scorpion |
| Dec 17 | (5-part serial) |

1933

Feb 25	The Master Magician
June 10 thru	The Sapphire Death
July 15	(6-part serial)

1934

Mar 31	The Octopus of Hongkong
Aug 25 thru	Kingdom of the Lost
Sept 22	(5-part serial)

1935

| Apr 6 | Over the Dragon Wall |

Sanders of the River by (Edgar Wallace)
(Listing covers only American magazine appearances and is incomplete.)
Action Stories

1949

| Summer | Drums of Treason |

Adventure

1913

Feb	The Crime of Sanders
June	The Tale Tellers
Aug	Arachi the Borrower

1914

| Oct | A Maker of Wars |

1918

| 1st April | The Fetish Stick |

1919
Aug 15   M'Gala the Accursed

All-Story Weekly

1916
July 22   The Devil Light

American Magazine

1912
Nov   Nine Terrible Men

1913
Feb   The Affair of the Lady Missionary

Blue Book

1914
Sept   The Queen of the NGombi

Canadian Magazine

1916
Dec 2   Northern Men

Colliers

1915
Jan 16   Bones
Jan 30   The Soul of the Native Woman
March 20   The Green Crocodile
April 17   The Stranger Who Walked by Night

1916
May 6   Bones, Sanders, and Another
June 3   Bones Changes His Religion
July 8   Bones and the Wireless
Sept 23   Bones: Kingmaker
Dec 2   Northern Men

Everybody's

1929
Feb   Keepers of the Treasure
March   In the Matter of Lipstick

Golden Book

1930

Jan	People of the River
Feb	Nine Terrible Men
Mar	The Maker of Spears
May	The Rising of the Akasava
July	Sanders Meets Love

Harper's Weekly

1911

Feb 18	The Devil Man
May 20	The Lonely One
Aug 26	Bosambo of Monrovia
Sept 23	Sanders of the River

1912

| Apr 20 | A Certain Game |
| Oct 19 | The Thinker and the Gum Tree |

Jungle Stories

1948

| Fall | The Clean Sweeper |

McClures

1910

| May | The Education of King Peter |

Metropolitan

1911

| March | Sanders of the River |

Munsey's Magazine

1928

| March | The Ghost Walker |

New Story Magazine

1915

May	The Education of the King
June	The Keepers of the Stone
July	Bosambo of Monrovia
August	The Drowsy One
Sept	The Special Commissioner
Oct	The Dancing Stones
Nov	The Forest of Happy Dreams
(becomes *All-Round Magazine*)	
Dec	The Akasavas

1916
Jan   The Wood of Devils
Feb   The Loves of M'Lino
Mar   The Witch Doctor
April   The Lonely One
May   The Seer
June   The Dogs of War

Short Stories

1926
March 10   The Five Words

(The considerable effort taken by John Hogan, Walker Martin, and Leonard Robbins to search out these stories is gratefully acknowledged.)

Hurricane Williams by Gordon Young
in *Adventure*

1918
May 1   The Unlisted Legion
                                             (short story)

1919
Mid-July thru First Sept   Savages
                                             (4-part serial)

1920
Mid-March thru First June*   Wild Blood
                                             (4-part serial)
Mid-Dec   Storm Rovers (novel)

1923
May 30,   Hurricane Williams' Vengence
June 10,20,30   (4-part serial)

1931
June 1, 15   If There Be Courage
July 1, 15   (4-part serial)
Adventure published no issues dated in May of 1920. Because of a printers' strike the preceding year, the magazine's dating had gone awry and the May dates were dropped to correct that situation. The omission did not affect volume numbering.

Index

Action Stories, 18, 30, 32, 71, 132
Adrian, Jack, i
Adventure, 1, 10, 16, 17,
  26-30, 54, 66, 71, 78, 79,
  95, 103, 106, 111, 123, 132,
  134, 135, 141, 148, 181n, 182n,
  205
—departments, 29
—editors, 182n
—issuance, 30
Alger, Horatio, 9
All-Story, The, 1, 10, 36, 46
Allal Quatermain, 63
American Legion, 29
American Magazine, 71
amnesia, 60
Argosy, The, 1, 9-10, 35,
  36, 46, 47, 61, 105, 112, 134,
  148, 149, 170, 171, 172, 173,
  174, 175
Argosy All-Story Weekly,
  46-47, 105, 114, 121, 130,
  170, 173, 174
Arietta, 49
"Ask Adventure," 29, 122
Asterix the Gaul, 55
*Avenger, The,*81
Ayesha, 12, 65

Bantam, Captain, 13-14, 15, 31, 190
Bardeen, Matt, 154
Baumhofer, Walter, 154
Bedford-Jones, H., 3
Big-Book Western, 135
Big Story Magazine, 118
Bill and Jim, 173-175, 177
Billy June, 95-98
Black Mask, The, 14, 18, 166
Black Star, 125
Blackwell, Frank, 87
Blake, Steve, 154-155

Bleiler, Richard, i
Blood, Captain, 16, 23-26, 31, 190
Blue Book, 1, 10, 54, 66,
  132, 152, 154, 169
Blue Jean Billy, 121
Bobbs, Faraday, 13
Bones, 67, 72-73, 77
Borria, Romola, 41-42, 44, 46
Bosambo, 67, 68, 69-70, 77
Bosambo of the River, 72
Botts, Alexander, 154
Bower, B.M., 12, 132
Boyd, Felix, 12
Bradley, Typhoon, 18, 31-32
Brand, Max, 133, 137
Breezy Stories, 116, 161-162
Brent, Loring (pseudonym for
  G.F. Worts), 36, 183
Bronson-Howard, George, 12, 33
Brown, Raymond, 168
Burroughs, Edgar Rice, 48, 52,
  58, 59, 60, 61, 65, 66, 85
Butterick Publishing Company, 28

"Camp-Fire, The," 29, 104
Campbell, Scott, 12
Captain Blood, 24
Captain Blood Returns, 25
Cardossa, Luigi, 180
Carr, Nick, i
Carter, John, 59
Carter, Nick, 105, 125, 170, 173
Cassidy, Hopalong, 85, 132, 142
Cavalier, The 1, 4, 10
Christie, Agatha, 85
Chronicles of Captain Blood, The 25
Clark, Red, 18
Clayton, Frederick, 87
Collier's, 36, 46, 71, 122
Corcoran, William, 29
Cordie, Jimmie, 61, 105, 179, 180

Cox, Randy, i
Crawford, Joan, 46
Current Literature, 86

Daly, John Carroll, 18
Davis, Elmer, 29
Davis, J. Frank, 159
Day, Holman, 156
de Grandlieu, Princesse
  Beatrix, 6-7, 9
de S. Horn, R., 87
Deadly Excitements, 186n
Delineator, The, 28
Dent, Lester, 50
Derlict Hunters, The, 13
Detective Fiction Weekly, 121
Detective Story Magazine,
  87, 105, 121, 130, 161, 163,
  164, 166, 175
Detective Tales, 166
Deveny, Jack, i
Deveny, Helen, i
Dime Detective, 172
Dockstader, Charlotte, 175
Doubleday, Page, and Co., 86-87
Douglas, David, 157
Doyle, Conan, 10, 78
Druke, Jericho, 81
Drummond, Bulldog, 180

Eddsfield, 159-60, 177
Eddis, Edward S., 9
Everhard, Don, 18, 85, 179, 181n
Everybody's Magazine, 28, 36
Fantastic Adventures, 54, 66
Field and Stream, 135
Finnegan, Frank, 152
Fire Fighters, 154
Fitzgerald, J.A., 154
Flynn's, 173, 174, 175
Forest and Stream, 122
Fortunes of Captain Blood, The, 25
Four Just Men, The, 71, 182n
Frete, Janie, 114, 121-131, 132,
  179, 190-191
Friedman, I.K., 169
Friel, Arthur Olney, 98, 103-105
From the Dark Side, 183n
Fu Manchu, 38, 50
Furber, Art, 169

Gentleman Prefer Blonds, 160
Gentleman's Magazine, 63
Geoff, 13
Gerald, Francis, 71, 184n
Glory Figures, 184n, 185n
Golden Argosy, The, 9, 66
Golden Book, 71, 123
gold-diggers, 160-163
Gotch, Shark, 18, 31
"Green Sachem, The," 125-126
Greene, L. Patrick, 18, 78, 79, 83, 88
Gregory, M.D. 88
Grey, Zane, 137
Gunnison, John, i

Haggard, H. Rider, 12, 48, 52,
  62-64, 81, 85, 91, 104, 105,
  178, 179
Hall, Wilbur, 95
Hamilton, Captain, 67
Hamilton, Patricia, 73, 74, 76
Hansen, Mother, 121, 130, 152,
  163-165, 191-192
Harper's, 122
Harper's Bazar, 160
Harper's Weekly, 71
Hart, William, 137
Hartley, Hashknife, 115, 133-
  151, 179, 191-196
Hawley, Frank, 155-156
Hazeltine, Gillian, 47
Hendryx, James B., 87
Heronhaye, Geoff, 93-94, 105, 196
Hersey, Harold, 154
Hidden Blood, 143-144
Hiji, 78
Hill, Harold, 154
Hock, Plantagent, 33-35, 196
Hoffman, Arthur Sullivant, 27, 28, 29,
  30, 182n
Hogan, John, i, 184n
Holly, Ned, 152
Holmes, Sherlock, 54
Howard, Robert, 66
Hubin Bibliography, Mystery
  Fiction, 195
Hurst's American Weekly, 63
Hyne, Cutcliffe, 14

I Love Lucy, 166

James, Henry, 64, 66
"Janie and the Waning Glories,"
    129-130
"Janie Frete Intrudes," 126
"Janie Pays a Debt of Honor,"
    128-129
Jim the Hottentot, 81-82
Johnson, Ginger, i
Johnson, Tom, i
Jungle Stories, 71
Justice of Sanders, The, 71

Keniston, Edward, i
Kettle, Captain, 14-15
Khlit, 180
"King of No Man's Land, The," 102
King Solomon's Mines, 63
Kirdy, 180
Kussman, Earl, i

Lai, Rick, i, 188
Lamb, Harold, 18
Lardner, Ring, 168, 169
LaTouche, Diggs, i, 200
Law of the River, The, 71
Legrand, Vivian, 121, 130
Leith, Lester, 180
Lewis, Henry Harrison, 12
Lewis, Sinclair, 29
Liberty Magazine, 135
Life of Caesare Borgia, The, 24
Lindsey, Cynthia, i
Lone Wolf, 6, 124
Loos, Anita, 160
Lorimer, Aileen, 39-40, 41, 43, 44, 45
lost race, 77
"Lost Trails," 29
Lost World, The, 78
Love and Mr. Lewisham, 12
Lowder, Christopher, i
Lybeck, A.H., 200
Lyte, Steer, 156

McClures, 71
McConaughy, Captain, 31
McCulley, Johnston, 79, 133
McGee, Spud, 152, 175-176, 197
McIlwraith, 87

McLaurin, Hamish, 169
McTurk, John Kelly, 14, 15, 31, 197-198
MacLean, Charles, 181n
Maisie, 165-166
Major, The, 78, 79-86, 88-92, 113, 179,
    198-200
Maroney, Rosie, 158-159
Marsh, Richard, 12
Martin, Nell, 165
Martin, Walker, 195
Mattis, Carlton, 153
Maule, Harry E., 87
Max Brand Western, 135
Merriwell, Frank, 152, 155
Metropolitan, 71
Miller, Steve, i
Minter, Richard, i, 173
Mission River Justice, 150
Modern Adventuress, 121
Monthly Story Magazine, 1, 10
Moore, Peter (see Peter the Brazen)
Moskowitz, Sam, 181n
motion picture influences on
    magazine fiction, 23, 39, 46,
    132, 136, 146
"Mountains of Mystery," 103
Mulford, Clarence, 87, 133
Mundy, Talbot, 18, 28
Munsey, Frank A., 9, 10, 105
Murray, Will, i

Narrative conventions: battle, 54-5;
    character, 10, 18, 32, 40, 47, 81,
    137-8, 145; dehumanization, 43;
    factual content, 28, 45, 70, 91;
    inspired fool, 79; masculinity,
    26-7, 86; moral ambiguity, 126;
    physical suffering, 8, 91;
    psychological torment, 22, 31;
    Oriental evil, 38, 42-3; WWI
    influence, 16, 23, 45, 100, 105, 179
narrative devices: battle, 101, 179;
    death presumed, 58-9; dialect,
    146-7; drugs, 56; exploration, 8,
    64-5, 98; humor, 146; lost race,
    65, 77, 101; pacing, 11, 27, 32, 47,
    48; problem story, 31, 177; public
    interest, 11, 169, 177; technology
    use, 11, 16, 154
National Geographic, The, 10

Nature, 123
New Story Magazine, 30, 63, 71
New York Herald, 122
New York Sun, 122
Night Wind, The, 125, 180
Norroy, 12, 33, 180
Norroy, Diplomatic Agent, 33
O'Gilvie, Susan, 48-49, 50, 51, 52, 53,
    54, 55, 56-59, 60
O'Leary, T.X., 180
O'Rourke, Terence, 6-10, 181n, 200-201
"Old Songs," 29
"One-Two" Mac, 31
Oppenheim, E. Phillips, 12, 180
Outdoor Stories, 30
Outing Magazine, The 122

Page, Norvell, 51
Paget, Blackstone, 157-158
Parisienne Monthly, The 161
"Pathless Trail, The," 98-100, 185n,
    201
Patten, Gilbert, 12, 155
People's Favorite, The, 1, 153,
    157, 159, 166, 170
Pep Stories, 161
"Pete Kelly's Blues," 172
Peter the Brazen, 35, 36-60, 92, 177,
    179, 201-202
Peter the Brazen, 36, 43, 112, 182n
Phantom Detective, The, 59
Picture Players, The, 170
Pivet, Barbe, 121
Popular Magazine, The, 1, 9, 10,
    12-13, 14, 33, 63, 66, 93, 110,
    123, 132, 152, 159, 166, 168, 169,
    170, 181n
Popular Publications, 30
Prichard, K. and Hesketh, 93

Quatermain, Allan, 63, 85, 92, 151, 180
Quinn, Seabury, 78

Railroad Man's Magazine, 1,
    166
Raine, William Macleod, 3, 87
Reader's Digest, 123
Red Book, 36
Red Legs, 168-169
Reddale, Frederic, 154

Return of Sanders of the River, The, 71
Ridgway Company, 28
River of Stars, The, 71
Robbins, Leonard, i
Rohmer, Sax, 52, 61
Romance, 30
Roxton, Lord, 78
Rud, Anthony, 29

Sabatini, Rafael, 4, 23, 24-5
Sad Sontag, 149
Sampson, Robert, 183n, 186n
Sanders of the River, 66-68, 85, 92,
    179, 184n, 202-205
Sanders of the River, 69, 72
Sandi the King-Maker, 71, 77-78
Saturday Evening Post, 36, 123, 168
Savage, Doc, 50, 59, 66
Savage, Patricia, 50
Scaramouche, 24
Scarlet Adventuress, 121
Scribner's 122
Sea Hawk, The, 24
Sea Stories, 4, 30, 166
Scientific American, 122
Shadow Magazine, The, 81
She, 63
Sheena, 121, 185n
Short Stories, 1, 66, 71, 78,
    86-88, 113, 132, 134, 135, 149, 152
"Shortage in Perfumes, A," 126-127
Singapore Sammy, 47, 61
Smith, Arthur D. Howden, 31
Smithers, Saxophone, 172
Snappy Stories, 117, 152, 160, 166
Solomon, John, 180
Somers, F.M., 86
Spears, Raymond, 121, 122-123, 131,
    160, 161, 162
Spider, The, 51
Sports Stories, 166
Sports Story Magazine, 166
Standish, Burt, 4, 155, 167
Stevens, Sleepy, 136, 139
Storey, Madame, 121, 130
Street and Smith, 4, 157
Stribling, T.S., 28, 30, 182n
Syncopatin' Kid, 171

Tankeray, Vernon, 162

Tarzan, 55, 58, 59, 65, 66, 78, 85, 86
Tavern Knight, The, 24
*Terence O'Rourke, Gentleman
  Adventurer*, 6, 200
Thomas, Henry Wilton, 155
Thoris, Dejah, 58
Thrill Book, 166
Thriller, The, 184n
Thrilling Western, 135
Thursday, Thomas, 170-171
"Tiger River," 101-102
Tip-Top Weekly, 155
Top Notch, 1, 10, 66, 132, 152,
  153, 155, 166, 167, 170, 171, 186n
*Torquemada and the Spanish
  Inquisition*, 23
"Trail Ahead, The," 29
"Trail of the Otter Pelts, The," 123
Transvaal, 63, 182n
Treasure Island, 13, 63
Trevor, 180
Triebault, Slash, 167-168, 177
Triem, Paul Ellsworth, 163
Trimble, Terry, 79
Tros, 180
Tuttle, W.C., 88, 133, 134-136,
  139, 145, 146, 147, 186n
Typhoon, 13

Ullman, Albert E., 158
Umslopogaas, 81, 179

Vance, Louis Joseph, 6, 12, 181n

Wallace, Edgar, 66, 67, 70-71, 85, 92
Webb, John, 31
Weekly Tale-Teller, 71

Weird Tales, 54, 78, 87, 166
Wells, H.G., 12
Wentworth, Richard, 59
West Magazine, 122
Western Story, 135, 166
Wetgen, Albert Richard, 18, 31-2
White, Pearl, 130
White, Trumbull, 28
Whitman, Vic, 153, 171
Wide-World Adventure, 78
Wild West Weekly, 49
Williams, Hurricane, 15, 16-23,
  31, 32, 85, 105, 177, 179, 205
Williams, Race, 181n
Windsor Magazine, The 71
Wirt, W., 61, 179
Wodehouse, P.G., 27, 182n
Women: adventurous, 49-50, 121, 130,
  160-163; dangerous, 16-7, 19;
  imperiled, 50, 85; liberated, 46, 127
Wood, William, 13
Wooster, Bertie, 78, 79
World War I, 15-16
  —effects on fiction, 16
Worts, George Frank, i, 35-36,
  46, 47, 51, 55, 58, 59, 60-61, 182n

Yellow Pup, 153
You Know Me, Al, 168
Young, Gordon, 17-18, 61, 179
Young Wild West, 49
Young's Magazine, 116, 162
Youth, 13

Zaire, 76, 92
Zing, 161
Zorro, 16, 180